PAINTING ◦ COLOUR ◦ HISTORY

COLLECTION PLANNED AND DIRECTED BY
ALBERT SKIRA

A handsome book is not the work of a single person, but a product of the collective, well-directed efforts of all who have contributed to its success.

HISTORY OF MODERN PAINTING

FROM

BAUDELAIRE

TO

BONNARD

THE BIRTH OF A NEW VISION

THE HONFLEUR SCHOOL - IMPRESSIONISM - NEO-IMPRESSIONISM
SYMBOLISM - POST-IMPRESSIONISM

TEXT BY MAURICE RAYNAL

INTRODUCTION BY HERBERT READ

HISTORICAL AND BIOGRAPHICAL NOTES
JEAN LEYMARIE

TRANSLATED BY STUART GILBERT

ALBERT SKIRA

GENEVA

COLLEGE OF ART
LIBRARY
30004
759.05 RAY
COVENTRY

As early as 1930 we had in mind the publication of a series of works in which colour reproduction was to play a novel and a leading part. No longer treated merely as a source of pleasure for the eye, it would (as we planned to use it) also serve a wider purpose and implement the systematic study of the history of art.

But the years went by and, for reasons of a technical order, our project had to be postponed. The series of portfolios of our " Trésors de la Peinture Française " (begun, it may be remembered, in 1934) was, seen from this angle, a laboratory experiment in view of an ulterior aim : that of exploiting all the possibilities offered by the most recent methods of colour reproduction, and of mastering a technique enabling us to turn them to best account. Our objective was the production of books which were more than mere anthologies of pictures, and furnished information no less accurate than complete. For it is clear that verbal description, however lucid and historically valid, cannot be enough ; it must be implemented by reproductions, and these should not be deprived of what is vitally essential to their expressive value : in other words, of their colour.

After many years of preparation and research-work we now feel qualified to lay as it were the foundation-stone of the vast edifice we propose to build, and it is under the auspices of Modern Painting that our collection " Painting — Colour — History " begins. It is intended to meet the wishes and requirements of all who, whether remotely or closely interested in art, would wish to possess a book which is at once a mine of information, a thing of beauty, and a source-book indispensable to both amateurs and connoisseurs ; a work containing all essentials and so arranged as to facilitate the study of the great movements, pointing out their landmarks, and showing the relations between these movements, their origins and their evolution. In short, a work which by making the approach easy and agreeable will stimulate both the public taste for art and a wider, more enlightened understanding of its masterpieces.

In carrying out this programme we have taken into account not merely the aesthetic value of the works reproduced but also their historical significance, their dates, and their importance both as regards the trends they stand for and the movements to which they belong, and as regards the style and personal evolution of the individual artists. Thus each reproduction serves as a pointer, helping the reader to find his way in the vast and complex field of art and familiarizing him with the problems of the creative process. With this in mind we have secured the collaboration of writers who have specialized in the period covered by each volume, and they have been invited, working in close contact, to supply an harmonious (but not arbitrary) presentation of the historical, critical and technical ambience of the works reproduced, while leaving readers free to form their own judgements, according to their predilections.

The title chosen for this first volume, "From Baudelaire to Bonnard," may perhaps cause surprise. Need we say that this choice was not due to the mere coincidence that the death of Baudelaire and the birth of Bonnard took place in the same year, 1867? The point we wish to emphasize is that Baudelaire, first critic of modern painting, who sponsored with his prophetic pen the most daring aspirations of his contemporaries, inaugurated that fruitful collaboration between poets and painters which has meant so much to art. Mallarmé, Apollinaire, Max Jacob and Eluard in turn have kept this fine tradition alive, and this is why we place our first volume under the aegis of a poet who was not only a friend of painters but one who, with the prescience of genius, discerned the course that modern painting was to take.

And now we invite the reader to prospect, pleasurably we hope and easefully, this colourful pageant of art in the second half of the XIXth century. It may be well to point out here that we make no claim to have given a full-length study of the impressionist movement; what we have sought to convey is that Impressionism constituted an all-important stage in the advance towards Modern Painting—whose entrance on the scene we place somewhere between Bonnard and Matisse. Our object is to show, with Impressionism, the notion of freedom, a legacy from Romanticism, breathed new life into traditional aesthetics, and how its "lyrical" technique led painting to that emancipation from the tyranny of the object, which, claimed in the second half of the nineteenth century, was achieved at the beginning of the twentieth . . .

It is a pleasure to record our gratitude to those whose whole-hearted and indeed enthusiastic co-operation has enabled us to bring our task to a successful conclusion. To Maurice Raynal, especially, we owe our thanks. In the making of this book he proved himself a wise adviser and a loyal friend, whose competence never failed us in the hour of need. We also tender our thanks to the Conservators of museums who so kindly facilitated our researches, and to whose expert aid our documentation owes so much. No less warmly do we thank the eminent collectors who have allowed us access to the treasures of their private collections.

Lastly, we would have all our collaborators know that we are gratefully conscious of their contribution to the making and success of the work now submitted to the public; indeed this brief acknowledgement does far less that justice to our gratitude.

A. S.

CONTENTS

THE COLOURPLATES

It will be noticed that while most of these titles are translated into English, some remain in French. The principle followed is that titles which have no quite satisfactory equivalent in English (e. g. **Poseuse***), or are universally accepted (e. g.* **Le Déjeuner sur l'Herbe***), or whose meaning is self-evident (e. g.* **Intérieur de Restaurant***) are left in French.*

THE MODERN EPOCH IN ART

BY

HERBERT READE

Discussing the origins of naturalism in the Middle Ages, Max Dvorak warned us against the folly of trying to fix a specific " beginning " to anything so underground as the first growth of an artistic style. The modern movement in art, which in general is a reversal of the movement discussed with such brilliance by Dvorak (in his *Idealismus und Naturalismus in der gotischen Skulptur und Malerei*), offers no exception to this rule. Its origins are extremely obscure, and, like roots, proceed from different levels and contradictory directions. One cannot exclude either the revolutionary romanticism of a Blake or the revolutionary classicism of a David ; Constable's scientific naturalism is certainly a factor, but so is the historical idealism of Delacroix (to Cézanne always " le grand Maître "). The realism of Courbet and Manet ; the expressionism of Van Gogh and Munch ; the symbolism of Emile Bernard and Gauguin—all these precede and in some degree predetermine the specifically modern movements of fauvism, cubism, constructivism and surrealism. Perhaps we should abandon our biological analogies and think rather of the complex " movement " of a chronometer ; for historical " time " seems to reduce, on analysis, to such an interlocking of gears and ratchets. It will be said that even the chronometer has a spring at the centre, but this is not necessarily true of the modern chronometer, which may be set and kept in motion by the simple alternation of night and day.

There is, of course, the further explanation offered by the theory of dialectical materialism. For night and day in our metaphor we may substitute rich and poor, bourgeoisie and proletariat, and in the circulation of élites see a sufficient motive power for all the stylistic changes of art. This is not an argument that can be ignored, for art never exists in a vacuum, but is inextricably entangled in the life of society as a whole. If we discover that the modern artist is relatively isolated from society we must not be led to suppose that such isolation is a characteristic of art itself—an island as such is only defined by reference to a neighbouring land-mass.

Nevertheless, economic facts and social movements can only have an indirect relation to the stylistic evolution of art. In the period that concerns us here, there is one broad economic development of the utmost significance—the gradual decline of private patronage consequent on the restrictions imposed on capitalist development. Private collectors still buy works of art in the open market—to that extent there are still patrons, if only through the medium of the art-dealer. But they no longer *command* the artist like the monastery or the guild, the court or the castle. The position has been so reversed that the contemporary artist must form the taste and recruit the public (through the intermediary of the art critic, in himself a modern phenomenon) on whose patronage he will then depend. The modern artist is miserably dependent on the media of publicity. That is his deepest humiliation.

There is another and a more limited sense in which the course of art is determined by economic factors. Scientific and industrial progress, particularly in the nineteenth century, threw out as by-products certain theories and inventions which had a direct impact on the technique and social significance of art. These have been too often discussed to need more than a passing reference. The formulation of a scientific theory of colour, which at first led to such aberrations as pointillism, has not had any permanent effect on artistic practice—the artist has discovered by now that he must rely on his sensibility and not attempt to particularize from laws of aesthetic effect. But more significant and more permanent in its influence on the development of art has been the invention of photography and of photographic methods of reproduction. The economic consequences of such inventions are serious enough—the public is provided with a cheap substitute for the plastic arts. It may not be aesthetically so satisfying, but it suffices for the low level of sensibility that seems to be a consequence of mass production and mass education. The effect on the artist has been even more profound, for it has relieved him of one of the social functions of art—that of "visual aid." It is true that certain subtleties of imaginative literature will still call for creative illustration ; but for instruction and clarification it is better to provide an *Orbis sensualium pictus* by means of the camera. What has been effected is a clear distinction between *illustration* and *interpretation*. This may not seem so significant at first, but implied in it is the distinction between *image* and *symbol*, which, as we shall see presently, is fundamental to an understanding of the modern movement in art.

What in general may be admitted in this connection is that economic and social trends determine and give their fluctuating shades to broad movements of thought and opinion in every epoch. The work of art cannot escape the ambience of such intangible effluences (the philosophies and theologies of the period). To the extent that a work of art is romantic or classical, realistic or symbolic, it will certainly be beyond the personal control of the artist. Even the structure of the work of art (the style of composition) may be a matter of taste or fashion determined by social contacts. But there comes a point in the evolution of art at which all these imponderable forces are but external pressures which result, not in a consequential " line of force," but in a leap into creative originality of quite incalculable kind. The dialectical materialist may still claim that social factors have determined that anamorphosis, but the quantum in art, as in physics, may be discontinuous. A brief examination of the concept of *originality* will perhaps make my meaning clear.

It has often been observed that if we have regard only for that quality we call " sensibility," which would throughout history seem to be the essential element in art, then no progress whatsoever is discernible between the cave drawings of the paleolithic period and the drawings of Raphael or Picasso. Sensibility is not the only value in art—as successive civilizations develop their cultures they invariably dilute this basic sensibility with other values of a magical or logical nature—they *use* sensibility in social contexts, and it is the variations of context that seem to explain whatever changes occur in the history of art. There is, of course, a degree beyond which the sensibility cannot be forced or prostituted—the result is then the *rigor mortis* of academicism, or the moral rot of sentimentalism. The vitality of art would seem to depend on the maintenance of a delicate balance between sensibility and whatever intellectual or emotional accretions it derives from the social element in which it is embedded.

The process is, it will be seen, a dialectical one, and it is certainly one in which tensions and contradictions inevitably develop. One way in which a tension may be relaxed takes the form of a decline of sensibility, and the tension must be restored if art is to survive. What precisely happens in such a crisis is in dispute. The alternative suggestions are : (1) the artist retraces the historical development of his art and resumes contact with the authentic *tradition* ; or (2) the artist resolves the crisis by a leap forward into a new and original state of sensibility—he revolts against the existing conventions in order to create a new convention more in accordance with a contemporary consciousness. We may admit that in doing so he merely recovers, in all its actuality, the original basic quality of art—

aesthetic sensibility in all its purity and vitality. But the context is new, and it is the synthesis of an untrammelled sensibility with a new set of social conditions which constitutes, in the evolution of art, an act of originality.

We must guard against interpreting " social conditions " in a sense narrowly economic or political. The artist's awareness of these conditions rarely assumes a politically conscious form, and certainly there is no correlation to be made between such consciousness in the artist and his degree of originality. Courbet, Pissarro, William Morris—these are the politically conscious artists and they have an important place in the history of modern art. But a more important place is taken by artists like Cézanne, Gauguin and Matisse, whose awareness of the social context of their work was never expressed in a political formula. It is only a primitive mind that can interpret the social context as Daumier's third-class railway carriage. The social context is the totality of our way of life and its impact on the artist may be through a philosophy or a science, or even through a pair of old boots (Van Gogh) or a heap of rubbish (Schwitters).

From this point of view a renewed contact with tradition may have as much revolutionary significance as any originality in style or technique. The validity of a tradition depends on its retention of the element of sensibility. We agree to find this element in the paintings of Poussin ; therefore, said Cézanne, let us go back to Poussin and try to recover, in front of nature, the element that made Poussin a great artist. Cézanne implied, not that the modern artist should imitate Poussin's style (which was personal to Poussin), but that a study of Poussin's art might lead to the recovery of sensibility—to the reanimation of his (Cézanne's) ability to " realize his sensations " in the presence of nature. " Nature " meanwhile had changed, because nature is but another word for the social context already mentioned. *To renew one's sensibility towards one's environment*—that is the method of both the traditionalist and of the revolutionary. Nevertheless, there is still a degree of originality which is not necessarily covered by the phrase.

The sense of " reality " is surely one of those conventions that change from age to age and are determined by the total way of life. Not only does the concept of reality differ as between a medieval philosopher like St. Thomas Aquinas and a modern philosopher like Bergson, but a similar difference also exists on the average level of apprehension (the difference between animism and theism, between supernaturalism and materialism, and so on). The " reality " of a citizen of the Soviet Union is certainly different from the " reality " of a citizen of the United States. We have now reached such a stage of relativism in philosophy that it is possible to affirm that reality is in fact subjectivity, which means that the individual has no choice but to construct his own reality however arbitrary and even " absurd " that may seem. This is the position reached by the Existentialists, and to it corresponds a position in the world of art that requires a similar decision. The interpretation (or even the " imitation ") of reality was a valid function for the artist so long as it was agreed that a general and basic reality existed and was only waiting for revelation. Once this sense of security is removed (that is to say, is destroyed by scientific analysis) then philosophy and art are public auctions in which the most acceptable reality commands the highest price.

This may be a passing phase in philosophy and the world may return to systems of faith and revelation in which art once more resumes its interpretative function. But Existentialism is but the latest phase of a development of thought that reaches back to Kant and Schelling, and it is difficult (from a point of view inside the stream) to see any other direction which philosophy can take (it already carries along with it the contradictions of Christianity and atheism). It is in this mental climate that contemporary art has shown a tendency to usurp the positivist role of philosophy and to present its own self-sufficient " reality." A certain type of modern artist claims to construct new realities (" réalités nouvelles "), and he will go so far as to assert that his construction is in no way determined even by such vague concepts as universal harmony or the collective unconscious, but is an act of creation in the almost divine sense of the word. Naturally such an artist has to use elements of form and colour which are common to all the arts, and the world has not shown any inclination to recognize his work as art unless it possesses some of the sensuous qualities of the traditional work of art.

The conclusion we are driven to is that originality can only be conceptual, thematic, structural—never sensuous. There are new ways of thinking and doing—we call them inventions; there are new ways of stimulating the senses. But sensation itself can only be modified—coarsened or refined. It has the physical limitations of our animal frame; stretched on that frame the nerve breaks if forced beyond its expressive compass.

At the same time we must recognize, with the Marxists, the historic nature of human consciousness; and, with certain psychologists, the ambiguous nature of this evolutionary acquisition. In terms of art it gave us the symbol where hitherto there had been only the image. Man in his first unreflecting unity with nature needed only the image to project his sensations. Man as a self-conscious individual separated from the rest of creation needed a language of symbols to express his self-ness. The elaboration of that need gave rise not only to conceptual symbols like " God " but also to a myriad of plastic symbols, some of them constant and archetypal, others temporary and even personal. If we could reconstruct the stages in human evolution which led from the eidetic, vitalistic art of the Paleolithic period to the symbolic, geometric art of the Neolithic period, we should have a clear conception of the rise of not only human self-consciousness, ethical conscience and the idea of a transcendental God, but also of the origins of that polarity in art which has caused a rhythmic alternation of styles throughout the history of art, and which now exists as an unresolved dialectical contradiction. It is the *co*-existence of the image and the symbol, as norms of art, which explains the apparent complexity and disunity of the modern movement.

The true understanding of art depends upon an appreciation of the nature and uses of symbolism. Symbolism is one of the two ways in which the human mind functions, the other being the direct experience of the external world (the " presentational immediacy " of sense perception). Since language itself is already symbolism, and the complicated forms of thought depend on a system of symbols such as we have in the science of algebra, it is natural to assume that there is something primitive and ineffective about the presentational immediacy of sense perceptions. This is far from being the case. It is much more difficult to be faithful to our direct experience of the external world than to " jump to conclusions " which are in effect symbolic references. The poet, said Gautier, is a man for whom the visible world exists; he wished, by this definition, to exclude from art those secondary elaborations of perception involved in the use of symbols. As the poet is condemned to use the symbolism of language, the ideal would seem to be quixotic. (Nevertheless poetry continues to reveal a fundamental strife between imagism and symbolism).

The special position of the visual artist may be illustrated by a quotation from Whitehead's *Symbolism: its Meaning and Effect* (1928). " We look up and see a coloured shape in front of us and we say,—there is a chair. But what we have seen is the mere coloured shape. *Perhaps an artist might not have jumped to the notion of a chair. He might have stopped at the mere contemplation of a beautiful colour and a beautiful shape.* But those of us who are not artists are very prone, especially if we are tired, to pass straight from the perception of the coloured shape to the enjoyment of the chair, in some way of use, or of emotion, or of thought. We can easily explain this passage by reference to a train of difficult logical inference, whereby, having regard to our previous experiences of various shapes and various colours, we draw the probable conclusion that we are in the presence of a chair."

This clearly illustrates the difference between a perspective experience (the immediate perception of an image) and the use of a symbol (the image plus its mental associations). Whitehead adds: " I am very sceptical as to the high-grade character of the mentality required to get from the coloured shape to the chair. One reason for this scepticism is that my friend the artist, who kept himself to the contemplation of colour, shape and position, was a very highly trained man, and had acquired this facility of ignoring the chair at the cost of great labour."

With this distinction in mind we can perhaps begin to understand what Cézanne meant by " realizing his sensations." We can understand what Van Gogh meant when he said that " a painter as a man is too much absorbed by what his eyes see, and is not sufficiently master of the rest of his life." (Letter 620.) Van Gogh's letters are full of descriptions of his intense concentration on what a philosopher like Whitehead would call " presentational immediacy." For example : " I myself am quite absorbed by the immeasurable plain with cornfields against the hills, immense as a sea, delicate yellow, delicate soft green, delicate violet of a ploughed and weeded piece of soil, regularly chequered by the green of flowering potato-plants, everything under a sky with delicate blue, white, pink, violet tones. I am in a mood of *nearly too great calmness*, in the mood to paint this." (Letter 650 written in Dutch.)

This " mood of nearly too great calmness " is the mood of direct experience, of instinctual awareness in which the eidetic image is, as it were, preserved from the contamination of symbolism—from the need for further reference to other elements in our experience. It has been claimed that the capacity for realizing and retaining the image in a state of perceptive vividness is the quality that distinguishes the artist from other men, but in fact it is the distinguishing quality of one type of artist—the imagist. It was by his insistence on the strict purity of this perceptive experience that Cézanne restored to art some degree of primal rectitude.

At the other extreme of artistic practice the artist abandons himself freely to a symbolic activity. Whitehead has said that " the human mind is functioning symbolically when some components of its experience elicit consciousness, beliefs, emotions, and usages, respecting other components of its experience. The former set of components are the ' symbols,' and the latter set constitute the ' meaning ' of the symbols." An artist of the symbolist type is creating a combination of forms and colours (or of sounds if he is a musician) which will convey a meaning, and in art this meaning always has an aesthetic or emotional tinge. Art of this kind may therefore be defined as " the symbolic transfer of emotion " and as Whitehead says, this definition is at the base of any theory of the aesthetics of art—" For example, it gives the reason for the importance of a rigid suppression of irrelevant detail. For emotions inhibit each other, or intensify each other. Harmonious emotion means a complex of emotions mutually intensifying ; whereas the irrelevant details supply emotions which, because of their irrelevance, inhibit the main effect. Each little emotion directly arising out of some subordinate detail refuses to accept its status as a detached fact in our consciousness. It insists on its symbolic transfer to the unity of the main effect."

This definition of symbolism agrees closely with those definitions of " synthétisme " which were formulated by Emile Bernard in 1888 and which, through the medium of Gauguin, were to have revolutionary effect on the whole development of modern art. Bernard wrote :

" Puisque l'idée est la forme des choses recueillies par l'imagination, il fallait peindre non plus devant la chose, mais en la reprenant dans l'imagination, qui l'avait recueillie, qui en conservait l'idée ; ainsi l'idée de la chose apportait la forme convenable au sujet du tableau ou plutôt à son idéal (somme des idées) la simplification que l'essentiel des choses perçues et par conséquent en rejette le détail. La mémoire ne retient pas tout, mais ce qui frappe l'esprit. Donc formes et couleurs devenaient simples dans une égale unité. En peignant de mémoire, j'avais l'avantage d'abolir l'inutile complication des formes et des tons. Il restait un schéma du spectacle regardé. Toutes les lignes revenaient à leur architecture géométrique, tous les tons aux couleurs types de la palette prismatique. Puisqu'il s'agissait de simplifier, il fallait retrouver l'origine de tout : dans le soleil, les sept couleurs dont se compose la lumière blanche (chaque couleur pure de la palette y répondant), dans la géométrie, les formes typiques de toutes les formes objectives."

This distinction between painting " devant la chose " and " en la reprenant dans l'imagination " expresses neatly the two ways open to the artist, and the further insistence on "simplification " (Bernard) or " unity of the main effect " (Whitehead) points to that characteristic in symbolic art which can involve a progressive modification of the " schema " in the direction of abstraction. There is nothing in the paintings of Gauguin which would seem to imply or justify the abstractions of a Kandinsky or a Mondrian ; nevertheless, there is what Whitehead calls " a chain of derivations of symbol from symbol whereby finally the local relations, between the final symbol and the ultimate meaning, are entirely lost." Thus these derivative symbols, obtained as it were by arbitrary association, are really the results of reflex action suppressing the intermediate portions of the chain. By such a chain of derivations we could conceivably establish an association between such apparently disconnected symbols as Gauguin's *Yellow Christ* and Mondrian's *Boogie-Woogie*. Mondrian was fond of describing his art as " a new realism," but it is clear from his writings that he had invented a new symbolism. Mondrian insists that art is a parallel experience, not to be identified in any way with our experience of the external world ; but in Whitehead's words we would say that such parallelism is an illusion due to the suppression of intermediate links. The creation of a " new " reality is not within the scope of our human, time-conditioned faculties.

Let us now leave the realm of theory and try to trace what has actually happened in the evolution of art in the modern epoch. We shall not be able to leave ideas entirely out of account, because my main contention is that art has developed in stages that are parallel of the development of thought, and that both developments have intimate connections with social movements. Perhaps a few words will make clear to what extent the formal evolution of modern art has been " conditioned " by social and economic forces.

I have already drawn attention to the relative isolation of the artist in modern society. The general effect of the industrial revolution on art has been a gradual exclusion of the artist from the basic economic processes of production. This development may be said to begin with the capitalist system itself ; that is to say, with the accumulation of individual wealth. The way in which, from the fifteenth century onwards, the " patron " gradually forces his own personality, even his own person, into the work of art has often been remarked. At first he is the pious donor, humbly kneeling in an obscure corner of the picture ; but he gradually grows in size and importance until, in a painting like Holbein's *Virgin and Child with the Burgomaster Meyer and his family* (1526), he is painted on the same scale as the holy figures. Man is as good as God—as a theme for the artist. This humanism gave rise to the development of schools of portrait painting and historical painting which, for three centuries, constituted the main substance of the plastic arts. But such a development left the artist in a precarious position—dependent, not on the social organism as such (his position during the Middle Ages), but on the patronage of a limited class within that organism. For most of this time he maintained vitalizing contacts with the general processes of production—in our sense of the word he was still an industrial artist who might on occasion turn his hand to the design of metal work, furniture or tapestries. But by the time the industrial revolution was complete, the artist was cut off from even these subsidiary activities and had become parasitically dependent on his patron.

In such a situation the artist might react in several ways. He might become sycophantic, adopting the point of view of his patron, supporting the existing structure of society, supplying works of art designed to satisfy the tastes and flatter the vanity of his clients. Such, in general, is the bourgeois art of the eighteenth and nineteenth centuries. But such, also, is a situation that implies the progressive degradation of art. No longer drawing any inspiration or force from the organic wholeness of society, the art in such a situation becomes anaemic and sophisticated, and, in any spiritual sense, purposeless. The basis of patronage may spread more widely, as it did throughout the nineteenth century, but the result will only be an art measured to the mean capacities of *l'homme moyen sensuel.* Just as according to the Marxists, capitalism contains in itself the seeds of its own inevitable destruction, so (more certainly, even) such a relation between the artist and society involves inevitable decadence.

The artist who resists such decadence may react in two distinct ways. If he is socially conscious, he may revolt against the social situation as such and become a revolutionary artist—that is to say, an artist who consciously uses his art to reform the social situation. That type of artist is rare—it implies a use of art in the service of preconceived *ideas* which the true artist cannot accept. Even Courbet, in a political sense probably the most revolutionary artist of the nineteenth century, held that " the art of painting can consist only in the representation of objects visible and tangible to the painter " and that " art is completely individual, and that the talent of each artist is but the result of his own inspiration and his own study of past tradition " (Open letter to a group of prospective students, 1861). But the same social situation produces in the artist a state of mind in which he turns from what he regards as the false aesthetic values of the past to seek new aesthetic values more consonant with the developing social consciousness of his fellow-citizens. Constable was not politically minded, but when he wrote (Notes for his lectures at the Royal Institution, May 26, 1836) that art " is *scientific* as well as *poetic* ; that imagination never did, and never can, produce works that are to stand by a comparison with *realities*," he was expressing a revolutionary sentiment, a revolt against the art of Boucher which in its turn had been the expression of another and very different social situation. This attitude is still more clearly expressed in a note of June 16, 1836 :

> I have endeavoured to draw a line between genuine art and mannerism, but even the greatest painters have never been wholly untainted by manner.—Painting is a science, and should be pursued as an enquiry into the laws of nature. Why, then, may not landscape be considered as a branch of natural philosophy, of which pictures are but experiments ?

On that " experimental " note the modern epoch is announced, and never from that moment until comparatively recently has the artist relented in his experimental attitude. Exactly seventy years later we find Cézanne writing in almost the same terms as Constable (letter of September 21, 1906) :

> Shall I ever reach the goal so eagerly sought and so long pursued ? I hope so, but as long as it has not been attained a vague feeling of discomfort persists which will not disappear until I shall have gained the harbour—that is, until I shall have accomplished something more promising than what has gone before, thereby verifying my theories, which, in themselves, are easy to put forth. The only thing that is really difficult is to prove what one believes. So I am going on with my researches...
>
> (Trans. Gerstle MACK.)

Research, experiment—these words describe the efforts of all the great artists that fall within these seventy years—Millet, Courbet, Manet, Degas, Monet, Pissarro, Renoir, Rodin, Whistler, Seurat, Van Gogh—it is all a persistent attempt to correlate art and reality. It is the research, not of the absolute, but of the concrete, of the *image*, and behind it all is not only the divorce of the artist from the processes of production, but also the concurrent attempt to establish a philosophy of reality, a phenomenalism that owes nothing to divine revelation or universal truths, but brings to the analysis of human existence the same faculties that the artist brings to the analysis of nature. Constable, Cézanne, Picasso—Hegel, Husserl, Heidegger ; these names represent parallel movements in the evolution of human experience.

But this movement, in art, was not to remain unchallenged. To the image as representation is opposed, as we have seen, the symbol as interpretation, and there is no doubt that the " synthétisme " of Bernard and Gauguin was a conscious reaction against the scientific attitude in art. The theoretical basis of this reaction was given in the definition of " synthétisme " by Bernard already quoted, but what that theory involved in practice was first shown by Gauguin. We can best appreciate the antithetical nature of the contradiction by considering what form and colour meant respectively for Cézanne and Gauguin.

Both artists went through an Impressionist phase, and their divergence developed as they felt dissatisfaction with the results of their practice of the impressionist technique. Both artists, incidentally, found a meeting-place in Pissarro, who is the chief *point de repère* for the whole revolution. What Cézanne learned from Pissarro was of fundamental importance for his subsequent development, but it did not affect the direction taken by that development. Cézanne felt that the analytical methods of the Impressionists had led to a certain dissolution of reality ; they had, as it were, realized the vitality of objects, the vibrancy of light, the vividness of colour, at the cost of the essential nature of those objects—their solidity—indeed, their reality. The analysis of light and colour had led to a separation of colour and form, and this Cézanne felt to be a betrayal of the painter's function. Without sacrificing the real advances made by the Impressionists, he set himself the task of realizing and presenting the solid structure of objects. He arrived at a method which he called " modulation " (as distinct from the Impressionists' " modelling ") in which volume was represented by local colour changes. His own words must be quoted :

> For progress towards realization there is nothing but nature, and the eye becomes educated through contact with her. It becomes concentric through observation and work ; I mean that in an orange, an apple, a sphere, a head, there is a focal point, and this point is always nearest to our eye, no matter how it is affected by light, shade, sensations of colour. The edges of objects recede towards a centre located on our horizon.
>
> (Letter of 25 July, 1904. Trans. Gerstle MACK.)

This rather obscure passage is illuminated by a letter of December 23 of the same year :

> This I declare to be indisputable—I am very dogmatic : an optical sensation is produced in our visual organ which causes us to grade the planes represented by sensations of colour into full light, half-tones and quarter-tones (light does not exist for the painter). Necessarily, while we are proceeding from black to white, the first of these abstractions being a sort of point of departure for the eye as well as for the brain, we are floundering, we do not succeed in mastering ourselves, in ruling over ourselves. During this period—we go to the great masterpieces the ages have handed down to us, and we find in them a solace and a support.
>
> (Trans. Gerstle MACK.)

One further quotation, for it is essential for an understanding of the origins of modern art to be quite sure that we first understand what Cézanne was after :

> Now the idea to be insisted on is—no matter what our temperament or power in the presence of nature—to produce the image of what we see, forgetting everything that has been done before. Which, I believe, should enable the artist to express his entire personality, great or small.
>
> Now that I am old, almost seventy, the sensations of colour which produce light are a source of distraction, which do not permit me to cover my canvas or to define the delimitations of objects when the points of contact are so tenuous, fragile ; the result is that my image or picture is incomplete. Then again the planes are superimposed on one another, from which springs the Neo-impressionist system of outlining the contours with a black line, an error which should be opposed with all our strength. Now if we consult nature we shall find a way to solve this problem.
>
> (Trans. Gerstle MACK.)

" I regret my advanced age, on account of my sensations of colour "—such was the recurrent complaint of Cézanne in his last years. He felt a certain opposition between the surface sensuousness of objects and their real nature—his eyes were, as it were, dazzled by the brilliance of light and colour. Light and colour were not the same thing as *lucidity*. (" I am becoming more lucid in the presence of nature, but—the realization of my sensations is always painful. I cannot reach the intensity which appears to my senses...")—(September 8, 1906.) And then, in his final letter to Bernard, who significantly enough was the *agent provocateur* in this struggle for theoretical expression (significantly, because he played the same role for

Gauguin), he says : " I am progressing towards the logical development of what we see and feel by studying nature ; a consideration of processes comes later, processes being for us nothing but simple methods for making the public feel what we ourselves feel, and for making ourselves intelligible."

There were, therefore, in Cézanne's final phase, two stages in the production of a work of art : first, the realization of sensations, by which he meant a " logical " analysis of percepts, of what the eye actually sees ; second, processes by means of which this analysis could be presented to the public.

Cézanne was an extremely intelligent but simple man, and his efforts to explain his intuitive processes are not very clear. What in his stumbling way he seems to have grasped is the principle of the " good Gestalt." Without going too far into the theory of perception than would be justified in a general essay of this kind, it is difficult to give a convincing account of this term, but the underlying idea is that visual perception itself only makes sense, only becomes coherent, by virtue of an organizing faculty within the nervous system. We should not be able to cope with the multiplicity of impressions which the eye receives were we not, at the same time, capable of organizing these impressions into a coherent pattern. In the words of a Gestalt psychologist : " Perception tends towards balance and symmetry—or differently expressed : balance and symmetry are perceptual characteristics of the visual world which will be realized whenever the external conditions allow it ; when they do not, unbalance, lack of symmetry, will be experienced as a characteristic of objects or the whole field, together with a felt urge towards better balance... the stimulations which under ordinary circumstances affect our eyes are perfectly haphazard from the point of view of the visual organizations to which they may give rise. The organism... does the best it can under the prevailing conditions, and these conditions will not, as a rule, allow it to do a very good job (good, from the point of view of aesthetic harmony). A work of art, on the other hand, is made with that very idea ; once completed it serves as a source of stimulation specifically selected for its aesthetic effect." K. Koffka. " Problems in the Psychology of Art." *Art : a Bryn Mawr Symposium, 1940.*

Before Cézanne the principle of composition in painting was architectonic—the picture-space was " organized " as an architect organizes his building, and inevitably questions of balance and symmetry were taken into consideration. Cézanne's paintings are analysed and criticised as if they conformed to this principle, and such a method does indeed " work," though it ignores the essential virtue in Cézanne's compositions. For architectonic composition is *a priori ;* it fits the objects of perception into a pre-conceived pattern, a system of perspective and elevation, which is not necessarily inherent in perception itself. A landscape by Claude or Turner is as artificial as a garden, and as much the result of intellectual preconceptions. But a landscape by Cézanne begins with no preconceptions—nothing but the direct contact of eye and nature, and the " composition " is determined by what happens " in the eye "—the automatic selection of a focal point, limitation of boundaries, subordination of details and colours to the law of the whole. The " whole " is the *Gestalt,* but the psychologists recognize that the process does not end there—that there are " good " and less good Gestalts. " It is characteristic of a good *gestalt* not only that it produces a hierarchical unity of its parts, but also that this unity is of a particular kind. A good *gestalt* cannot be changed without changing its quality... in a masterpiece of painting no line, no form, no colour, can anywhere be changed without detracting from the quality of the picture." (Koffka, *op. cit.,* 247-48).

I think there is no doubt whatsoever that Cézanne was trying to realize the good *gestalt.* By intuitive processes he has hit upon a scientific truth which psychology subsequently discovered by experimental research. Cézanne, therefore, still remains within the characteristic development of nineteenth century art—as much as Constable he is an artist who regards landscape painting as a branch of natural philosophy. But Cézanne's natural philosophy was not destined to be understood by many of his followers, and it was largely on a misinterpretation of his purpose that cubism came into being (its subsequent development is another question). But before we discuss the influence of Cézanne let us return to the challenge to the scientific attitude in art made by Gauguin.

One's first inclination is to treat Gauguin as an artist altogether inferior to Cézanne. We cannot doubt his integrity or his sincerity, and the sacrifices he made for his art were certainly as great as Cézanne's. The contrast between the two artists lies in the field of sensibility, of technical accomplishment. Certainly some hard things can be said about Gauguin's technique. He despised the whole business of what he called "counting the hairs on the donkey." He had been an Impressionist and had sat at the feet of Pissarro; but his reaction was violent. "The impressionists study colour exclusively, but without freedom, always shackled by the need of probability. For them the ideal landscape, created from many different entities, does not exist. They look and perceive harmoniously, but without aim. Their edifice rests upon no solid base and ignores the nature of the sensation perceived by means of colour. They heed only the eye and neglect the mysterious centres of thought, so falling into merely scientific reasoning."—(*Intimate Journals*, trans. Van Wyck Brooks, p. 132-34). Form was not to be found in nature, but in the imagination. "It is well for young men to have a model, but let them draw the curtain over it while they are painting. It is better to paint from memory, for thus your work will be your own; your sensation, your intelligence, and your soul will triumph over the eye of the amateur." (*Ibid.*, p. 71, New York Edition, 1936). At every point Gauguin contradicts Cézanne, a fact understood better by Cézanne than by Gauguin. "He never understood me," said Cézanne. "I have never desired and I shall never accept the absence of modelling or of gradation; it's nonsense. Gauguin was not a painter, he only made Chinese images." To which Gauguin would have replied (in words he wrote to Daniel de Monfreid): "The great error is the Greek, however beautiful it may be... Keep the Persians, the Cambodians, and a bit of the Egyptians always in mind." (October 1897.) Or: "It is the eye of ignorance that assigns a fixed and unchangeable colour to every object... Practice painting an object in conjunction with, or shadowed by—that is to say, close to or half behind—other objects of similar or different colours. In this way you will please by your variety and your truthfulness—your own. Go from dark to light, from light to dark. The eye seeks to refresh itself through your work: give it food for enjoyment, not dejection... Let everything about you breathe the calm and peace of the soul. Also avoid motion in a pose. Each of your figures ought to be in a static position... Study the silhouette of every object; distinctness of outline is the attribute of the hand that is not enfeebled by any hesitation of the will... Do not finish your work too much..." One could go on building up the contradictions, but they all amount to this: *the laws of beauty do not reside in the verities of nature.* The work of art is in some sense a suggestive symbol, stirring our emotions rather than stimulating our sensations.

Between these two points of view, these two distinct conceptions of art, there can be no compromise. Most of the contradictions and varieties of modern art spring from their antithetical opposition. No synthesis within the realm of art seems to be possible; it is not obvious why it should be desirable.

The situation as it developed towards the end of the century was not, however, to remain a simple antithesis. If, for the sake of brevity, we describe the aim of Cézanne as the representation of the real, and that of Gauguin as the creation of beauty, there still remained another ideal of which Van Gogh became the leading exponent. Provisionally we might call it the expression of emotion, but the phrase needs a particular definition. The word *express*, however, inevitably recurs in all our attempts at definition, and Expressionism is the name which has been given to this tendency in modern art. " To *express* the love of two lovers by a marriage of two complementary colours, their mingling and their opposition, the mysterious vibrations of kindred tones. To *express* the thought of a brow by the radiance of a light tone against a sombre background. To *express* hope by some star, the eagerness of a soul by sunset radiance. Certainly there is nothing in that of stereoscopic realism, but is it not something that actually exists ? "—these words of Van Gogh written at Arles in 1888 show the beginnings of a divergence of aim which in the years to follow was to modify profoundly the evolution of modern art.

Such a humanistic ideal in art was, of course, no new thing. It goes back to Rembrandt, if not farther, and in this tradition are such painters as Delacroix, Millet and Israels—all favourites of Van Gogh. Even Courbet and Manet contribute to the tradition, though their main significance lies elsewhere. Another quotation from Van Gogh's letters will serve to define this tradition and separate it from contemporary trends like Impressionism :

> What a mistake Parisians make in not having a palate for crude things, for Monticellis, for clay. But there, one must not lose heart because Utopia is not coming true. It is only that what I learned in Paris is leaving me, and that I am returning to the ideas I had in the country before I knew the impressionists. And I should not be surprised if the impressionists soon find fault with my way of working, for it has been fertilized by the ideas of Delacroix rather than by theirs. Because, *instead of trying to reproduce exactly what I have before my eyes, I use colour more arbitrarily so as to express myself forcibly.* Well, let that be as far as theory goes, but I am going to give you an example of what I mean.
>
> I should like to paint the portrait of an artist friend, a man who dreams great dreams, who works as the nightingale sings, because it is his nature. He'll be a fair man. I want to put into the picture my appreciation, the love that I have for him. So I paint him as he is, as faithfully as I can, to begin with.
>
> But the picture is not finished yet. To finish it I am now going to be the arbitrary colourist. I exaggerate the fairness of the hair, I come even to orange tones, chromes and pale lemon yellow.
>
> Beyond the head, instead of painting the ordinary wall of the mean room, I paint infinity, a plain background of the richest intensest blue that I can contrive, and by this simple combination of the bright head against the rich blue background, I get a mysterious effect, like a star in the depths of an azure sky.
>
> In the portrait of the peasant again I worked in this way, but without wishing in this case to produce the mysterious brightness of a pale star in the infinite. Instead, I think of the man I have to paint, terrible in the furnace of the full harvest, the full south. Hence the stormy orange shades, vivid as red hot iron, and hence the luminous tones of old gold in the shadows.
>
> Oh, my dear boy... and the nice people will only see the exaggeration as caricature.
>
> (Letter 520).

The whole theory of Expressionism, in its strength and weakness, is in this letter. Its strength lies in its humanism—in the fact that art cannot be limited to the search for any absolute, whether of reality or beauty, but must ever return to the essential dignity of our common human qualities, our human nature. It weakness lies in the imprecision of its terminology—in words like mystery and infinity which, when it comes to the point of translation into practice, into terms of form and colour, have no real meaning. There are no " infinite " shades of blue, and brightness is no mystery—that, at least, would have been Cézanne's opinion. Gauguin would have been more in sympathy with this language, but he was not really interested in painting a postman, for example, " as I feel him," but rather in using any suitable model for the creation of an independent aesthetic entity, a work of art which creates and contains its own emotional values and is not dependent on the evaluation of a human context. For Gauguin the work of art, as a symbol, must be detached from any particular occasion, just as a crucifix is detached from the Crucifixion.

Van Gogh had no immediate following in France. It was in the far North, in Scandinavia and later in Germany that Expressionism had its widest expansion. Here the dominant figure is the Norwegian Edvard Munch. Munch was born ten years later than Van Gogh (in 1863) and he may to some extent have been inspired by the Dutchman. There is certainly a close affinity of aim, and even of style, between the two artists. But a countryman of Ibsen's had really no need of external inspiration, and though Munch modified his style after his visits to France, he may be said to have been born with the desire to express himself forcibly. His scope, however, is not quite the same as Van Gogh's ; it is more objective. It is true that he could write in his diary in 1889 words which are quite reminiscent of those we have quoted from Van Gogh's letter of the previous year : " No more painting of interiors with men reading and women knitting ! They must be living people who breathe, feel, suffer and love. I will paint a series of such pictures, in which people will have to recognize the holy element and bare their heads before it, as though in church." (Quoted by J. P. Hodin, *Edvard Munch,* Stockholm—Neuer Verlag—1948, p. 28.) But in Munch's subsequent paintings, as in the work of the expressionist school generally, there is an element of despair, leading to remorseless analysis and masochism, which was not characteristic of Van Gogh. This Kierkegaardian morbidity in Expressionism is a sufficient explanation of its failure to appeal more strongly to the Latin races. There is plenty of wonder in Expressionism, but little joy.

Und ich wiederhole : naturferne Kunst ist
publikumsfremde Kunst. Muss es sein.

Wilhelm WORRINGER.

It has not been my aim in this Introduction to mention every artist of importance, or even to produce one of those charts in which every movement has its appropriate graph. The truth is obscured by such rigid complexities. It is the broad effects that are significant for my present purpose, and these are complex enough. If I have succeeded, the reader will be conscious of a stream which runs fairly consistently through a tract of time measuring about a century, widening as it approaches the sea. But this stream is carrying down with it the sands and pebbles that have ineffectually opposed its progress. This silt accumulates as the river is about to attain its end, blocks the flow and creates a delta—the one stream becomes many separate streams. But here the metaphor breaks down, for the separate streams do not make their way fanwise to the ultimate sea ; some turn inland again and are lost in the deserts of futurity.

This diversion in modern art is due to the failure of the scientific attitude in art. It has not proved possible, or at any rate finally satisfying, to consider art as " a branch of natural philosophy, of which pictures are but experiments." In art, " l'exactitude n'est pas la vérité." " We all know that art is not truth. Art is a lie that makes us realize truth, at least the truth that is given us to understand." (Picasso.) Art is a closed system, and it is " true " in the degree that its rhetoric convinces us, pleases us, comforts us. It has no spiritual mission ; it is accused of having no social function.

The artists themselves have recognized their isolation. " Uns trägt kein Volk," cried Klee—the people are not with us. But it is useless to blame the artist for that isolation —we might as well blame the weathercock for not turning in the wind. (It is true, there is a kind of weathercock that does not turn because its hinges are rusty—the academic artist.) The climate of the age (Zeitgeist, usw.) is the creation of a thousand forces, and perhaps the Marxists are right in giving priority, among these forces, to economic trends. But the failure of the Soviet Union, after more than thirty years of strenuous effort, to produce a new art on the basis of a new economy proves that the inspiration of the artist cannot be forced. We must wait, wait perhaps for a very long time, before any vital connection can be re-established between art and society. The modern work of art, as I have said, is a symbol. The symbol, by its nature, is only intelligible to the initiated (though it may still appeal mysteriously to the uninitiated, so long as they allow it to enter their unconscious). The people can only understand the image, and even this they distrust in its eidetic purity, for even their vision is conventional. It does not seem that the contradiction which exists between the aristocratic function of art and the democratic structure of modern society can ever be resolved. But both may wear the cloak of humanism, the one for shelter, the other for display. The sensitive artist knows that a bitter wind is blowing.

HISTORY OF MODERN PAINTING

BY

MAURICE RAYNAL

DOCUMENTATION
HISTORICAL AND BIOGRAPHICAL STUDIES
BY

JEAN LEYMARIE

1858-1870

1858 Eugène Boudin meets young Claude Monet at Le Havre; guides his early efforts.

1859 Meeting of Monet and Pissarro at the **Académie Suisse.**
Courbet, Boudin and Baudelaire at "Mère Toutain's" Ferme Saint-Siméon, at Honfleur.
Baudelaire's review of the 1859 Salon. He speaks in praise of Boudin, "roi des ciels."
Birth of Georges Seurat, Paris (December 2).

1860 Large-scale private exhibition of Modern Painting (Delacroix, Corot, Courbet, Millet).

1861 Edouard Manet's début at the Salon **(Le Guitarrero)**: he meets Baudelaire, exhibits at the Galerie Martinet.
Paul Cézanne's first stay in Paris. He meets Pissarro at the Académie Suisse.
Degas paints academic compositions: **Sémiramis** (Louvre, Paris).

1862 Manet paints his **Musique aux Tuileries** (National Gallery, London), strikes up a friendship with Degas.
Monet at Le Havre with Boudin and Johann Barthold Jongkind. Monet, Renoir, Sisley, Bazille meet at **Gleyre's studio.**
Degas paints **Horse Races** at Longchamp, for the first time.

1863 **Salon des Refusés.** Violent attacks on Manet: **Le Déjeuner sur l'herbe** (Louvre, Paris).
Death of Eugène Delacroix (August 13). Fantin-Latour pays him a tribute.
Renoir, with Fantin-Latour, spends much time at the Louvre.
Reorganization of the Ecole des Beaux-Arts.

1864 Pissarro exhibits at the Salon; describes himself as 'Corot's pupil.' Stays at Montfoucault.
Monet at Honfleur with Boudin, Jongkind; he invites Bazille to join them.
Renoir, painting in the forest of Fontainebleau, meets Diaz and undergoes his influence for a while.
Birth of Toulouse-Lautrec at Albi (November 24).

1865 Proudhon's death. Posthumous publication of his **Principe de l'Art.** Zola visits Courbet.
Manet exhibits **Olympia** (Louvre, Paris), travels in Spain, meets Duret in Madrid.
Monet with Bazille at Chailly (forest of Fontainebleau), with Courbet at Trouville.
Renoir and Sisley at Marlotte (forest of Fontainebleau).

1866 Meeting at the **Café Guerbois**. Zola's articles in the newspaper "L'Evénement."
Monet finds favour at the Salon **(Camille),** meets Manet, works at Sainte-Adresse and Le Havre.
Renoir shares Bazille's studio, at Marlotte paints his **Cabaret de la Mère Anthony** (Stockholm).
Monet paints his **Women in the Garden,** Bazille his **Family Gathering** (Louvre, Paris).
Cézanne, persistently rejected by the Salon, protests to the Director of Fine Arts.
Pissarro breaks away from Corot, settles at Pontoise.

1867 **World's Fair.** Manet and Courbet give one-man shows in special "pavilions."
Extreme severity of the Salon Jury: all Impressionists, save Degas, banned.
Renoir at Chantilly and Fontainebleau. Sisley at Honfleur. Monet at Sainte-Adresse.
Deaths of Charles Baudelaire and Jean-Dominique Ingres.
Birth of Pierre Bonnard, at Fontenay-aux-Roses (October 13).

1868 Manet exhibits **Portrait of Zola,** stays at Boulogne; in England; meets Berthe Morisot.
Monet in Paris with Renoir and Bazille; at Etretat, Fécamp. Poverty: attempted suicide.
Renoir's success at the Salon: **Lise** (Folkwang Museum, Essen); he paints Bazille's, Sisley's portraits.
"International Maritime Exhibition" at Le Havre (Boudin, Manet, Monet, Courbet).
Degas begins to go to the theatre for his subjects: **Mlle Fiocre** (Brooklyn Museum, New York).

1869 Manet exhibits **The Balcony** (Louvre, Paris); again spends summer at Boulogne (seascapes).
Renoir and Monet at Bougival. **La Grenouillère.** Birth of the Impressionist technique.
Pissarro moves with his family to Louveciennes. Cézanne paints **The Black Clock.**
Birth of Henri Matisse at Le Cateau (Nord) (December 31).

1870 **Franco-Prussian War.** Proclamation of the Third Republic.
Death of Bazille in the Battle of Beaune-la-Rolande (November 28).
Manet serves in the National Guard, Degas in the Infantry, Renoir in the Cuirassiers.
Cézanne at Aix, then at L'Estaque, near Marseilles.
Monet, Sisley, Pissarro in England; discover Turner, Constable; meet Durand-Ruel.

The Legacy of Courbet

While readily admitting the influence of Ingres, Delacroix, Constable and Corot on the course of Modern Painting, we have thought it best to place the name of Gustave Courbet in the forefront of this History, the reason being that, of all the masters of form and colour, Courbet is the one as to whose eminent priority all painters are in agreement. None, indeed but sees in him a past-master in that excellence of craftsmanship which is the lodestar of every professional artist. The daring and the power, the delicacy of execution and the sheer gorgeousness of his art opened up so many new vistas that even artists with radically different temperaments, such as Matisse and Picasso, join in regarding his work with that slightly envious deference which is accorded only to what is permanent in the *métier*.

The first-named, and chief, of these qualities—daring—has played a determining part in the evolution of modern painting. Courbet's zest for freedom—it was second nature with him never to make concessions to the narrowly traditional—acted as a vital ferment in the art of all who followed him. But he did not live to see Impressionism. He died in 1877 in Switzerland where he had been living in exile since 1873, the French police "wanting" him for his alleged participation in the dismantling of the Vendôme Column. Perhaps, however, he foresaw Impressionism's coming when he forgathered with Boudin and Monet in 1859, usually at the *Brasserie des Martyrs*, where Baudelaire, Daudet, de Banville and Jules Vallès also were often to be seen. It was his influence which led the young painters to that exaltation of the instinct (as above the intellect) which has determined the whole course of modern art. In any case by pointing to the absurdities of the then fashionable "Idealism," Courbet forced painters to face up to the *reality* of human bodies, of earth and sky and flowing water, and his programme was far bolder and more drastic than the half-hearted ventures of such men as Constable and Bonington. Thus Impressionists and, after them, Expressionists were far readier to fall in with his injunctions, all the readier for being more thorough, for an ever closer analysis of the visible world. It was Courbet who led them on to scrutinize reality with the objectivity and clean-cut precision which are now among the chief concerns of the world we live in, and especially of painting. So much so that many of his successors called in science to help them in exploring the new field of forms and colour Courbet had opened up, though on empirical, "unscientific" lines. If Baudelaire, esthete though he was, and preferring Delacroix to Courbet, so much admired him, this was because he had been swept off his feet by the sheer driving force of Courbet's art ; this revelation of the creative power of instinct had overwhelmed, for once, his deference to the rational.

Not that Courbet invariably rejected the dictates of the intellect. But Courbet's intellect was that of the countryman—he came of a farming family—and differed from Baudelaire's as does a plain man's simple faith from the faith of a theologian. Due, indeed, to his faith in painting was his regard for that perfect craftsmanship which in the last analysis lies at the base of art, the painter's "one thing needful." But it was left to Modern Art to discover that no renewal of the art of painting can dispense with painstaking research-work into the *matière*, the physical stuff of painting.

That is why, beyond all methods and consciously planned techniques, Courbet stands out as the harbinger of the *matière* of modern painting, as Victor Hugo was of that of words. And the habit of the *morceau* the subject chosen in the living world around him, which he inaugurated (and to which the "liberties" taken by the Impressionists were to owe so much), freed art from the thrall of a tradition which looked to Courbet as effete as the social order it had sponsored.

G. COURBET (1819-1877). PORTRAIT OF BAUDELAIRE (DETAIL), 1853. 24×20¾". MONTPELLIER, MUSÉE FABRE.

BAUDELAIRE (1821-1867), POET AND MASTER-CRITIC, FRIEND OF ALL GREAT ARTISTS FROM DELACROIX TO MANET, FORESAW AND DEFINED ALL MODERN SENSIBILITY, STARTING FROM "ROMANTIC" AESTHETICS. "WHAT," HE ASKED, "IS PURE ART ACCORDING TO OUR MODERN CONCEPTION? IT IS THE CREATION OF A SUGGESTIVE MAGIC CONTAINING AT ONCE THE OBJECT AND THE SUBJECT, THE WORLD OUTSIDE THE ARTIST AND THE ARTIST HIMSELF."

CONTACTS AND INFLUENCES

It was under Courbet's dynamic influence that the young innovators destined to go down to history as " Impressionists " broke with the past. Feeling ill at ease in the gloomy Parisian studios (in which they soon marked each other out amongst the nondescript crowd of academic-minded students, and accordingly joined forces), they migrated, once the weather had turned fair, first to the Forest of Fontainebleau, and then to the Channel coast, where they could work in the open and rub shoulders with two precursors of the older generation, Boudin and Jongkind, who were ushering in a new kind of painting, flooded with limpid light. And Courbet in person presided at these stimulating gatherings of what came to be known as the Saint-Siméon pre-Impressionist School, at Honfleur.

THE " SUISSE " ACADEMY

Thus named after its founder, a M. Suisse. A squalid room, located on the Quai des Orfèvres near the Pont Saint-Michel, in which artists could work from the living model for a small sum, without tuition or examination, it provided a sort of free training for the Ecole des Beaux-Arts. *It was here that Pissarro, the oldest of impressionist group, who had been frequenting this establishment since 1855, made Monet's acquaintance in 1859 (before Monet left for his spell of military service in Algeria), and, in 1861, that of Cézanne, who had just come to Paris from his hometown, Aix-en-Provence, and whom he promptly and powerfully influenced.*

GLEYRE'S STUDIO

Here the master was authentically Swiss, a pillar of academicism and a severe teacher. In 1862 four young men, all under twenty-five and all destined to become famous, met here and struck up a friendship that was to endure : Monet hailing from Le Havre, Bazille from Montpellier, Renoir a Parisian, and Sisley an Englishman. On one occasion Gleyre asked young Renoir sarcastically if he painted "just to amuse himself." Renoir replied that he had never dreamt of painting for any other reason. Rebellious by nature and realizing that there was nothing to be learned here, the four artists left this studio after a year, and migrated in the spring of 1863 to the Forest of Fontainebleau, and next summer to Normandy. It is significant that Monet, boldest of the group and leader-to-be, was already recognized as their moving spirit, and actively promoted contacts between the Gleyre studio and the " Suisse " Academy on the one hand, and the Honfleur group on the other.

THE FOREST OF FONTAINEBLEAU

Brought into fashion by the Romantics, the Forest of Fontainebleau was now the favourite resort of independent landscape-painters of the Barbizon School (Rousseau, Diaz, Millet). It was in contact with them, and in this romantic setting of trees and crags, that the Impressionists tried their 'prentice hands at landscape. Their style was still naturalistic, combining the influences of Corot and of Courbet, both of whom knew this forest well.

1863. *Monet and Bazille take their holidays at Chailly, near Barbizon, on the outskirts of the forest.*

1864. *At Monet's instigation the four young rebels from Gleyre's studio meet at Chailly, where Renoir now makes Diaz' acquaintance.*

1865. *Monet starts painting his* Déjeuner sur l'herbe *(a sketch for which is in the Modern Art Museum, Moscow), for which Bazille poses. Courbet introduces them to Corot. Renoir is staying near by, with Sisley, at Marlotte.*

1866. *Monet finishes his composition. Renoir paints his* Cabaret de la Mère Anthony, *now in the National Museum, Stockholm, while Sisley paints views of the village.*

1867. *Still under the influence of Courbet Renoir does figures in the open : his* Lise *(Folkwang Museum, Essen), which won approval in the next year's Salon, and his* Portrait of Sisley and his Wife *(Walraf Richartz Museum, Cologne).*

Pissarro did not actually work at Fontainebleau, but sometimes visited his friends there. Cézanne, last, it seems, to " discover " the forest, was to remain faithful to it the longest; every time he came to Paris, up to his last visit (in 1904), he never failed to make a trip to Fontainebleau.

The Seine estuary, so popular at the beginning of the century with British watercolour painters and thereafter with the Romantics (Huet, Bonington, Delacroix), and finally with Corot, was, between 1860 and 1870, the true cradle of Impressionism. It was in this environment of sea and limpid light that the new technique and the new way of seeing took their rise, under the influence of two precursors, Boudin and Jongkind.

1858. *Boudin (1825-1898), a painter of sunlit, shimmering seascapes, dubbed by Baudelaire "Monarch of the Sky," hailed from this part of France, Honfleur being his birthplace. There he met his young neighbour Monet, who hailed from Le Havre and had made something of a name locally with his caricatures. This meeting decided Monet's vocation. "It was as if a veil had been torn from my eyes," Monet was to say in later years. "In a flash I saw what painting really meant."*

1859. *Courbet, on a visit to Le Havre accompanied by Schanne, another painter, "discovers" Boudin, who takes him to Mère Toutain's famous inn at the Ferme Saint-Siméon. When out walking together they meet Baudelaire who, like Courbet, is greatly struck by Boudin's painting, and praises it in his review of the 1859 Salon.*

1862. *Jongkind (1819-1891), a Dutch painter, famed for his luminous, boldy executed sketches, returns to these parts (where he had previously stayed, in 1850). Monet makes his acquaintance, introduces him to Boudin and the three painters work together.*

1863. *Jongkind spends the greater part of this year at Honfleur.*

1864. *Bazille, Monet, Boudin join forces with Jongkind at Honfleur. "Boudin and Jongkind are here," Monet announced to a friend. "We get on splendidly together—and there's much to be learnt in such company."*

1865. *Monet is painting, in Courbet's company, at Trouville.*

1867. *Monet is now at Sainte-Adresse (near Le Havre); Sisley at Honfleur.*

1870. *Monet returns to Trouville and Le Havre; then crosses over to England.*

IN JONGKIND AND IN MOST LANDSCAPE-PAINTERS OF THE EARLY XIXth CENTURY WE FIND A CONTRAST BETWEEN THEIR PAINTINGS WHICH ARE STUDIO-MADE, AND THE SKETCHES THEY MADE STRAIGHT FROM LIFE, ON THE SPOT, THESE LATTER BEING MUCH FREER, MORE PROGRESSIVE. AND THE ACHIEVEMENT OF IMPRESSIONISM WAS PRECISELY THIS, THAT IT RETAINED IN THE PICTURE THE VIVACITY AND FRESHNESS OF THE SKETCH, AND GENERALIZED IN PAINTING THE SPONTANEITY OF THE WATERCOLOUR. THE GONCOURT BROTHERS NOTED HOW DECISIVE WAS JONGKIND'S INFLUENCE AND OBSERVED IN THEIR *JOURNAL*: ALL LANDSCAPES OF ANY VALUE TO-DAY STEM FROM THIS PAINTER, BORROW HIS SKIES, HIS ATMOSPHERE, HIS SCENES.

J. B. JONGKIND (1819-1891). VIEW OF ROUEN, WATERCOLOUR, 1864. 11¾×18¾". LOUVRE, PARIS.

"For a figure see that you have full light, full shade; all the rest will come naturally; it often amounts to very little."

MANET

As member of a well-established family—his father was a magistrate—, Manet may have felt a little out of place in the Impressionist group, who made no secret of their revolutionary leanings. While frankly ambitious and no mean wit, he was always readily accessible and never " let down " a friend. He was not discouraged by the ill success that dogged him. Endowed with a well-balanced mind, he never set up to be a prophet or precursor. His life, which was simple, crystal-clear, is mirrored in his straightforward way of painting in full light with his subjects lit up from in front ; and in his habit of using those local colours which his Impressionist friends were soon to abolish utterly.

As a young man respectful of tradition, Manet began by visiting the chief art museums of Europe. He developed a liking for the interplay of blacks and white, the *arcana* of light-and-shade, and those silver-fox greys which so well accorded with his personal refinement. Throughout his life he was held by the charm of these neutral hues, and his impressionist friends' quest of pure tones never lured him from them.

One of Daumier's lithographs shows us two artists painting the same subject, one behind the other, with the caption : " The man in front is copying nature, the man behind is copying the man in front." Behind the obvious jest Daumier may well have had in mind a not uncommon form of aesthetic practice, and we might say, without the least wish to disparage the artist, that in a way it sums up the dazzling art of Manet—who had a taste for paradoxical procedure. Thus he began by taking over subjects already treated, from Titian's day to Goya's ; but he neither copies, nor imitates—he *remakes*. For him—and this was a sign of the times—the subject was losing its importance. But all these past-inspired canvases bear the stamp of Manet's personal and unique genius.

Soon he became very friendly with the Impressionists, though less enamoured of their programme. For one thing, he fought shy of their cult of painting in the open, which conflicted with his notions of studio-produced art. However, he deferred to the advice of Monet, who urged him to get rid of the black of which he was so fond. But as to drawing and composition he stood his ground ; he was determined to keep his black contour-lines, his broad tracts of white. His friendship with Baudelaire led him to share, though with extreme caution, in his friend's taste for the " Satanic," which certainly influenced his *Berthe Morisot* (1872), *Olympia* (1863) and *Absinthe Drinker* (1859), amongst other canvases.

But this mild dalliance with the dark side of life was shortlived. His true personality found a new and brilliant outlet in his handling of perspective—so severely condemned by Courbet who insisted that " a picture must not be a playing-card." From now on Manet spreads his backgrounds with a thin coat of semi-transparent colour. When handling foregrounds and objects in full light he makes a point of using the local tone. Here we have, in effect, a rendering of space purely in terms of the relations between tones. Hence his uniformly bright surfaces, and planes superimposed in a calculated clash of tonal " dissonances." Manet was perhaps the first artist to attempt to endow colour and colour alone with the power of setting form free from the shackles of the past with its over-emphasis on the strictly " plastic "—by endeavouring to suppress the third dimension.

Here we certainly see the influence of Japanese art for which Manet had such enthusiasm that he included Japanese prints in some of his pictures. Debatable as always is the problem of " anticipation," one thing is certain : Manet must be regarded as a precursor of the developments in the handling of colour and composition which Gauguin, then Matisse (with " Fauvism ") and, lastly, Abstract Art, were to press to their utmost limit.

E. MANET (1832-1883). LE DÉJEUNER SUR L'HERBE, 1863. 84¼×106¼". LOUVRE, PARIS.

THIS IS THE MOST FAMOUS OF THE THREE "SCANDALOUS" PAINTINGS EXHIBITED BY MANET AT THE SALON DES REFUSÉS (THEN WITH *THE BATH* AS TITLE), THE EMPEROR HIMSELF DECLARING IT "IMMODEST." YET IT IS ONLY A RESTATEMENT OF A CLASSICAL THEME DEAR TO GIORGIONE AND TITIAN. WHAT SHOCKED WAS ITS MODERN, DARINGLY LIFELIKE PRESENTATION, WITHOUT ANY MYTHOLOGICAL "JUSTIFICATION"; ALSO ITS WHOLLY NOVEL TONAL CONTRASTS. A PRELIMINARY SKETCH IS IN THE COURTAULD COLLECTION (TATE GALLERY, LONDON). TWO YEARS LATER MONET PAINTED THE SAME SUBJECT ENTIRELY IN THE OPEN AIR (IN THE FOREST OF FONTAINEBLEAU), AND TWO OTHER VERSIONS, BY CÉZANNE, ARE EXTANT.

1863

Delacroix *dies in the very house (in the Place de Furstenberg) in which, two years later, Monet and Bazille were to share a studio. Fantin-Latour paints a "Homage" to the dead Master, placing Baudelaire and Manet in the forefront. Delacroix's intuitive discoveries in the field of colour had a compelling influence on the course of modern painting, and on the most diverse temperaments. Seurat, like Renoir, Matisse and Redon, admitted his debt to him. His direct influence on Impressionism and its aftermath was well brought out by Signac in the remarkable essay he published in 1899,* From Eugène Delacroix to Neo-Impressionism.

Aside from the official Salon a Salon des Refusés *was now instituted, as an exceptional measure, in which figured amongst others, Manet, Pissarro, Jongkind, Whistler and Cézanne. The breach between living art and the general public now became absolute. The same people who raved about Cabanel's luscious* Venus *(bought by the Emperor) in the Salon guffawed or waxed indignant when confronted by Manet's luminous masterpieces. Manet, who had given a one-man show, previous to the Salon, at the Martinet Gallery, came to be regarded, rather against his wishes, as the "ringleader" of the group of young enthusiasts at Gleyre's studio. Thus, too, he was regarded by Cézanne and his friend Zola, when they visited these memorable Salons. In 1866 Cézanne and Zola were, as a result of the ruthless ostracism of the official Jury, to solicit the revival of the* Salon des Refusés, *but in vain.*

I. 4

E. MANET (1832-1883). PORTRAIT OF ZOLA, 1868. 43¾×31½". LOUVRE, PARIS.

IT IS TO ZOLA (1840-1902) THAT WE OWE THE FAMOUS DEFINITION: "A WORK OF ART IS AN ASPECT OF CREATION SEEN THROUGH THE MEDIUM OF A TEMPERAMENT." HIS CAREER AS AN ART-CRITIC BEGAN ON APRIL 27, 1866, WITH A BRILLIANT VINDICATION OF MANET'S ART (IN THE NEWSPAPER *L'ÉVÉNEMENT*), AND ENDED LAMENTABLY ON MAY 2, 1896, WITH A REPUDIATION OF IMPRESSIONISM, PUBLISHED IN THE *FIGARO*.

PAINTERS AND CRITICS. THE CAFÉ GUERBOIS. ZOLA

Though this tradition seems to be dying out, we must not overlook the important part that cafés used to play in the exchange of views between artists and men of letters. In those days most aesthetic theories were born in cafés. Manet, cynosure of youth since the uproar caused by the Salon des Refusés, *abandoned in 1866 the fashionable Café de Bade and took to visiting the famous Café Guerbois. Its most active period was 1868-1869 when every Friday evening there gathered around Manet, Astruc, Zola, Duranty, Duret, Guillemet, Braquemond, Bazille, Degas, Constantin Guys, Stevens, Renoir, Nadar the photographer, and, when they were in Paris, Pissarro, Monet and Sisley. To begin with Duranty took the lead at these meetings; then, from his first dramatic appearance, Emile Zola, who launched a strenuous press campaign on behalf of Manet and the young school—though later he abjured them. One wonders if he ever understood his friends, and if he could really appreciate their painting; considering that he once said, " I have no use for that word ' art '; what I want of you is Life." The result was that even well-meaning critics, misled by Zola's dogmatic* ... *inality and purely pictorial aspirations of Impressionism.*

PANESE COLOURPRINTS

ussions at the Café Guerbois, and none of the group failed ... *ir. The discovery of Japanese prints counted for as much* ... *pture in the shaping of Cubism. It was to Braquemond*

SUGATAMI SHICHI NIN KESHO (ONE OF THE " SEVEN WOMEN ... IIRROR "), C. 1790. 10×11". FORMER MUTIAUX COLLECTION.

· 5

foundly affected by it (note the boldly Japanese setting in the Portrait of Zola *here reproduced), and, in the next generation, Gauguin, Van Gogh and Lautrec. In 1873 Théodore Duret returned, full of enthusiasm, from a trip to Japan. " The Japanese," he said " are the first, and the supreme Impressionists."*

E. DEGAS (1834-1917). THE ORCHESTRA AT THE PARIS OPERA, C. 1868. 22½×18½". LOUVRE, PARIS.

"THE AIR WE SEE IN THE GREAT MASTERS' PICTURES," DEGAS SAID, "IS LITERALLY UNBREATHABLE." ANALYTIC-MINDED AND A SUPERB DRAUGHTSMAN, HE HAD NO INTEREST IN LANDSCAPE; HE APPLIED HIS KEEN VISION TO OBSERVING HUMAN BEHAVIOUR AND THE MECHANISM OF BODIES; TO EXPLORING PROBLEMS OF COMPOSITION AND THE "EFFECTS" OF ARTIFICIAL LIGHT. HIS FAVOURITE THEMES WERE THE THEATRE AND THE BALLET; THIS CANVAS SHOWS HIM AT A TURNING-POINT IN HIS CAREER. IN IT DEGAS DELIBERATELY FACED, AND SOLVED, A SERIES OF TECHNICAL AND PSYCHOLOGICALP ROBLEMS: HOW TO COMBINE A GROUP OF PROFESSIONAL PORTRAITS—THOSE OF THE MUSICIANS IN THE ORCHESTRA PIT OF THE PARIS OPERA—, WHILE BRINGING OUT EACH INDIVIDUALITY, AND STRESSING THAT OF HIS FRIEND DÉSIRÉ D'IHAU, THE BASSOONIST, WITHOUT IMPAIRING THE ENSEMBLE.

The anomaly of Degas

Courbet, and he alone, championed vigorously the supremacy of instinct, which could not fail to provoke reprisals from upholders of the " divine right " of the intellect. The strange career of Degas is an illustration of the consequences of this clash.

In Degas we have a highly intelligent man who from early youth haunted the great art galleries and knew Italy by heart. Fastidious, sophisticated and mistrustful of the world at large, he was also cantankerous and disdainful. He spoke of himself as " a die-hard, incorrigible reactionary." Nevertheless he struck out new lines ; notably he deliberately broke up classical composition, lowered the horizon-line, and scored surfaces with horizontal strokes. He discovered a new kind of space—unless this was a borrowing from Japan ; yet this procedure fits in so well with his temperament that we may give him the benefit of the doubt. His inordinately keen eye, impartial as a camera lens, registered qualities and defects alike with merciless fidelity. Thus he recorded less the reality of the subject in itself than attitudes and poses " snapped " in hundredths of a second. One of the most baffling elements in his technique—baffling because it seems so wantonly unimaginative—was his device of sketching the model in attitudes approximating to each other ; then tracing them and superimposing these tracings so as to obtain a synthesis ; in other words, a *résumé* embodying them all. But when he rode his hobby of " precision," he set no limits to his analysis.

Misogynist though he was, he bent his mind and his amazing powers of observation to finding out all the secrets of a woman's body. For him it was but a pretext for analysing movement, as true Impressionists analysed light. In this sense Degas might be regarded as an Impressionist of *form* ; for he was not particularly interested in nature or in colour. He loathed his friends' Impressionism, because it dissolved line, outlines and composition. To his mind, the essential should rank before the "accidental." Intent on setting down the truth and nothing but the truth, he saw to it that the firmness of his line repressed all promptings of his instinct, which, taking him unawares, might relax his self-control. During most of his career, colour was for him merely a filling-in for his superb drawing and added little of expressive value. Nevertheless some of his canvases suggest that he might have been a great colourist—if at the cost of being taken for one of Manet's disciples.

In the last analysis, Degas' reactionary tendencies derive from an excess of intelligence. He wanted to understand everything in a field of human activity in which it is best not to seek overmuch to understand. For intellectualism when pressed too far gets but a " dusty answer," and may easily lapse into fatuity or worse. Aware of these perils of the soul, Degas struggled to extricate himself. That is why in the last years of his life, he tried to react against his intellectual self and allow a touch of instinct, that great liberator, to intervene. Always disliking oils—he had had so many setbacks in this medium—, he took to pastel as a compromise. Then, exasperated by its limitations, he mixed oil with it, and counteracted the insipidity so frequently observed in pastel drawing by using tones harsh to the point of crudity and often clashing with each other. Likewise he corrected the rigidly analytical precision of his drawing by hatchings, lines slashed across the texture, that sometimes achieve extremely powerful effects. There is an element of tragedy on the grand scale in the rageful frenzy of Degas' last phase. With his passion for exactness Degas did much to determine a new trend in painting by choosing the most commonplace objects as his models. The " subject " of the picture, whose importance Manet had already queried, had none at all for him. Thus, by his renewal of the stock-in-trade of the traditional *décor* he cuts an almost revolutionary figure, but revolutionary chiefly *qua* technician.

Figures in the open

Victor Hugo wrote in one of the poems of *Contemplations* (1852), entitled *La Fête chez Thérèse* (in words deliciously impressionist, though anticipating Impressionism by two decades) :

> " ... Et sur leurs gorges blanches
> Les actrices sentaient errer l'ombre des branches." [1]

Do not these lines bring to our minds Renoir's *Moulin de la Galette,* and Monet's *Women in the Garden ?*

But, to begin with, the future Impressionists were still all for Realism. The hour of " pure painting " had not yet struck, and while they followed the old traditions regarding figures in the open air (to which the greatest painters of an earlier age, from Fouquet to Watteau, had deferred), and while they had before their eyes the examples of Delacroix' *Marphise,* of Corot's *Petite Jeannette,* of Courbet's *Demoiselles au bord de la Seine,* Manet, Cézanne, Monet, Bazille and Renoir kept no less faithfully to the artificial light of the studio, to the old rules of perspective, of local colour, and of light-and-shade.

However, the figure is not incorporated in the landscape, it remains a silhouette. The air does not flow around it ; done in flat colours, the trees look like stage sets ; the costumes of elegant young women suggest a " still " of some charming ballet stuck upon backgrounds erected for the occasion, like those of photographers. We realize this when we look at Manet's *Déjeuner sur l'herbe* or Cézanne's (1869) at Renoir's *Diana* (1866) or the brilliant pageantries of Bazille, such as *The Terrace* (1860), or Pissaro's *Maid* (1867), or Monet's *Women in the Garden* (1867)—in all of which the " open air " is still studio-conditioned. In the last-named canvas it is noteworthy that we find no hint of Impressionism as yet. What we find is Manet's influence—in the wide planes of the dresses, the strip of pathway, the patches of grass, and also in the bouquets, of which there had been " previews " in *Olympia* and *Le Déjeuner sur l'herbe.* In general, though we cannot but be impressed by the splendour of these works, they still lack something of that atmospheric unity which Impressionism was to achieve ; they resemble sumptuous tapestries. Manet's influence is still preponderant. Indeed there is little incentive to display originality, in view of the hostility of official art, and of a press and public that make no secret of their prejudices. These were indeed hard times for the young artists. In 1869 Monet attempted to kill himself. Not until after the shock administered by the war of 1870-1871 were temperaments able to express themselves in relative freedom and bold innovations countenanced. And soon the conventional treatment of the figure in the open was to give place to a vigorous examination of light and its effects.

It was about 1870-1871 that Impressionism began to give a new significance to the figure placed in the light of day. The break with studio painting was made gradually—with, for example, Pissarro's *Jeanne in the Garden* (1872), Manet's *Game of Croquet* (1873), Renoir's *Moulin de la Galette* (1876).

From now on the figures in a landscape are not as it were posed for the photographer in a convergent glare of spotlights, but are themselves sources of radiant light. The landscape is no longer a background ; figures and nature coalesce ; and thus the proudly heralded " impressionist pantheism " at last comes into its own, in a symphonic richness of which even the loftiest traditional art had no inkling.

[1] "And the actresses felt shadows of the branches straying on their white bosoms."

C. MONET (1840-1926). WOMEN IN THE GARDEN, 1867. 100¼×81¾″. LOUVRE, PARIS.

PAINTED ENTIRELY IN THE OPEN AIR, PROBABLY AT VILLE-D'AVRAY, THIS CANVAS WAS REJECTED BY THE 1867 SALON. IT WAS BOUGHT BY BAZILLE, WHO PAID FOR IT BY MONTHLY INSTALMENTS, SO AS TO HELP HIS FRIEND THROUGH A DIFFICULT PERIOD. THE CHARM AND ORIGINALITY OF THIS FINE WORK LIE IN ITS DECORATIVE BEAUTY, THE ELEGANCE OF THE WOMEN'S FORMS, THE FLUENT RHYTHM OF HIGHLIGHTS AND POOLS OF SHADOW, AND A GRACIOUS DELICACY ALL ITS OWN—HERE WE HAVE ALL THE POETRY OF SPRINGTIME IN A GARDEN. THERE IS A FORETASTE OF IMPRESSIONISM IN ITS CANDID TREATMENT OF THE OPEN AIR, BUT THE TECHNIQUE OF FLAT TONES COVERING LARGE UNIFORM SURFACES, THOUGH LESS UNCOMPROMISINGLY APPLIED, STILL SHOWS MANET'S INFLUENCE.

A. RENOIR (1841-1919). LA GRENOUILLÈRE, 1869. 26×32". NATIONAL MUSEUM, STOCKHOLM.

SEVERAL TIMES IN THE SUMMER OF 1869 MONET AND RENOIR PAINTED "LA GRENOUILLÈRE," AN IDEAL MOTIF, READY TO THEIR HAND, FOR THE BEGINNINGS OF IMPRESSIONISME ONE OF MONET'S VERSIONS IS IN THE METROPOLITAN MUSEUM, NEW YORK, AND ANOTHER OF RENOIR'S VERSIONS IN THE OSCAR REINHART COLLECTION, WINTERTHUR.

LA GRENOUILLÈRE

Monet and Renoir spent the summer of 1869 together, at Bougival, working in friendly rivalry and with vast enthusiasm. One of the local attractions was the restaurant of "La Mère Fournaise" at Croissy (which Renoir often revisited in later years), and they also frequented the celebrated bathing-place, La Grenouillère, then much in vogue. Maupassant has described it in several of his short stories; notably in Paul's Wife. *"At La Grenouillère crowds of people were strolling under those giant trees which make of this corner of the island the world's most delightful park." Monet and Renoir often painted the picturesque little islet, with its solitary tree, round which there was a constant stir of boats, a flutter of gaily coloured dresses, while sunbeams strewed the river with a haze of broken lights. Monet and Renoir never grew tired of feasting their eyes on this entrancing scene, and it was here that the methods, later to be incorporated "officially" in the doctrines of Impressionism—the division of tones, the use of small patches of colour—came to them spontaneously, without any conscious effort on their part. A new way of seeing had come into being, owing nothing to any theory, and all to the direct observation of nature, of the play of sunlight on the Seine. True, the unity of the impressionist style was not a* fait accompli *until round about 1873; yet we may well think that neither Monet nor Renoir ever surpassed the inspiration of this, their "first fine careless rapture." After painting at least two versions each of La Grenouillère and several other local scenes, the two artists parted company in October. Monet stayed at Etretat and Le Havre before returning with his wife and his young son to Saint-Michel, near Bougival, while Renoir joined forces with Bazille in Paris.*

IMPRESSIONISM

A NEW WAY OF SEEING THE WORLD

We have ample evidence that revolutions in the field of art, as in other fields, are the result of slowly working processes, a sort of underground movement whose progress is glimpsed now and then in the light of flashes of inspiration—or of deliberate provocativeness, when a spirit of contradiction goads artists to assert their independence.

Beginning in 1866, Monet had formed a habit of making a yearly stay on the Normandy coast, where, in his fifteenth year, he had met Boudin, who made him acquainted with open-air painting. To this young man, enamoured as he was of movement, the methods of the Barbizon school seemed unduly static. Also it seemed to the young leader-to-be of the Impressionists that the lessons of Courbet's realistic, tempestuous art had had no real influence on the art of Daubigny, Troyon and Rousseau, or even on that of Boudin, his mentor. For them landscape was still merely a romantic *décor*. Corot, first to use the word "impression," was aware of this. In the 1866 Salon Monet had been greatly struck by Jongkind's *Sortie du Port de Honfleur,* in which air and light seemed no longer static but freely moving ; and this movement was destined to be the vital element in Impressionism. This way of seeing the world ruled all Jongkind's art. Variations of the light according to the hour, atmospheric changes, ripples on water and the broken gleams that play across its surface, the ever-changing clouds, dim recessions of sails across the sea, the gliding movements of skaters—all these evoked the notion of the fleeting moment which must be grasped at all costs, an exquisitely fugitive sensation which eager youth, breaking from the trammels of the Schools, longed to express and glorify. Jongkind, moreover, painted in small separate touches, which somehow conjured up the idea of movement, or else by modulations which achieved an amazing luminosity. In his *Beach at Sainte-Adresse* (1867), Monet was already trying to discover the secret of that clear radiance which was subsequently to illumine his noblest achievements. But it was only by degrees that he made this light his own. At this stage his colour is laid on in broad, sweeping brushstrokes which accurately reflect light ; but it still lacks those *nuclei* of shimmering intensity which constellate his later works. Thus he has not yet created light ; only copied it. Nevertheless he has made great strides ; the brilliant intricacies of his master Boudin are far behind and have given place to a spacious ease of execution. But he has not yet definitely broken with the Honfleur School.

In 1869 Monet settled at Saint-Michel (near Bougival), and Renoir came to join him there. This is the " Grenouillère " period, when the two artists in friendly rivalry tried their hand at the same subject, a small bathing-place and restaurant on the Seine. Here both artists made the discovery of reflections, even distinguishing the " reflections of reflections " in running water. By reason of the eddies in the current these reflections take the form of minute, juxtaposed surfaces which when they clash together emit flashes of intensely vivid light. Similarly, in wind-ruffled leafage curious vibrations are set up, and these, too, studied by the keen eyes of our Impressionists-to-be, opened portals of discovery. We are now witnessing the preamble of Impressionist technique, with its tiny patches of colour, and breaking-up of tones. But the two young pioneers had not realized as yet the value of their discoveries ; nor had they formed theories—theories always come later. They were still feeling their way ; and all such tentatives are more spontaneous than deliberate. This may be why their *Grenouillères* have qualities which neither artist was ever to surpass.

Yet, though we find the impressionist way of viewing the world taking form in Monet's art, it was accepted only with restrictions, due to differences of temperament, by other members of the group. Thus, though Renoir, Pissarro and Sisley were much taken by this ingenious conception of light and movement, it seemed to them a little too abstract. Renoir was far from being a blind adorer of nature ; in fact he once declared that it was not looking at nature that made the artist, but looking at the masterpieces in the museums.

Pissarro demurred for different reasons. His love of nature was essentially the artist's ; he loved nature for what he had learned of her from Courbet to begin with, then from Troyon and Daubigny; from the whole Barbizon School and especially from his master, Corot. Thus at first he felt some qualms about this notion of brutally dissecting certain aspects of the visible world—of which his masters had made so much ; for example that majestic order in diversity, which his still essentially classical outlook led him to admire in nature. Thus, deeply loving nature for herself, he felt some consternation when he saw Monet putting her, as it were, on the operating-table. Hence the adherence to the Corot tradition that we see in his *View of Louveciennes*. When Monet gives a name to a picture, even one of a well-known place, we feel that he attaches no importance to it. Whereas we feel, with Pissarro, that this is a spot of earth which he has singled out and loves ; he names his picture " Louveciennes " for example, with much the same feelings as has a townsman choosing a name for his country cottage. And he gives as much loving care to his canvas as does the townsman to the upkeep of " his little place in the country." He scrupulously respects the unity of the scene, plots everything out in advance, and encloses it within quite definite limits. The lines of streets, rivers, trees and houses are used as solidly constructive elements, countering any risk of fragility in the composition. And he takes these precautions at the very time when Monet and Renoir, in their *Grenouillères*, are scattering light-heartedly upon their canvases those multicoloured vibrancies borrowed from the glints on water and flashes of refracted light, building up with these an image of nature that (we must admit) has something a trifle artificial, almost robot-like about it—anyhow if we view it from the angle of the classical landscape. But Pissarro, in whom the principles of the Barbizon School, combining romantic spontaneity with strictly disciplined execution, were deeply ingrained, held, thanks to them, an admirable balance between his sensibility and his intellect.

While Pissarro was still faithful to this sense of construction—which, indeed, never left him—Sisley, too, held off for yet a while from the impressionist adventure. He, too, loved nature and was set on keeping to his programme of being nature's servant and not using her for his own ends. Moreover, the restlessness and dazzle of impressionist art somehow offended both his natural delicacy and his very sensitive vision. Thus his *Montmartre* is the picture of a place where we feel he would have wished to live. This is why he, too, never broke with the Barbizon tradition. His feeling for the permanent was always at strife with the ephemeral, and, conscious of his temperamental instability and his unresolved conflicts, he preferred to throw in his lot with the constructivists. Also his natural discretion warned him off over-bright tones. Thus we find Corot's silvery tonalities in his poplars and willows ; indeed, the art of the two masters is always pitched in the same key.

Sisley was the least intransigent of the Impressionists precisely because, being endowed with an exceptionally delicate sensibility, he elected, on the promptings of a vaguely wistful romanticism, to keep to a manner which already in the days of Monet seemed a shade out of date.

C. PISSARRO. THE GISORS ROAD.

PAINTER OF THE COUNTRYSIDE AND RURAL LIFE, PISSARRO IS MORE REALISTIC THAN MONET AND RENOIR, MORE MINDFUL OF CONSTRUCTIVE VALUES. COTTAGES ON THE OUTSKIRTS OF A VILLAGE, THE RECESSION OF A COUNTRY ROAD (A HERITAGE FROM COROT), WITH THE NEW-DISCOVERED VIBRATION OF LIGHT AND SHADOWS, ARE HIS FAVOURITE THEME.

A. SISLEY. VIEW OF MONTMARTRE.

FOR THIS FINE VIEW OF MONTMARTRE SISLEY SET UP HIS EASEL ON THE PLAINE MONCEAU. THE FAMOUS HILL, SOON TO BE OVERRUN BY HOUSES, WAS STILL A COUNTRY VILLAGE WITH A FEW SURVIVING WINDMILLS. GEORGES MICHEL, DEAN OF THE PAINTERS OF "LA BUTTE" JONGKIND, COROT AND THÉODORE ROUSSEAU, HAD ALREADY TURNED ITS PICTURESQUENESS TO ACCOUNT; NOW THE IMPRESSIONISTS WERE TO ADOPT IT, AND MAKE IT ONE OF PAINTING'S "HIGH PLACES."

C. PISSARRO (1830-1903). PONTOISE, THE GISORS ROAD, 1868. 15×18″. BELVEDERE, VIENNA.

A. SISLEY (1839-1899). VIEW OF MONTMARTRE, 1869. 27½×46″. MUSÉE, GRENOBLE.

I. 11

C. MONET (1840-1926). THE BEACH AT TROUVILLE, 1870. 15×18". TATE GALLERY, LONDON.

BEACHES AND PARASOLS

We have seen Monet and Renoir at Bougival, in 1869, painting their Grenouillères, *the first distinctively impressionist canvases. But Monet had not yet attained a wholly personal style, and in the summer of 1870, at Trouville and Le Havre, he still was painting (if for the last time) in the manner of Courbet and Manet. In September he went to England; the atmosphere of London, his discovery of Turner and Constable, followed by two successive trips to Holland, speeded up the evolution of his art. On his return from Holland in 1872, abandoning the Channel coast for the banks of the Seine, he settled at Argenteuil, where his friends came to join him. The Channel seaside resorts were a " creation " of the Second Empire, and especially the Duc de Morny, who launched Deauville and Trouville. It was to Trouville that the Goncourts took the painters in their* Manette Salomon *(1866). These coastal resorts played an important part in the shaping of Impressionism, under the aegis of Boudin and Jongkind. They were also playgrounds reserved for the upper classes, and as such appealed to Manet, whose palette was always keyed to elegance. But, for very good reasons, the young painters preferred the less elegant and far cheaper joys of boating on the Seine and staying at the little riverside inns near Paris, which likewise came into vogue around 1870.*

This new-found delight in open-air life and sunlight led to the appearance, at the seaside, in gardens and on country walks, of that charming adjunct of feminine excursion, the parasol—and the Impressionists were not slow to turn it to account. These many-hued, gracefully rounded forms, dappling faces with sudden gleams and shadows, admirably fell in with their programme. Amongst well-known masterpieces in which the parasol plays its charming part, we may cite Courbet's Woman with the Shawl, *Degas'* Women at the Races, *Manet's* Spring, *Pissarro's and Sisley's* Garden *scenes, Renoir's and Monet's numerous pictures entitled* Woman with a Parasol.

Discovery of London

At the very moment when their researches were beginning to take shape, the 1870-1871 War broke on the Impressionists, and it had far-reaching effects on their work. Bazille volunteered for active service and was killed in the fighting at Beaune-la-Rolande (1870). Cézanne took refuge at l'Estaque, near Marseilles. Renoir was posted to the Xth Regiment of Light Cavalry at Bordeaux. Manet served as a Staff Officer in the National Guard. Meanwhile Monet, Pissarro and Sisley joined forces and migrated to London. There they met Daubigny, who proved a friend in need, and introduced them to Durand-Ruel. This famous picture-dealer, who had hitherto confined his patronage to the works of the romantic painters, now took the new school under his wing, and gave them material aid.

The peculiar quality of the London light fascinated the three painters, and had an influence on them which profoundly affected the subsequent course of Impressionism. A tenuous, faintly misted light, it was already doing what the young Impressionists were presently to do deliberately: "volatilizing" forms. Daily from the window of his bedroom, which overlooked the Thames, Monet watched a billowy pall of smoke and fog spreading across the sun. Outlines softened, buildings grew blurred, and this feeble light struggling to pierce the famous "pea-soup" fog of London conjured up an eerie sort of reality — a wholly new experience for the eyes of young artists used to the clearer air of France.

Also, they discovered Turner. Despite his obvious romanticism, he came as a vast surprise to Monet and Pissarro (Sisley knew him already). His lyrical emotion, his feeling for the prodigious, sometimes a little strained and aiming more at theatrical effect than at the realistic precision dear to Impressionism, revealed to them a new aspect of light. Nevertheless, despite the progress made by Turner, they recognized in his work a survival of the classical types of lighting against which Watteau and Claude Lorrain had tried to contend. But it was the great English master's watercolours that most impressed the young artists. In them light is evoked with a sensitive immediacy; whereas Turner's oil paintings retain traces of studio-produced work.

It would seem that Constable's art held their attention even more than Turner's. That radiant evocation of the sheen of windy mornings, of dew, of coolness and young flowers, gave them the assurance they so greatly needed of the legitimacy of their quest. What, like Sisley, Pissarro appreciated in Constable was, primarily no doubt, his rejection of the "noble features" of a landscape; but also his respect for the classical composition from which they could never break away. We may also be sure that Monet, Sisley and Pissarro saw that famous canvas to which Constable gave a title stating the time of day at which he painted it. What better precedent could they desire for their quest of sensations born of the fleeting hour? And Monet certainly had this in mind when he added to his famous *Sunrise* the sub-title *Impression.*

During his stay in London Pissarro resolved to give light that primacy which subsequently Impressionism was "officially" to confer on it; all his canvases, while still somewhat leaden-hued and dull, now definitely tended to grow lighter.

Monet, on the other hand, found in Turner an endorsement of his leanings toward decoration. London's influence on him was even more decisive than that of Japanese art. As we watch the evolution of his work we find that, though often faithful to memories of his first teacher, Boudin, he also employs Turnerian methods — using large tracts of flat colour; a practice in which he persisted longer than in that of the juxtaposition of tones. And, in his last works, it still was memories of Turner that led him to press his "poetry of light" to an extreme which, for all its extravagant intensity, does not lack grandeur.

J. F. BAZILLE (1841-1870). THE ARTIST'S STUDIO, 1870. 31¼×50". LOUVRE, PARIS.

IN HIS NEW STUDIO IN THE BATIGNOLLES DISTRICT, NEAR THE CAFÉ GUERBOIS, BAZILLE, A WARM-HEARTED YOUNG MAN, KEPT OPEN HOUSE TO HIS FRIENDS. HERE WE MAY IDENTIFY EDMOND MAITRE AT THE PIANO, ZOLA LEANING ON THE BANISTER, RENOIR SEATED ON THE EDGE OF A TABLE, MANET WEARING A HAT AND, BEHIND HIM, MONET, BOTH OF THEM LOOKING AT THE CANVAS THAT BAZILLE, PALETTE IN HAND, IS SHOWING THEM. THE TALL FIGURE OF BAZILLE IS SAID TO HAVE BEEN SKETCHED IN BY MANET. APART FROM THE DOCUMENTARY INTEREST OF THIS PICTURE, ITS FRIENDLY ATMOSPHERE AND ITS HARMONY OF GREYS, PINKS AND BLACKS ARE PARTICULARLY EFFECTIVE.

BAZILLE

It was a visit to the collection of Alfred Bruyas, friend of Delacroix and Courbet, at Montpellier (his birthplace) that decided Bazille, who was intended for the medical profession, to become a painter.

The memory of this affectionate, warm-hearted young man, of whom Renoir made so touching a portrait (1868), who helped his friend Monet through a period of extreme financial straits, and, having enlisted for active service as a volunteer, fell at the Battle of Beaune-la-Rolande on November 28, 1870, raises the question of what might have been the future course of a career so rich in promise. When he died, Impressionism had not yet come into its own and painting out-of-doors was, comparatively speaking, in its infancy. The most that was being done at this stage was to use a palette featuring light colours, which merely gave an illusion of sunlight and the open air.

But in his *Family Reunion* (1866), an excellent portrait of Sisley, another of Renoir, of a boldness at once novel and compelling, and *The Artist's Studio* (1870), which perhaps owes something to the influence of Degas—in all these canvases Bazille made proof both of a fine feeling for construction and a subtle treatment of colour. What course would his art have taken, had he lived ? We have an impression that his natural trend was towards a broadness of treatment and a tectonic handling of volumes that might well have given his " Impressionism " that architectural quality in which Cézanne was destined to excel.

1871-1880

1871 The **Commune.** Courbet President of Art Commission. Birth of Rouault.
Manet with his family near Bordeaux, Degas with his friends the Valpinçons, Sisley in England.
Monet visits Holland for the first time, perhaps with Daubigny: Views of Zaandam.
Renoir in Paris, then near by, at Louveciennes and Bougival. Delacroix' influence.
Pissarro returns to France in June and finds his studio looted.

1872 Degas' trip to New Orleans. **The Cotton Office** (Pau Museum).
Manet at Haarlem, admires Franz Hals. Durand-Ruel buys 40,000 francs' worth of pictures from him.
Monet's second visit to Holland. On his return settles at **Argenteuil.**
Pissarro at **Pontoise,** where Guillaumin and Cézanne join him.
Renoir in Paris, rue Notre-Dame-des-Champs. Views of the Pont-Neuf and the Seine quays.

1873 Degas returns. Studies of dancers. The Opera burnt down.
Great success of Manet at the Salon, Le Bon Bock (Collection Carroll J. Tyson, Philadelphia). Summer at Berck-sur-Mer.
Monet at Argenteuil, sets up studio in a boat, paints river-scenes, regattas.
Cézanne at Auvers, with Dr Gachet. **La Maison du Pendu** (Louvre).
Pissarro: **Les Coteaux de l'Hermitage.** Sisley at Louveciennes, Marly, Bougival.
Renoir, helped by Durand-Ruel, settles into No. 35, rue Saint-Georges, announces he has "arrived."

1874 **First Group Exhibition** (April 15 - May 15) in Nadar's Galleries, boulevard des Capucines.
165 pictures, 30 artists. Manet stands out. Difficulties over Cézanne's participation.
Manet and Renoir at Argenteuil, with Monet. Caillebotte, artist and connoisseur.
Manet at Venice, Sisley in England, Pissarro at Montfoucault.

1875 **First Impressionist Sale, at the Hôtel Drouot** (March 24). Chocquet, the picture-lover. Death of Corot.
Cézanne at Paris, Quai d'Anjou. **Portrait of Chocquet.** Meets Père Tanguy.
Monet at Argenteuil, Pissarro at Pontoise, Sisley at Bougival, Marly, Saint-Germain.

1876 **Second Group Exhibition** (April. 19 exhibitors), 11, rue Le Peletier.
Cézanne stands out, retires to L'Estaque for the summer. Dispute with Monet.
Duranty publishes **La Nouvelle Peinture,** the first study of Impressionism.
Manet gives receptions in his studio. **Portrait of Mallarmé,** whose friend he has become.
Renoir in Montmartre, rue Cortot: **La Balançoire, Le Moulin de la Galette** (Louvre).
Pissarro at Pontoise; in summer at Montfoucault and at Malleraye (Mayenne).
Monet in Paris: begins painting **Saint-Lazare Station series.**
Gauguin exhibits at the Salon; in touch with Pissarro; collects impressionist works.

1877 **Third Group Exhibition** (April. 18 exhibitors), 6, rue Le Peletier.
Rivière edits "l'Impressionniste." Article by Renoir, "Decorative and Contemporary Art."
Manet, Degas, George Moore at the **Café de la Nouvelle-Athènes,** Place Pigalle, Montmartre.
Cézanne at Pontoise with Pissarro; then at Auvers and at Issy.
Sisley at Sèvres, Saint-Cloud, Saint-Mammès on the Loing Canal.
Second Impressionist Sale at the Hôtel Drouot (May 28). Death of Courbet.

1878 **World's Fair.** Duret publishes "Les Impressionnistes." Zola settles at Médan.
Pissarro at Pontoise, Cézanne at Aix and L'Estaque. Monet at Vétheuil, Sisley at Sèvres.
Seurat enters Ecole des Beaux-Arts; studies under Ingres' pupil, Lehmann.

1879 **Fourth Group Exhibition** (April 10 - May 11. 15 exhibitors) at 28, avenue de l'Opéra.
Charpentier launches "La Vie Moderne," with drawings by Renoir. Daumier's death.
Renoir's success in the Salon. One-man show at "La Vie Moderne." **Portrait of Madame Charpentier.**
Cézanne returns to Paris. Long stay at Melun. Visits Zola frequently at Médan.
Pissarro at Pontoise, where Gauguin joins him. Sisley at Veneux-Nadon.
Odilon Redon publishes an album of lithographs entitled **Dans le Rêve.**

1880 **Fifth Group Exhibition** (April. 18 exhibitors, including Gauguin) at 10, rue des Pyramides.
Monet and Manet have one-man shows at "La Vie Moderne."
Degas: **Portrait of Duranty** (Lewisohn Collection, New York); travels in Spain. Manet ill at Bellevue.
Pissarro works at decoration; does etchings with Degas, Mary Cassatt.
Sisley at Suresnes, Louveciennes, Moret. Deaths of Flaubert and Duranty.
Renoir lodges with "La Mère Fournaise" at Croissy. After much self-communing breaks with Impressionism.
Cézanne back in Paris. Meets Huysmans. Spends summer with Zola at Médan.

ARGENTEUIL

IMPRESSIONIST THEMES

Amongst the cities of the world whose names are permanently associated in our minds with certain great art periods, the little township of Argenteuil must not be denied a place ; for it was the cradle of an art movement of extreme importance : of Impressionism. As well as its " place of origin," an exact date may be fixed as that when the new aesthetic theory touched highwater-mark in the way of truly creative achievement : the year 1874. It was then that the rendering of light and movement, the Impressionists' great discovery, was brought to a pitch of precision and a plenitude never to be surpassed — though the painters, haunted as all creative spirits are by dreams of bettering their best, still pressed forward on the path of discovery, until indeed they were " in wandering mazes lost." Thus it was when Monet, carried away by not unjustifiable pride, tried to carry his researches into the *texture* of light still further, and to achieve the impossible in painting. And, in later days, since evidently genius and imagination alone could not suffice, the Neo-Impressionists called in science, and pressed the exact analysis of colour and light-rays to a point where they came up against that *ne plus ultra* which is the end of all art movements that have worked themselves out. But art goes on, though " movements " end. Their discoveries are not lost, but serve as starting-points for new discoveries.

Argenteuil shows us that Impressionism is beginning to build up a new aesthetic theory, derived from technical *data* that were not, strictly speaking, new. But it pressed its realistic observation of nature to a point at which its very excesses, coupled with its scientific analyses of the *matière* — the material on which the artist works — raised what was to be the central problem of modern art. Meanwhile, however, the new school stood by the doctrine of the imitation of nature. They noticed that the masters of the past had practised it, though with an eye to extra-pictorial considerations of many kinds. So had done the Romantics ; not only those for whom the " story " of the picture was everything, but also those who specialized in landscape pure and simple, such men as Brascassat, Marilhat or Georges Michel (whose art, at bottom, always was far less instinctual than intellectual). So it was that Impressionism began by pressing literal realism to an extreme precision, surpassed only by photography — the recent discovery of which had certainly caught the attention of the Impressionists at this stage.

Thus they soon realized they must outdo mere nature-imitation. To use a term soon to come into fashion, and one which our contemporary artists were to adopt with still bolder ends in view, they tried to create *a new reality*. And theirs was no traditional or slavish realism, but a very personal interpretation of nature — on the lines of Zola's famous definition of art as " an aspect of creation seen through the medium of a temperament."

It was a new conception of Space and Time that lay at the origin of impressionist aesthetics. Traditional art was based on a concept of permanence ; it aspired to the timeproof and unchanging. A gratuitous concept, indeed (to use a modern expression) a piece of wishful thinking, due to a very human longing to cling to the felicities of this present world, or the comforting assurance of a super-world of things eternal. But, nothing if not realistic, the Impressionists perceived the fragility of things, and it was this transient Here and Now they sought to picture. Naturally they were accused of embarking on " a wild-goose chase " ; actually they were but endorsing the adage : " All things flow... You cannot cross the same river twice." True, their intentions were in a sense contradictory (but is

C. MONET (1840-1926). ARGENTEUIL BRIDGE, 1874, DETAIL. LOUVRE, PARIS.

MONET LIVED AT ARGENTEUIL, ON THE BANKS OF THE SEINE, FROM 1872 TO 1878. DURING THIS PERIOD HE PAINTED, USUALLY IN A BOAT FITTED UP AS A STUDIO, HIS MOST SPONTANEOUS MASTERPIECES AND WAS THE UNDISPUTED LEADER OF IMPRESSIONISM. CAILLEBOTTE, MANET, RENOIR, SISLEY CAME HERE AT VARIOUS TIMES AND WORKED UNDER HIS INFLUENCE.

not all art a game played with logic ?) since they proposed to " fix " for all eternity the fugitive, the mournful glamour of the fleeting. In this respect it was only too easy for the pundits of classicism to tax the new aesthetic with a lack of spirituality and an addiction to the merely sensuous. " The spirit forms, but the senses deform," it was pointed out, and you can build nothing lasting with the fugitive. And since form persists behind and beyond the colour that is subject to decay, the notion of " coloured sensations " which informed impressionist theory was preposterous. But the men who were raising these objections were, for obvious reasons, unable to foresee that the notion of " coloured sensations " would give rise one day to constructive themes and that Impressionism, itself " fugitive," would come to mark but one stage more in art's long pilgrimage.

Obviously this new aesthetic called for an appropriate technique. Since light was the source of all sensations, light must dominate the artist's palette. Each fleeting aspect of the world needed a technique capable of isolating its coloured moment, and it was thus the artist's task to analyse the vibrations of the air and of light, and to break them up into parts. In the movement of running water, the drift of clouds, the ripple of leafage, the keen eyes of the young Impressionists perceived a juxtaposition of pure colours, and a clash of pure tones, without the intervention of intermediate tonalities. These tones, each acting independently, led to new groupings, much as each individual contributes to the aspect of the group he lives in. Thus, more even than the sight of everchanging nature, it was an organic compulsion to build up a coherent whole that led the Impressionists to the system of dividing up tones and sprinkling the canvas with disconnected spots, splitting up light prism-wise into the seven component colours. Thus, too, they abolished " local tone," which necessitates a respect for contours binding forms together within fixed, unchanging limits. Hence the presentation of the subject as an *ensemble* of vibrations generating waves of light, which affect the eye like the images on a cinema screen. The consequence was that form (or anyhow form in its traditionally accepted sense) became totally dispersed, volatilized, and it was against this annihilation of form that soon the post-impressionist reaction took arms.

No doubt there was something slightly mechanical in this procedure ; in impressionist technique we often seem to hear as it were a click of turning cogs. And then we think approvingly of Delacroix's comment on a Ruysdael seascape — that it was " the perfection of art because the art was so completely hidden." But rare are the works, even great ones, of which we could say this ! Nor must we forget that we are now at the early, analytic phase of Impressionism — and it is a habit of young enthusiasts to lay down the law.

Essentially this method of juxtaposed touches of pure colour was not wholly new. In tracing the sources of Impressionism, art-historians have not failed to point out anticipations of its technique in the work of the old masters. Several of the Men of the Renaissance dallied with it. Nearer our times, it was used by Watteau and by Chardin, of whom a contemporary writer, Bachaumont, wrote, " He puts on his colours one after the other, hardly mixing them, the result being like a mosaic or embroidery in which a square stitch *(point carré)* is employed." Goya, too, sometimes used a narrow, vibrant brushstroke. And Delacroix' transverse strokes showed his knowledge of the uses of complementary colour in bringing out a given hue. Constable, Bonington and Jongkind had contributed to the shaping of the new technique. And, finally, Corot on his deathbed had predicted the coming of Impressionism.

Nevertheless these excellent precedents did not prevent critics and public alike from heaping derision on the new school, whose principles were formulated round about 1872. The war being over, the young artists met again in Paris, but soon retired to the suburbs ; notably to the banks of the Seine where regattas, country inns and sunlit foliage quickened their inspiration. Sisley stayed at Marly, Renoir at Croissy, and Monet at Argenteuil, where he was joined by Caillebotte and Manet and, later, by Renoir. During this period Manet painted his *Rowers at Argenteuil* (1874), Caillebotte his *Boats at Argenteuil* (1875), Renoir *The Seine at Argenteuil* (1873), Monet his *Regatta at Argenteuil* (1873). Thus this charming little town may well be regarded as the " Barbizon " of Impressionism. For better than all else, skies and flowing water bespeak the " fugitive."

Never quite converted to the technique of divided tones, Manet kept to the small, slightly elongated strokes in which his amazing manual dexterity could operate to greater advantage than in the microscopic analysis involved in the use of tiny specks of colour. Moreover, protagonist though he was of bright tones, he never liked painting in the open. Also he had little use for new-fangled theories and felt at home with not a few conventions of the older art. He went so far in the way of estrangement from his friends as to persist in canvasing the approval of the " official " Jury. Of course Manet was well-to-do (as, too, was Degas), and a rich man tends to fight shy of perilous adventures. Also he was more interested in figures than in scenery ; thus he often put figures in his landscapes, procuring from them those effects of light and shade whose quest he always advocated. " All the rest," he said, " comes naturally, and it often amounts to very little." Renoir, too, was no fanatical admirer of nature ; his view was that a man becomes a painter not by gazing at nature but by contemplating the masterpieces in museums. The " division of tones " as practised by him consisted in the use of small, fluttering, richly coloured dabs of pigment. Moreover, he was no servile follower of Monet's dynamic methods ; his cult of light, in figures and landscapes alike, never took precedence of his sensuous delight in colour. Sisley restricted his palette to tones of blue, pink and golden-yellow—expressive of his delicate sensibility. Thus Monet cuts the figure of the group-leader, strictly applying as he did, the principles implicit in his method, and painting in strong, luminous, resolute " touches." For he never wavered in his life's endeavour—to re-create light on canvas.

Thus we see that the Impressionists (as was only to be expected) would not be bound by cut-and-dry rules. Nor need we be surprised if, after the Argenteuil phase, during which all were ready to make concessions in the common cause, each individual temperament struck out for itself. And we shall see that with Pissarro and Cézanne, at Pontoise and Auvers, a rift within the ranks of Impressionism began to show itself.

A. SISLEY (1840-1899). BOATS AT BOUGIVAL LOCK, 1873. 18×25½". LOUVRE, PARIS.

I. 15

A. RENOIR (1841-1919). LE MOULIN DE LA GALETTE (DETAIL), 1876. 51¼×69″. LOUVRE, PARIS

THIS FAMOUS WORK, IN WHICH THE RHYTHM OF THE LIGHT, WITH ITS EDDYING SHEEN, IS SUPERBLY WEDDED TO THE RHYTHM OF THE WALTZ, WAS PAINTED ENTIRELY IN THE OPEN, ON THE SPOT. GEORGES RIVIÈRE HAS DESCRIBED HOW EACH EVENING THE ARTIST'S FRIENDS HELPED HIM TO CARRY BACK HIS PARAPHERNALIA TO HIS NEAR-BY STUDIO, AND HAS GIVEN US THE NAMES OF THE PRINCIPAL FIGURES, CHOSEN FROM AMONGST THE ARTIST'S FRIENDS AND WOMEN FREQUENTING THE "MOULIN." IN THE CENTRAL SECTION, HERE REPRODUCED, WE SEE, LEANING ON A BENCH, ESTELLE, SISTER OF JEANNE, THE MODEL FOR *THE SWING*. A PREMILINARY SKETCH AND A FIRST VERSION OF THIS PICTURE ARE EXTANT.

E. MANET (1832-1883). ARGENTEUIL, 1874. 58½×51½". MUSÉE DES BEAUX-ARTS, TOURNAI.

DURING THE SUMMER OF 1874. MANET STAYED FIRST AT GENNEVILLIERS, THEN AT ARGENTEUIL WITH MONET, AND LIKE HIM MADE SEVERAL OPEN-AIR PICTURES OF REGATTAS AND BOATING ON THE RIVER. THIS, THE FIRST OF THE SERIES, AND ITS MASTERPIECE, WAS REJECTED BY THE 1875 SALON. THE COUPLE IN THE BOAT ARE MANET'S BROTHER-IN-LAW RUDOLPH LEENHOFF THE PAINTER, AND A MODEL FOUND ON THE SPOT. A FEW DAYS LATER MANET MADE ANOTHER TREATMENT OF THIS SUBJECT, *BOATING AT ARGENTEUIL* (METROPOLITAN MUSEUM OF NEW YORK), IN WHICH WE SEE THE SAME FIGURES, BUT NOW IN PROFILE, STANDING OUT SHARPLY AGAINST THE BLUE WATER.

I. 18

C. MONET (1840-1926). ST. LAZARE STATION, 1876-1877. 20¾×28¼".
COLLECTION HON'BLE CHRISTOPHER MCLAREN, ENGLAND.

AT THE THIRD GROUP EXHIBITION, IN APRIL 1877, MONET SHOWED NO LESS THAN SEVEN VIEWS OF SAINT LAZARE STATION SEEN FROM DIFFERENT ANGLES; THESE MADE UP THE FIRST AND THE MOST STRIKING OF HIS "SERIES." THAT NOVEL THEME, THE RAILWAY (DEEMED VULGAR, UNAESTHETIC AT THE TIME) WAS OFTEN TREATED BY THE IMPRESSIONISTS (BY PISSARRO IN 1871, MANET IN 1873, SISLEY IN 1878, MONET ON SEVERAL OCCASIONS). LESS FOR ITS MODERN AND "SOCIAL" IMPLICATIONS (STRESSED BY DURANTY) THAN FOR THE MARVELLOUS PICTORIAL EFFECTS WHICH IT AFFORDED AND WHICH SERVED MONET'S DYNAMIC LYRICISM SO WELL.

THE FOUR ELEMENTS

During the period when Impressionism was at its apogee, we find that the Still Life was temporarily — and significantly — out of favour. Cézanne alone, like the prudent countryman he was, kept some apples and fruit-bowls in reserve. The truth was that this theme lacked the dynamism which meant so much to the genuine Impressionists. A new convention was now directing painters' attention to the most fleeting aspects of the visible world.

We have mentioned the theme of the figure in the open air. But the impressionist quest of light turned all four elements to account.

Air is intrinsically the vehicle of light ; the location of the horizon-line is determined by the aerial texture, so to speak, that the artist's sensation necessitates. It is the sky that, of its very nature, regulates the distribution of the light. Sometimes, indeed, in Monet's seascapes, water and sky are mingled in an intricate interplay of reflections, whose impacts likewise become sources of vivid light.

The water of seas and rivers is treated as a mirror multiplying the light-waves, and in the ceaseless movement of the water is found a supreme example of the dynamic juxtaposition of tones.

The clashes between the fires of locomotives, the smoke of trains of steamboats and the clouds overhead, which Monet, Pissaro and Sisley had witnessed on the Thames and Charing Cross bridge, as well as in Turner's pictures, served well the impressionist theme of the "fleeting moment." Now that the railway train had replaced the diligence and the stagecoach, the countryside near the capital was being "discovered" by Parisians, with its possibilities for cheerful picnic-parties and all the pleasures of a rural Sunday afternoon *en famille* or with friends. Thus for many town-dwellers the flying trails of smoke of passing trains came to be a symbol of these brief escapades into the open and, by the same token, of the swift and evanescent. The painters were quick to grasp this and were delighted by the effects that were produced by the clashes already mentioned between the wisps of smoke and steam and the statelier movement of the clouds above. And their clouds were no longer the feather-bed clouds of classical paintings, or the black, ragged cloudwrack dear to the romantics. The impressionist artist neither asked of them that they should help to build up his composition, nor that they should increase the emotional tension of a scene. They played a part in the visual impression he was putting on to his canvas, and nothing more.

Earth, least "impressionist" of the elements, stood for the solid and enduring. A mere strip of sand or some furrows were called on to support the crushing weight of a boundless sky, the soaring bulk of trees, the structural mass of walls. These constituted the indispensable foregrounds. Snow, too, was used to play this basic part. (Surely the inventor of the *dictum* that "there is no white in nature," left snow out of account.) Not to mention the Dutch, who were specialists in snow, the Old Masters found good use for

THE ANIMATION (THEN BEGINNING) OF THE BOULEVARDS, THE MOTLEY BUSTLE OF THE CROWD, VISTAS OF MINGLED TREES AND HOUSES, QUAYS, BRIDGES, CHANGING SKIES, THAT BLUE-GREY LIGHT WHICH HOVERS OVER PARIS—ALL WERE MOTIFS "MADE" FOR THE IMPRESSIONIST PALETTE, AND SO IT WAS THAT THE MASTERPIECES OF RENOIR (*LE PONT-NEUF*, 1872), OF MONET (*BOULEVARD DES CAPUCINES*, 1873), OF MANET (*LA RUE MOSNIER*, 1878), OF PISSARRO (*AVENUE DE L'OPÉRA*, 1898) REVEALED THE HITHERTO UNNOTICED BEAUTIES OF THE PARISIAN SCENE.

A. RENOIR (1841-1919). LES GRANDS BOULEVARDS, 1875. 19¾×24". PRIVATE COLLECTION, U.S.A.

white, always so useful for contrasted variations, in the wings of angels, in winding-sheets, in the tablecloths of their Last Suppers, or, more prosaically, on dining-room tables. The Impressionists did not fail to turn to account winter's white amenities for the free play of reflected light, and for telling contrasts between snow and black trees fretting a grey sky. Snow in fact supplied an ideal undertone for the boldest chromatic variations. But the snow-scape's lack of colour as a standby called for careful handling and a " style "—which never failed such men as Sisley, Monet, Renoir and Pissarro, who delighted in the problems of the winter scene, even using smears of silver, lead or ashes to heighten their effects.

In the urban scene the Impressionists found contrasts to their hearts' content, and the colour vibrations they excelled in rendering, admirably brought out the dynamism of the tonal patterns of city streets. Paris, above all, inspired Renoir, Pissarro and Monet to vivid renderings of the feverish life of a great modern city ; and when they depict the hurrying crowds on the sidewalks, the busy traffic, and windswept trees along the boulevards, they evoke movement with an easy competence far more telling than the laboured compositions of the Futurists.

Gardens were another theme much favoured by the Impressionists. Monet, Manet, Renoir, Sisley and Cézanne had gardens of their own at Vétheuil, Rueil, Argenteuil, Giverny, " Les Colettes," and elsewhere, and some famous canvases bear these names. The painters kept up their gardens, or had them kept up, with loving care ; they were pretexts for brilliant *bravura* pieces or sketches including technical " notations " for future use, since obviously their exiguity did not lend itself to big compositions. The painters' gardens supplied material for highly elaborate analyses of colour, and, needless to say, the flower theme bulked large in their experiments. Flowers supplied the *data* of dazzling colour symphonies for which the artists' visual sensations provided an endless range of brilliant improvisations. Renoir said of one of his coruscating bouquets, "Isn't it almost as colourful as one of Delacroix' battle-scenes ? "

THE MOTIF OF SNOW, ALREADY TREATED BY COURBET AND JONGKIND, STILL GAVE SCOPE FOR SUBTLE VARIATIONS. IN 1865, AT HONFLEUR, MONET PAINTED SNOWSCAPES IN WHICH UNDER THE EXTERNAL REALISM WE ALREADY FEEL AN IMPRESSIONIST " VIBRATION." IT WAS THAT DELICATELY PERCEPTIVE ARTIST SISLEY WHO MADE THE MOST OF THIS THEME ; THANKS TO THE SENSITIVE PRECISION OF HIS PALETTE, SNOW INSPIRED HIM TO THE SUBTLEST COLOUR EFFECTS.

A. SISLEY (1839-1899). BOUGIVAL WEIR UNDER SNOW, 1876. FORMER A. LINDON COLLECTION.

THE 'CLIMATE' OF THE IMPRESSIONIST PERIOD

It was in or about the years 1870-1871 that the ideas behind Impressionism took more or less coherent and explicit form. On the political and social plane this was a momentous epoch, but the painters do not seem to have been seriously perturbed. As we have seen, the Impressionists were dispersed during the war, in France and abroad, and do not seem to have been much disturbed by it; nor did the proclamation of the Third Republic affect them greatly. Such indeed was their normal financial plight that they had failed to notice some excellent reforms brought in under the Second Empire; so slightly had these benefited them. Nor did they perceive that, almost immediately after the defeat, France entered on a phase of quite unlooked-for prosperity. Even the picture-dealing business, too, made a forward stride, and the activities of the famous Durand-Ruel family of picture-dealers, especially in opening up new markets in Great Britain and the United States, gave an unexpected fillip to the investment value of works of art.

A period of great inventions and discoveries now set in. Renan published his Future of Science. *Bell invented the telephone, Edison the incandescent electric lamp, Pasteur began his series of epoch-making discoveries, and railways spread their iron tentacles across the whole of France. Under the auspices of science a new world was coming into being. Yet, though the Impressionists, too, were inaugurating a wholly new way of viewing the world and were as truly pioneers as the great scientists, these discoveries of science left them cold. None the less they could not help being affected by the prevailing 'climate' and by the almost universal feeling that the world was on the brink of a new age, in which the secrets of nature were to be scientifically probed and exploited for the common good. Yet, though they formed a clan apart, they responded to that revolutionary atmosphere which, after the upheavals of 1789, 1830, 1848 and 1871, once more prevailed in France. For one thing, most of them were of humble origin and the middle class often made them painfully aware of this; as when they taxed the younger painters' work with vulgarity, and blamed them for preferring subjects unsuited for the 'noble' academic style, and for concentrating on rustic and lower-class life. Yet it was precisely because they refused to be bound by the static, cut-and-dry conventions imposed by the Academy — conventions which the Academy, now as ever a loyal servant of officialdom and decorum, accepted as in duty bound, and indeed in which it rejoiced — that the Impressionists instinctively accepted that notion of evolution whose laws had been established by such men as Darwin, Spencer and Lamarck. It was perhaps partly this awareness of evolution as an instinctual drive that led these highly gifted artists to resist constraints deriving from an outlook too purely intellectual and sophisticated. Nor must we forget that the natural desire for liberty, born with the Revolution, had been promoted by the increasing influence of Rousseau's doctrines, which sponsored a scheme for living congenial to their social status — in most cases that of the worker, employee or small farmer. Lives passed in contact with nature, not to mention the reasonable self-interest of those who have to earn laboriously their daily bread, had inspired them with a classical devotion to the soil, to* Terra Mater, *and likewise a sturdy independence, for which art offered a very favourable field. Thus we soon find the Impressionists desisting even from their short stays in the capital, moving out to the country and settling there. No such notion would ever have crossed the minds of the academic painters, tethered to Paris, as being the centre for the distribution of medals, for making a reputation and for cultivating people who might commission portraits. This 'society' clientèle knew nothing of the French countryside except what it had seen in Bastien-Lepage's landscapes, which were exactly to its taste. Before making their new, direct approach to nature, the Impressionists duly studied it in the landscapes of Corot, Courbet, Rousseau, Dupré, Boudin, Jongkind and the rest. And thus it was they lit on their great discovery. For now the young artists compared nature as portrayed by the Masters with the actual scene before them — and were amazed at the discrepancy. What they discovered furnished that challenge to excel their predecessors that painters always stand in need of; and they now brought to bear that 'analytical' observation which, as we have seen, lies at the root of all impressionist technique. In short, discarding all conventions of the past, they looked at nature with new eyes. Like the first observers of the phenomena of electricity, steam-power, or some new element, the Impressionists, too, made far-reaching discoveries, though as yet they had no idea of their possibilities. In pursuing these investigations each man followed the line best suited to his temperament. Men like Monet sought to see exactly* what *it was that happened; those like Cézanne,* why *it happened thus. Thus analysis was the order of the day, Degas analysing movement, Monet light and Cézanne form. They studied life and nature with an application sometimes wildly enthusiastic, sometimes almost painfully intense. We can picture these young painters poring intently on the book of nature, like a schoolboy bent over his exercise-book, puckering his brows or putting out his tongue in the effort to control his novice pen. Whereas the successful painter of the day merely applied himself to burnishing his hero's helmet, while dreaming of the gold medals awaiting him.*

Thus the impressionist period encouraged both the fervour of young sensibilities and the scientific precision dear to neophytes, and it was through the interaction of these that the new way of viewing the world came into being. Thus it always has been, and always will be when youthful aspirations join forces with freedom of expression and a gift for technical innovation. And despite the divergencies which subsequently led the Impressionists each to go his personal way, it is to these qualities shared in common that their contribution to art and the 'climate' of their time owes its indubitable unity.

E. DEGAS (1834-1917). THREE DANCERS (BETWEEN 1875 AND 1877). 10½×8½″.
PRIVATE COLLECTION, PARIS.

A. RENOIR (1841-1919). HER FIRST OUTING, 1875-1878. 25½×19¾". TATE GALLERY, LONDON.

C. PISSARRO (1830-1903). THE HERMITAGE AT PONTOISE, 1875. 21¼×25½″. PRIVATE COLLECTION, PARIS.

FROM 1872 TO 1883, PISSARRO LIVED AT PONTOISE, WHERE CÉZANNE AND GUILLAUMIN OFTEN VISITED HIM. IT WAS HERE HE PAINTED HIS MASTERPIECES, INSPIRED ALMOST ALWAYS BY THE HERMITAGE HILLSIDE, THE STABLE QUIETUDE OF THE OLD COTTAGES CONTRASTING WITH THE RIPPLES OF THE LEAFAGE FAINTLY STIRRING IN A SUMMER BREEZE, IN A PERFECT EQUILIBRIUM OF LIGHT AND MASSES.

PONTOISE

On his return from London Pissarro went first to Louveciennes (1871), then settled at Pontoise (1872). It was a great change from the suburban scene of the Seine banks ; here were cultivated fields, woods and ploughlands—a genuine, unspoilt countryside, and one which appealed especially to Pissarro. In his technique we always find reminiscences of Corot and Courbet. Pissarro, too, began by setting up his easel " no matter where." Landscapes " arranged " by man, in other words, ready-made masterpieces only waiting for the painter's brush, do not interest him. With a tumbledown cottage, some hedgerows and a few more or less luxuriant trees, he composes pictures in which nature, analysed piecemeal, yields not a " naturalistic," that is to say, theatrical truth, but one that is quick with emotion, vibrant with life. Pissarro was a born poet of the woods and fields, a painter afterwards. Throughout his work we see him poring on the book of nature with a zest that reveals itself in the extreme vivacity of his brushstrokes. In his case the constructive element is more a matter of deliberate planning than spontaneously arrived at ; he is rather like a novelist who, lacking the storyteller's craft, feels the need of a style. All his life he bethought himself of Corot's lessons, but he also turned to good account such tectonic methods as came to his notice, whether those of Cézanne or those of Seurat, both architects-born.

P. CÉZANNE (1839-1906). THE HANGED MAN'S HOUSE, 1873. 21¾×26". LOUVRE, PARIS.

IN 1873, CÉZANNE LEFT PONTOISE AND SETTLED AT AUVERS-SUR-OISE, A SMALL VILLAGE NOT FAR DISTANT, WHERE HE PAINTED THIS, HIS FIRST WORLD-FAMOUS MASTERPIECE. IT MARKS A TURNING-POINT IN HIS CAREER: THE ABANDONMENT, UNDER PISSARRO'S INFLUENCE, OF HIS FIRST LOWTONED, TENSELY EMOTIONAL *FACTURE*, AND THE BEGINNING OF HIS NEW METHOD OF CONSTRUCTION IN TERMS OF COLOUR.

AUVERS

After the 1870 war Cézanne came back from Provence and joined Pissarro, whom he much admired, at Pontoise. Next, he settled down at Auvers. Pissarro's example, like Monet's, now encouraged him to enter into a communion with nature more intimate than that inspiring his romantic landscapes of round about 1860. He abandoned the passionate, not to say Baroque " vision " which had led to his *Modern Olympia* and *Temptation of Saint Anthony*. Under Manet's influence he had tried to curb his natural turbulence, and now, under the influence of impressionist theory, he imposed a new discipline on himself, while his art found a new objective, one which had never yet occurred to him—the quest of luminous atmosphere. During this phase he gave up the rather slapdash technique of palette-knife painting, saw the advantages of associating light hues, and tentatively employed juxtaposed " touches." Later on he was to discard the new aesthetic theories; meanwhile, however, he spoke with modest satisfaction of his " small impressionist personality," and lets himself be carried away by the impetuous enthusiasms of his friends and the brief glamour of the " fleeting." But soon he was to retrieve his bearings—when his native prudence urged him back to that solid framework of which his self-confessed " weakness " stood in need.

Dissensions and Disruption

When an art movement reaches a point where researches can be pressed no farther, and all that remains to the artists is to repeat themselves with sterile pertinacity, we know that its last hour has struck. Its members separate, and each pursues his chosen path. Some—the leaders—refuse to own defeat and frantically try to strike out in new directions, in a desperate attempt to keep the flag flying. Others make shift to live on their capital of acquired experience, thus giving a clear field to every kind of "mannerism." Lastly, there are those who try to refashion past discoveries, and this work of synthetic creation is usually the most rewarding, since it paves the way to new achievements.

Thus it was with Impressionism. Classicism, Romanticism and Realism had known this fate, which neither Neo-Impressionism nor Fauvism, neither Cubism nor Surrealism was to escape.

Manet had never whole-heartedly adopted the tenets of Impressionism. The juxtaposition of small patches of colour could not satisfy the sensibility of an artist always inclined to the use of those broad planes and large tracts of colour which naturally appeal to a temperament averse from meticulous analysis and minute attention to detail. His manner was broad, swift and forthright ; he *synthesized*. To him much of the theorizing of

PROBABLY PAINTED IN 1877, HIS LAST YEAR IN PARIS, THIS COMPOSITION, WITH ITS RESTLESS MOVEMENT OF LIGHT AND SHADE, REVEALS A LIGHT, VIBRANT TECHNIQUE STILL IMBUED WITH IMPRESSIONISM.

P. CÉZANNE (1839-1906). SUBURBS IN THE SPRING, C. 1877. 19¾×23½".
HAHNLOSER COLLECTION, WINTERTHUR.

Impressionism was frankly tedious. His natural facility and virtuosity would have been inhibited by any sort of system. Though he never doubted the interest of the new discoveries regarding light, and turned them to account in many admirable canvases, he took much less trouble over his light effects than did the true Impressionists with their elaborate manipulations of pigment. Moreover it is no secret that he was ambitious ; J. E. Blanche, who knew him well, once said, "He always works with an eye to the official Salon." But though he turned his back on impressionist theory—one reason being that his training on classical lines prevented him from breaking with the discipline of drawing and precise form—he kept in touch with his friends and often visited the *Nouvelle Athènes* café.

Renoir abandoned the countryside and came to Paris. He was soon to say that you learn to paint not by looking at nature but by looking at the masterpieces in the museums. He never loved nature for herself ; at most she served him as a stimulus, or else he saw her as a superb example of life at its most exuberant, whose secrets it were well to learn, for other ends. The dispersal of the Impressionists took him to Italy in 1881 and his discovery of the great Renaissance masters helped to confirm his natural bent. His preference went to the human figure, and he was now by way of becoming " the poet of Parisian life." Portraits, nudes, interiors were his favourite themes. He "re-interpreted " tradition, and his predilection for building, so to speak, in slabs of colour, while remaining an architect of forms, led him to shun all that savoured of the " dissolving view." Thus gradually, in his work, the permanent ousted the fugitive. By a natural reaction he harked back to that period of his art which others have called Ingresque, but he himself called " harsh." Nor did the juxtaposition of tones appeal to him, and, during this phase, his break with Impressionism became apparent, notably in his practice of laying on colour in smooth surfaces, as opposed to the others' " flakiness," as he called it.

It is worth recording that he now had a period of extreme discouragement, due to his poverty, and in 1880 said in a letter to Durand-Ruel : " There are eighty thousand so-called art-lovers, who won't buy even an eyebrow, if the painter doesn't figure in the Salon."

A naturally touchy, not to say cross-grained man, Cézanne was offended by the poor reception his work encountered at the impressionist exhibitions in 1874 and 1877, in which he took part. Greatly embittered, he was now on friendly terms with Monet and Renoir only. In his novel *L'Œuvre* Zola took Cézanne as his model for the character of an unsuccessful artist, and the two men were within an ace of a duel. Henceforward Cézanne ceased exhibiting with his friends. In 1879 he retired to his birthplace, Aix-en-Provence ; thereafter rarely left it, and it was there he died (in 1906).

But his flight from the North had other causes. Impressionism had disappointed him. The analytical excesses of this painting, all in little dabs of pigment, were incompatible with the firm structure and design that his yearning for the permanent required. He wanted " to make Impressionism something solid and abiding, like the old masters." But, above all, Cézanne was a truly Mediterranean artist ; the hazy, almost evanescent landscapes of north and central France could not satisfy his taste for solidity and clean-cut form ; whereas Provence, with its crystal-clear atmosphere, its changeless skies and sharply defined contours, gratified his desire for perduring Space. Also, he had never relished the endless palaverings of the cafés, and Provence suited his taste for silence, solitude—and self-reliance. Here, in the Aix countryside he could realize his dream of combining his realistic way of seeing nature with the idealism of his concepts. Little by little he gave it form, setting it up against those impressionist theories, which now, in his heart of hearts, he judged not so much revolutionary as sloppily undisciplined.

Sisley setteled down at Moret. He had to struggle to keep afloat and naturally lost heart. Thus he wrote to Duret : " The time is still far off when one will be able to dispense with the prestige that only ' official ' exhibitions can confer. So I am dutifully sending in a picture to the Salon." None the less Sisley, Monet and Pissarro were still convinced that the technical possibilities of the juxtaposition of tones were not yet played out, and tried to press Impressionism yet farther. But though various experiments were made, Impressionism wore itself out in laboured self-repetition, and dwindled into a sterile mannerism.

Monet, despite adversity, put up the stoutest resistance. In 1880 he wrote to Duret: "I learn that the pictures I sent to the Havre exhibition have annoyed the local connoisseurs, and indeed have been laughed out of court." Moreover, differences of opinion in the group led Renoir, Sisley and Monet to refuse to join in the 1880 and 1881 exhibitions. Monet had a one-man show at the *Vie Moderne*. And, naturally enough, he too sought salvation in escape, migrating to Brittany (Belle-Ile), then visiting Italy (Bordighera) and even Norway. He was trying to forget the hostility of the public and the savage attacks on him in the press, in which, to make things worse, some friends who had once seemed favourable to the new school, now took part.

Their gradual estrangement from novelists and literary men in general was a severe blow to the Impressionists, who had come to count on their support. And the fact that these persons had shown such almost extravagant enthusiasm in the early days made their present hostility still more distressing and inexplicable. Thus Zola, turned "defeatist," now abjured his former comrades, declaring that none of them had "effectively or decisively implemented the new theory of art. The man of genius has not emerged, the modern artist is a mere fumbler, he stammers without finding his words," and so forth. His ground for this attack was his beloved "naturalism" (which he had naïvely thought the Impressionists were championing), and the fact that painters were turning their back more and more on the "subject" and the set theme.

Huysmans had begun by writing: "All honour to our little band of Impressionists for having swept away all the old prejudices and made havoc of conventions!" Now, however, he spoke of their "lack of talent and brutal clumsiness of execution." Elsewhere he wrote that "their works seem to bear out Dr Charcot's remarks regarding the falsified perception of colours that he has noted in the cases of many victims of hysteria."

Novelists have, in fact, a habit of misunderstanding the purely aesthetic, "plastic" side of art. And in the present case it was only natural that they should feel no liking for an art so little disposed to pander to their literary preconceptions, and, because it tended less and less to hold a mirror up to nature, so obviously unsuitable for illustrating any literary "text" and, so to speak, pictoralizing ideas.

To make things worse, the painters at this time were labouring under grave material difficulties. Their first sale at the Hôtel Drouot auction rooms (in 1875) proved how slender were their prospects of making a living by their art. The sale took place in a veritable pandemonium. "People did not merely roar with laughter," Gustave Geffroy tells us; "they brandished sticks and umbrellas and would have slashed the pictures to pieces, had they had the chance!" Canvases by Monet, Berthe Morisot and Sisley fetched prices ranging from fifty to a hundred and sixty francs, and ten of Renoir's went for less than a hundred francs a-piece. Monet actually attempted to commit suicide. Sheer fiasco was averted only by direct action on the part of Manet, who commissioned friends to bid for some of his pictures.

Now, since the painters had "to sell to live," it is not surprising that experiences like this, coupled with the venomous attacks on them in the press and the hostility of the public, led to a split in their ranks, which was not wholly due to differences of temperament. When a catastrophe occurs, everyone takes to his heels carrying away the most precious of his belongings. All the Impressionists carried away with them on their dispersal was their individual personalities, the theories of the past surviving only as a memory. The one thing they retained in common was that deep-rooted love of freedom which was now to lead them towards new avatars, untouched by outside influences, whether naturalistic or ideological, and to a determination to make good that "plastic autonomy" — the claims of form and colour to reign unquestioned in their own right — to which they had so brilliantly pointed the way.

1881-1884

1881 **Sixth Group Exhibition** (April 2 - May 1. 13 exhibitors) at 35, boulevard des Capucines.
Monet settles at Poissy; Sisley makes a stay in the Isle of Wight. Birth of Picasso.
Cézanne comes to Paris (January-April); stays at Pontoise (May-October), where he meets Gauguin and Pissarro.
Renoir visits Algeria in the spring; leaves for Italy in the autumn, "to see the Raphaels."

1882 **Seventh Group Exhibition** (March. 8 exhibitors), organized by Durand-Ruel.
Great Retrospective Courbet Exhibition at the Ecole Nationale des Beaux-Arts (May, 193 exhibits).
Manet exhibits his **Bar aux Folies-Bergère** (National Gallery, London). Seriously ill, spends summer at Rueil.
Monet at Varengeville and Pourville, both near Dieppe. Sisley sets up house at Moret.
Cézanne at L'Estaque; then in Paris (February-September). Accepted at the Salon. At Le Jas de Bouffan, near Aix.
On his return from Italy Renoir visits Cézanne at L'Estaque. Visits Algeria for the second time.

1883 **One-man show at Durand-Ruel's :** Boudin, Monet, Renoir, Pissarro, Sisley (February-June).
Huymans publishes **L'Art Moderne.** Exhibition of Japanese Prints at the Galerie Petit.
Monet settles at Giverny, with Mme Hoschedé. Stays at Etretat, Le Havre, in Provence (with Renoir).
Pissarro at Osny near Pontoise and at Rouen, with Gauguin. Sisley settles at Saint-Mammès.
Renoir in Guernsey (September), on the Riviera with Monet (December). Beginnings of his Ingresque period.
Cézanne roams Provence with Monticelli. **Gardanne.** Visited by Renoir and Monet.
Gauguin gives up stockbroking and decides henceforth to devote himself to painting.
With his Portrait of Aman-Jean Seurat makes his début at the Salon; paints **La Baignade** (Tate Gallery, London).
Manet's death (April 30).

Manet's abrupt disappearance from the scene synchronized with:
1. the emergence of a new generation (Gauguin, Seurat, Van Gogh) and
2. the complete split, despite Durand-Ruel's efforts, of the Impressionist Group; it had been foreshadowed by their differences of opinions as early as 1880. Their geographical dispersal (with Pissarro at Eragny, Monet at Giverny, Sisley at Saint-Mammès, Cézanne at Aix, and Renoir sharing his time between travels and stays in Paris, before finally settling down, too, in Provence) was accompanied by like divergences in their art. Now, as Lionello Venturi puts it, "Monet leaned towards a symbolism of light and colour, Pissarro was attracted by Pointillism, Renoir set to acquiring the elements of academic form, Cézanne concentrated on problems of construction, and Sisley found his way out in 'mannerism'" (Cézanne, 1936, p. 29). While guided by their innate genius, Renoir and Cézanne reached, without faltering on the way, their plenitude—in a steady ascent, which is illustrated by the colourplates that follow; Monet, Sisley and Pissarro, having been more closely involved in Impressionism, and therefore feeling more at a loss as to their future course, passed through various phases, hesitant, mannerist or decorative, without being able to regain the equilibrium and spontaneity which had been theirs in the early days of the movement.

Monet. At Vétheuil (1878-1881). Scenes of the village; beginning of his "free" Series: **The Breaking up of the Ice.** At Poissy (1881-1883). In April, 1883, settled at Giverny, where he lived until the end of his life. Busied himself with his flower-beds, water-gardens, boat-shed. Took more and more to painting "Series," which he exhibited at Durand-Ruel's, then at Bernheim's Gallery: in 1891 the **Haystacks** series, in 1892 the series of **Poplars,** in 1895 of the façade of **Rouen Cathedral,** of views of **London** in 1904, and of **Venice** in 1912, of **Waterlilies** in 1909. Died at Giverny on December 5, 1926.

Pissarro. Settled at Eragny in 1884. Exhibited in the Salon des Indépendants, took up Seurat's Divisionism. After 1888 reverted to the free impressionist technique, indulging in a new, often most happily inspired, lavishness of colour. Stayed in London in 1890, 1892, 1897; in Belgium in 1894; at Rouen in 1896; at Dieppe in 1900 and 1901; at Le Havre in 1903. His views of Paris, done like Monet's later works in "series," are his last masterpieces; **Place du Théâtre-Français** (1898), **Les Tuileries** (1899), **Pont-Neuf** (1900), **Quai Malaquais** (1903). Died in Paris on November 13, 1903.

Sisley. Withdrew to Saint-Mammès, on the edge of Fontainebleau Forest, in 1883. The banks of the Loing were still his favourite subject, but the disturbing influence of Monet affected for the worse the native ease and delicacy of his responses. Travelled in Normandy in 1894, in Wales in 1897. Died alone and almost penniless on January 29, 1899, without having been able to obtain his French naturalization, applied for in 1895.

AUGUSTE RENOIR (1841-1919). NUDE, 1880. 31¾×25½". MUSÉE RODIN, PARIS.

LIKE RUBENS AND BOUCHER, RENOIR WAS A GREAT MASTER OF THE NUDE. THE SENSUOUS APPEAL OF THIS FIGURE ENCHANTED RODIN; ITS FULL GRACE COMBINED WITH THE SHARPENED COLOUR SHOWS THAT THE ARTIST WAS MOVING FROM IMPRESSIONISM TOWARD THE MANNER OF INGRES.

"The Earth, Paradise of the Gods, that's what I want to paint."

RENOIR

Though there is no dispute as to the eminence of Renoir's genius, his work has had no influence at all on Modern Painting. It is regarded as something apart, unique, inimitable, the expression of a prodigious sensibility, defying all analysis. Also its highly personal, instinctual qualities do not fit in with any aesthetic theory of our times. While Cézanne's art had long-lasting repercussions, whose end is not for to-day nor to-morrow, Renoir's brought him no disciples. Yet, under its outward aspect of smiling, serenely voluptuous hedonism, the art of this great French painter concealed, like that of so many others, a secret unrest, an inner conflict—almost a tragedy—of divided purposes, which lasted from his beginnings (influenced quite normally by the old masters, Raphael and the Venetians, as well as by relatively modern masters such as Delacroix and Ingres) down to his last phase. In that last phase the rapturous exuberance of forms posed in full light gives place to an amazing starkness, all extraneous aspects of reality being pruned away ; the artist has reached the stage when memories, refined by age, suffice, " all passion spent."

Throughout its course Renoir's work was governed by the promptings of an intensely vivid, almost animal sensibility. Nevertheless, unlike Courbet, he was no votary of instinct pure and simple ; time and again he talked of his " research-work." Splendidly aware of the outside world, and impressionable as he shows himself to be in the dazzling profusion of his colour, Renoir made no secret of his opinion that it is not by looking at nature that a man learns to paint but by looking at the masterpieces in museums. Thus we find in Renoir a constant struggle between his instinct and his intellect. This might have led him to a nicely tempered eclecticism like that of Chassériau ; but his genius was on the alert, ever ready to interpose that " personal touch," which gives short shrift to reasoning and discretion. However it well may be that, had Renoir been given a classical—instead of a very rudimentary—education, that phase of his art when he was studying it almost " intellectually," and which he called his " harsh " period (1883), might have led to different results. Perhaps that scepticism, or caution, which comes of reasoning, would have prompted him to investigate for himself, like Ingres (whose fervent admirer he was for many years), the problems of style. But, for lack of an advanced education, he fell back on the examples of the Old Masters, and applied himself more to discovering the secrets of their power than to literally expressing his own optical sensations. " In 1883," he said, " there was a sort of break in my work." But what great artist has not experienced such " breaks " ? No artist escapes that inner conflict which he tries to camouflage as best he may by throwing off witty remarks, much as the traveller on a lonely road whistles to conceal his nervousness. And Renoir often made such remarks. He was well aware that equalling the Masters of the past was one thing ; surpassing them, another. And Renoir saw that perhaps he might achieve that other thing by cultivating the personal freedom which bade him refrain from imitating the externals and rather make his own those vital qualities of their art which his own surging vitality, his sense of splendid plenitude, justified him in annexing. This was doubtless owing to an innate, unreasoned feeling for the essential stuff of painting, which was ever leading him on towards those masterpieces of his last phase. That his personality developed on such normal lines was due to the fact that he never deliberately set out to innovate. In fact he vigorously repudiated any such intention. We have said that he never disdained the lessons of Tradition ; quite otherwise, the great Flemish masters, no less than the Renaissance Italians, always were his exemplars. But here we come on a rather paradoxical aspect of his development. Needless to say, he went to Italy and came back " bowled over " by what he saw there. He adored Rubens, but he had now discovered Raphael, who dazzled him no less. Here lies the origin of that " break " which gave him so much anxious thought. Though his education was sketchy, Renoir was highly intelligent, and also extremely sensual. There was doubtless much of Courbet in his make-up, but also a good deal of Degas. Thus he had an instinctive awareness of the advantages of balanced composition, and it led him to mistrust the shimmering vagueness of Impressionism. It was in observing traditional classicism that he discerned the stabilizing influences he needed. So now his problem was to strike a just measure between the teeming chaos of his sensual self and the disciplinary counsels of his intellect ; to find a common ground in which the two aspects of his temperament could combine, allowing neither to take the lead. By way of reflection and experiment, he became convinced that colour is but a raw material so to speak, not an end in itself ; it is like the plaster or cement used in buildings whose lay-out an architect has planned. Thus he assigned colour a secondary rôle, that of contributing to the set-up of a structure ; but the working plan was his, the architect's primary concern. With the result that his pictorial edifice was built to last ; it was no more like those houses of mud and clay, run up in haste and at the weather's mercy, than it was like the frail, precarious structures of impressionist composition. Renoir visited Italy not as an academic tourist, but because an inner voice had told him he would find there a solution of his problem. He was quick to see that Raphael, like Ingres whom he admired for the same reasons, had a nature as profoundly sensual as his own, but expressed his sensuality by way of what were later to be called " distortions "—their origin being an emotional and temperamental drive much like his own. His first step (of whose inadequacy he soon became aware) was to discipline his colour and tone down the seething brilliancy of his palette. This was his " harsh " period ; but though his colour gives an impression of being somehow overlaid and hidden under a coating (almost like stucco), the composition still fell short of the solidity which he aimed at. For, in this phase, his intellect alone was in the saddle. And a hostile critic writing of the work of his 1883 " harsh " period observed : " These Renoirs are sour fruits that will never ripen."

There was a grain of truth in this. And Renoir certainly realized that if he continued on this path he would end up in academicism. Very likely his memories of Gleyre and the dim exhibits of the official Salon emphasized the danger.

Happily, Renoir had genius, and his genius lit on a solution of his quandary. He now assigned to colour the task of creating its own solidity ; he learned the uses of *constructive* deformations which, from now on, gave his compositions all the balance, weight and natural density that could be desired, without letting us have glimpses of an over-rigid underlying structure—like that of which we are sometimes reluctantly aware in the mechanical lay-out of such artists as Degas.

But the fact that several times in the course of his career Renoir spoke of his " research-work " implies that this was not the only problem on his mind. Almost on his deathbed he declared, " I am just beginning to learn how to paint "—which means that he was seeking for something unattained as yet. Was it technical perfection ? This seems unlikely. Though he spent much time in art museums and conned assiduously Cennini's *Treatise on Painting*, Renoir's knowledge of all a painter needs to know was innate. His *Grande Baigneuse* of 1880 is as well painted as his 1916 *Baigneuses*. Renoir may not be a modern painter in the current meaning of the word. He is, rather, one of the great masters of all time. If he joined in the Impressionists' cult of light, this was because he wished to place his expression of life in a setting as much " alive " as life itself ; for him light was to play a more vital part than that of an accessory of realism. In Renoir's art, colour is treated not as a lucky-bag of handy flummeries for milliners (as Courbet put it, with Delacroix in mind), but a solid substance like flesh or earth, fitted to serve the building of the dream of the master-builder that he was. Hence, doubtless, the " weight " of his Nudes, so solidly planted in the light, which seems to encase them closely, indeed to shape them, as does the water round a floating swan. Hence, too, perhaps, that often uniform " script " employed by Renoir, in which colour, reduced to a few tones, becomes for him solely a plastic substance to manipulate—like that plastic substance whose shaping in his last phase, when paralysis

A. RENOIR (1841-1919). IN THE LUXEMBOURG GARDENS, 1883. 25½×21¼". PRIVATE COLLECTION, SAINT-PREX, SWITZERLAND.

THIS WAS PAINTED IN THE SAME YEAR AS THE FAMOUS THREE VERSIONS OF *THE DANCE*; A YEAR IN WHICH RENOIR HIMSELF NOTICED THERE WAS "A BREAK" IN HIS WORK. HE HAD RENOUNCED IMPRESSIONISM, VISITED ITALY AND BEEN CAPTIVATED BY RAPHAEL'S ART. HE NOW EXHIBITED IN THE SALON, MIXED IN "HIGH SOCIETY" AND INDULGED FOR A WHILE IN A SLIGHTLY SELF-CONSCIOUS ELEGANCE, WHICH, HOWEVER, THANKS TO HIS FINE INSTINCT, NEVER LAPSED INTO MANNERISM.

A. RENOIR (1841-1919). LANDSCAPE WITH BATHERS, 1916. 15×19".
NATIONAL MUSEUM, STOCKHOLM.

RENOIR'S "INGRESQUE" PERIOD WAS BUT A PASSING PHASE. THE POETIC FERVOUR OF HIS ART NOW DEEPENS AND INTENSIFIES. AROUND 1916 HE REVERTS FREQUENTLY TO THIS THEME OF BATHERS IN A LANDSCAPE (OTHER VERSIONS ARE IN THE BARNES FOUNDATION, MERION), ENDOWING IT WITH A SPLENDOUR OF FORMS, LIMNED IN LIGHT, EQUALLED BY TITIAN ALONE.

immobilized his hands, his eye alone could guide in making that mighty statue, his *Venus Triumphant.*

What, then, was Renoir's aspiration ? To elevate his realism to the nobility of classical art ? Had he not said *à propos* of Raphael's *Venus entreating Jupiter* : " What arms ! It's lovely, but one thinks of a good housewife, about to go back to her kitchen ! "

Herein lies, perhaps, Renoir's secret. Some days before his death he exclaimed : " What splendid men those Greeks were ! The earth, the Paradise of the Gods—that's what I want to paint." May we not deduce the goal of his " research-work " from this remark ? If we study attentively the evolution of his colouring, from the extreme smoothness of 1883 down to the so-called " rubicundities " of his last manner, we feel in Renoir a steadily increasing need for freeing himself from all over-realistic associations. Thus the goal of his researches may well have been that grandiose, poetic art of his dreams, in which the divine and the human merged into each other, in an ecstasy of radiant joy whose intimations pervade his long life's work. This was the ideal which Renoir, perhaps naïvely, pursued and in whose service he stripped his art persistently of all that seemed extrinsic or impure, at the risk of losing all touch with reality in the service of an ambition transcending the utmost scope of the imagination.

P. CÉZANNE (1839-1906). L'ESTAQUE: THE VILLAGE AND THE SEA, 1878-1883. 20½×25¼". PRIVATE COLLECTION, SWITZERLAND.

CÉZANNE LIVED AT L'ESTAQUE, NEAR MARSEILLES, FOR MANY YEARS, AND NEVER WEARIED OF PAINTING IT UNDER ITS DIVERS ASPECTS (CHIEFLY IN 1878 AND 1883-1885). NOTEWORTHY HERE IS THE HIGHLY PERSONAL TREATMENT OF THE SUBJECT, IN SLANTING, PARALLEL, STILL SOMEWHAT IMPRESSIONIST BRUSHSTROKES, AND THE RHYTHMIC VALUE OF THE FACTORY CHIMNEYS.

"I want to paint the world's virginity..."

CÉZANNE

Thus said Cézanne. Undoubtedly the desire to "make pictures" goes back to infancy. Not merely to the phase when the youngster tries his hand at drawing human figures, but to that earlier period of wholly "abstract" scrawls (like "doodling") which precedes any conscious imitation of reality. Due primarily to a purely physical desire for movement, it comes also of an urge to "*make*," to create something. And here we have an origin of Abstract Art which, when the time comes, we must not fail to consider.

But, with literal awareness of reality the child begins to draw his "little men"; this is conscious art. And likewise it means that an element of make-believe is now involved. He takes to playing games, and says to his small friends, "You'll be this, and I'll be that." According to the originality of their imaginations—the extent to which instinct masters intellect or *vice versa*—some children imitate reality, while others, a gifted few, transpose it into inventions of their own, which can be, as we all know, quite amazing.

I. 30

P. CÉZANNE (1839-1906). THE TWISTED TREE, 1882-1885. 18×21¾". PRIVATE COLLECTION, ARLESHEIM.

FOR PISSARRO A TREE REMAINS AN ISOLATED, SELF-SUFFICIENT MOTIF; WITH CÉZANNE IT IMPLEMENTS THE UNITY OF THE COMPOSITION, AND IS BUT A PRETEXT FOR RHYTHMICAL INFLEXIONS.

When he lets his instinct speak, the artist is always something of a child living in a fairy-tale world. This is especially true of Cézanne. He conjured up a world in the likeness of his sensibility. "I have tried to find the geological substructure," was how he put it. Far more a painter than a bucolic poet (à la Corot), he saw nature uniquely as the stuff of pictures. But the childish propensity to make-believe, coupled with his exceptional imagination, led in this case to a systematization of his truth. Instead of assembling the pictorial *data* of nature in a literal portrayal which he does not feel, he uses them for the creation of a new-born aspect of his personal response, embodying the "geological substructure."

That Cézanne has influenced, and long will influence, painting is due to the fact that his view of art, for all its novelty and boldness, is intensely human, and legitimately encourages artists to hark back to that state of childish grace for which all hanker more or less in their heart of hearts. Fortunately, thanks to the haunting dissatisfaction that never left him, Cézanne never achieved the aim of the artist in quest of a personal "manner"; he never "found himself." Nor indeed have we, nor our artists, "found" him. Cézanne's world was in constant gestation; always he was looking for his world and his world was seeking him. If Cézanne has given us, "for to admire," the picture of a world virgin he would have it be, this is due to the unifying force of an aesthetic system not purely intellectual, but warmly sensitive in its responses. For the first time painting is not a translation but has a language of its own (like mathematics); not the Esperanto of a traditional universal art, but with a

vocabulary unknown to grammarians and more like cries wrung from the heart. We are reminded of Constable, that other pathfinder, who said that whenever he sat down, pencil or brush in hand, and gazed at a scene of nature, the first thing he did was to forget every picture he had seen. Though Cézanne, in his early days, may not have thus forgotten previous painting, one thing is sure—that when he literally fled from Paris and took refuge in his beloved Provence, he had realized that neither what he saw in art-museums nor even the works of his contemporaries meant much to him.

There are so many facets to Cézanne's art and such is its complexity that its commentators have formed very different views of it ; much as, when several artists paint the same subject, their pictures are usually quite different. But all agree in holding that amongst the many " fathers " ascribed to Modern Painting, Cézanne is the most authentic and the greatest.

His enormous influence on the course of the painting of to-day (and doubtless of to-morrow) is due to the fact that he was at once an incomparable colourist, boldly architectural in his composition, and, by common consent, inventor of the most strikingly new rhythms.

After his venture into Impressionism, he left the neighbourhood of Paris and went South to Aix-en-Provence (his birth-place), then to l'Estaque. Here he had a wholly Latin atmosphere, congenial to the Southerner he was, and was no longer tempted by the faintly misted skies of the Ile-de-France to forgo his natural penchant for clean-cut form, and yield to the lure of a Nature before which, as Corot recommended, the artist should be humble, thus forfeiting the freedom of his brush. Turning his back resolutely on Impressionism (of which he retained little but a few aesthetic pointers), he set out methodically to ascertain in the scene before him—Nature at her most candid, and denuded—not how it was, but how it acted. And he applied the same method to the masterpieces in the museums,

CÉZANNE HAS FULLY MASTERED HIS STYLE, AT LAST HE TRULY INTEGRATES HIS FIGURES IN THE LANDSCAPE (THE DREAM OF EVERY PAINTER) IN HIS LONG SEQUENCE OF "BATHERS," MEN AND WOMEN, IN WHICH THE HUMAN ELEMENTS FORM PART OF A VAST ARCHITECTURAL SCHEME.

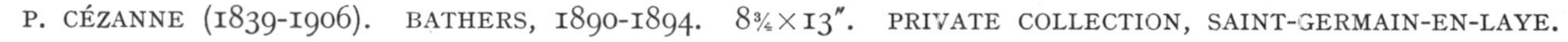
P. CÉZANNE (1839-1906). BATHERS, 1890-1894. 8¾×13″. PRIVATE COLLECTION, SAINT-GERMAIN-EN-LAYE.

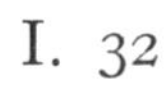

I. 32

P. CÉZANNE (1839-1906). THE BOY IN A RED WAISTCOAT, 1890-1895. 36¼×28¾". PRIVATE COLLECTION, ZURICH.

CÉZANNE DID FOUR SEPARATE PORTRAITS OF THIS YOUNG ITALIAN MODEL, DRESSED AS A PEASANT OF THE CAMPAGNA; THEY ARE RANKED AMONGST HIS MASTERPIECES. IT WAS WITH REFERENCE TO THIS ONE THAT GEFFROY WROTE IN 1895 THAT "IT CAN BEAR COMPARISON WITH THE MOST BEAUTIFUL FIGURES IN ALL PAINTING." NOTEWORTHY IS THE EXPRESSIVE DEFORMATION OF THE ARM.

which likewise he regarded as simple natural expressions, whose essential organic structure it was for him to detect.

Instead of following in the logical order one would expect, Cézanne's aesthetic and his technique are so closely bound up together that it is hard to decide which led to the other. This is, perhaps, due to a contradiction lying at the root of his work. A shy, devout, circumspect countryman, he liked solitude and was instinctively drawn to the solid and enduring ; in short, his outlook was conservative. Nevertheless he set out to build a private " universe " all by himself. Naturally he took a look at what others had built ; thus he approved of Rubens and Veronese. Still, after seeing them, he politely raised his hat and went his way ; he had his own ideas on the subject. Cézanne was a self-taught builder who insisted on following his own bent—meaning the use of new materials and avoidance of all standardization. So now we have our staunch conservative turning revolutionary ! Thus he constructed his universe on his own lines, out of the visual sensations he registered when viewing the world of nature less as a static landscape than as a living being. The new conception of reality called for wholly new methods — which led his friend, Schuffenecker, to say of him, " Cézanne has never made a picture or a work of art," but Cézanne himself to say, " I shall remain the primitive of the path I have opened up."

The construction of Cézanne's " world " called for new technical methods :

1. Cézanne viewed nature solely through his own eyes, the literal realism of traditional painting meant little to him, and his so-called distortions (which led Huysmans

THIS LITTLE STATUETTE, ASCRIBED TO PUGET, FIGURES IN TWO OTHER PAINTINGS BY CÉZANNE, AS WELL AS IN SEVERAL DRAWINGS AND WATERCOLOURS. CÉZANNE WAS MUCH TAKEN BY ITS INNOCENT GRACE.

... PLASTER CAST C. 1895. 24¾×31¾". NATIONAL MUSEUM, STOCKHOLM.

P. CÉZANNE (1839-1906). LE CABANON DE JOURDAN, 1906. CÉZANNE'S LAST PAINTING.
25½ × 31¾". KUNSTMUSEUM, BASEL.

ON OCTOBER 15, 1906, WHEN WORKING ON THIS, HIS LAST MASTERPIECE, IN THE COUNTRY NEAR AIX, CÉZANNE WAS CAUGHT IN A RAINSTORM, COLLAPSED AND WAS TAKEN HOME IN A CART. HE DIED ON OCTOBER 22.

to say he must be suffering from eye-disease) are due to a scrutiny of nature far keener than the normal.

2. His chief, most fruitful discovery was, to his mind, that of " modelling with colour," and " rendering form with the brush," instead of by the classical light-and-shade.

3. His method of rendering form modelled in colour was first to mix up and lay on a thick foundation ; then skilfully stripping his palette down to bare essentials, to put on light touches (calling to mind watercolour technique), disposed in small constructive masses like the stones in a building. One day when Cézanne and Pissarro were painting side by side, a peasant stopping to watch them said of Pissarro, " He prods ! " and of Cézanne, " He smacks! "

4. The constructional planes are allocated with an eye to associations of warn and cool tones, following the interplay of vertical and horizontal lines, so dear to Raphael. Cézanne also conjures up in his landscapes such geometrical figures as the cylinder, the cone, the sphere, which play a basic part in many forms of architecture.

These observations may, it is hoped, suggest why a picture by Cézanne gives a sensation of depth quite different from that given by classical perspective, which is based on receding lines and distance-marking objects.

1884-1891

1884 A new association, **Les Vingt,** is founded in Brussels by Octave Maus (January).
Foundation of the Salon and **Société des Indépendants:** Seurat, Signac, Cross, Redon, Angrand, Dubois-Pillet.
Seurat exhibits his **Baignade à Asnières** (Tate Gallery, London). Divisionism.
Foundation of **La Revue Indépendante** (edited by Félix Fénéon).
Manet Memorial Exhibition at the Ecole des Beaux-Arts. Manet auction sale at the Hôtel Drouot.
Monet at Bordighera (January-March), Menton (April), Etretat (August).
Renoir paints **L'Après-midi des Enfants** at Wargemont. (Nationalgalerie, Berlin).
Gauguin at Rouen (March-October); goes to Copenhagen (November).

1885 Renoir at Wargemont (July and November), at Essoyes (September, October). **Les Grandes Baigneuses** (C. S. Tyson Coll., Philadelphia).
Seurat at Grandcamp. Gauguin returns (June); meets Degas at Dieppe (August).
Van Gogh at Nuenen. **The Potato Eaters** (May). Leaves for Antwerp (November).
A new departure: the Montmartre cabarets. Aristide Bruant at **Le Mirliton.**

1886 **Eight and Last Group Exhibition** (May 15—June 15. 17 exhibitors), rue Laffitte.
Renoir, Monet, Sisley stand out. Degas shows 10 pastels of nudes.
Great **Impressionist** Exhibition at **New York** organized by Durand-Ruel.
Seurat at Honfleur. Exhibits **La Grande Jatte** (Art Institute, Chicago).
Fénéon publishes **Les Impressionnistes en 1886;** and Zola, **L'Œuvre.**
Monet at Haarlem, then at Belle-Ile (September-November), where he meets Geffroy.
Gauguin's first stay at Pont-Aven in Brittany (June-November).
Vincent van Gogh comes to Paris (March). Meets Lautrec, Pissarro, Degas, Gauguin, Seurat.
Le Douanier Rousseau exhibits for the first time, at the Salon des Indépendants.
Moréas publishes his Manifesto; founds the **Symboliste** review with Gustave Kahn.

1887 Antoine founds **Le Théâtre Libre.** Exhibition of "Les Vingt" at Brussels.
Vincent van Gogh meets Emile Bernard. Landscapes at Asnières. Pointillism.
Gauguin in Martinique with Charles Laval (April-December).
Toulouse-Lautrec paints his first scenes of Montmartre life.
Juan Gris, Marc Chagall born. Death of Jules Laforgue.

1888 Van Gogh leaves for **Arles** (February). Gauguin's eventful stay there (October-December).
Gauguin has a one-man show at the Galerie Boussod et Valadon.
Gauguin's second stay at **Pont-Aven,** Emile Bernard. Synthesism, Cloisonnism.
Bonnard, Vuillard, Denis, Ranson, Sérusier meet at the Académie Julian. The **Nabis.**
Seurat at Port-en-Bessin. Exhibits **Les Poseuses** (Barnes Foundation, Merion) and **La Parade** (Stephen C. Clark Collection, New York).
Cézanne at Paris. Meets van Gogh and Gauguin.
James Ensor paints his large-scale work: **Entrance of Christ into Brussels.**

1889 **World's Fair in Paris.** The Palace of Machinery. The Eiffel Tower.
Impressionist and Synthesist Group Exhibition at the Café Volpini.
Two-man show by Rodin and Monet at Galerie Petit.
Verlaine publishes **Parallèlement;** Bergson, **Les Données immédiates de la Conscience.**
Lautrec's first appearance at the Salon des Indépendants: **Au bal du Moulin de la Galette** (Art Institute, Chicago).
Gauguin at Pont-Aven, then at **Le Pouldu** (October). The Yellow Christ (Albright Art Gallery, Buffalo).
Van Gogh, victim of intermittent attacks of insanity, enters the **Saint-Rémy** Asylum (May 9).

1890 Foundation of La **Société Nationale** des Beaux-Arts by Puvis de Chavannes, Rodin, Carrière.
Foundation by Paul Fort of **Le Théâtre d'Art;** by Vallette, of **Le Mercure de France.**
Bonnard, Vuillard, Lugné-Poë at 28 Place Pigalle — Lautrec at the **Moulin-Rouge.**
Long stay by Gauguin at Le Pouldu with Seguin, Filiger, Meyer de Haan. Returns to Paris in December.
Seurat at Gravelines. Exhibits **Le Chahut** (Rijksmuseum Kröller-Müller, Otterlo).

1891 Retrospective Van Gogh Exhibition at Salon des Indépendants.
Death of Seurat (March 26). **Le Cirque** (Louvre).
Gauguin auction sale at the Hôtel Drouot (February 23). He leaves for Tahiti (April 4).

" Painting is the art of hollowing a surface."

SEURAT

As we have seen, the original creators of Impressionism had now drifted apart. Nevertheless their influence made itself felt on a new generation that was to exploit their undoubted discoveries, either by carrying them further, or by reacting against them and using them as a springboard for various new tendencies, very different but always having that purely and exclusively pictorial quality, defined by Cézanne, and named in the jargon of French studios *la peinture-peinture*. Around 1884 new names emerge, destined to become world-famous: Seurat, Redon, Van Gogh, Gauguin.

On June 30, 1884, was founded the *Société des Artistes Indépendants*. Amongst the four hundred artists figuring in this new organization were Cross, Dubois-Pillet, Luce, Angrand, Signac and Seurat. Their exhibition, housed in a temporary structure in the Cours des Tuileries, evoked fierce attacks in the press and general hostility amongst the public, recalling the darkest days of early Impressionism. In 1886 there was an attempt to organize an " Eighth Exhibition of Impressionist Painting." Requests by Signac and Seurat to take part in it met with a bad reception. Monet, Renoir, Caillebotte and Sisley withdrew. Eugène Manet — Edouard, his brother, had died in 1883 — who was one of the organizers was also hostile to the admission of Signac and Seurat. Degas himself was non-committal; however, he insisted that the word " Impressionist " should be omitted from the poster. In the end Degas, Berthe Morisot, Guillaumin, Pissarro and, at the eleventh hour, Schuffenecker, Odilon Redon, Signac, Gauguin and Seurat were allowed to take part. The last-named artist exhibited his *Sunday Afternoon on the Island of La Grande Jatte*, which was fiercely attacked by some, hailed with enthusiasm by others. The writer Félix Fénéon now became the spokesman of the new generation. In this same year he published a pamphlet, *Les Impressionnistes en 1886*, in which he expounded the theories behind the movement, then known under the name of " Neo-Impressionism."

Seurat described painting as " the art of hollowing a surface." He had in mind a new sort of space appropriate to the light that he was trying to place on canvas in terms of its reactions to the subject of the picture. What he wanted was to "make a picture," and (this, for the times, was a new venture) he aimed at a constructive lay-out. In this respect his classical turn of mind stood him in good stead. The constructive problem for Seurat was that of including three dimensions on a surface that had only two—obviously without literally boring a hole in it. (With twentieth-century painters this idea of the " hole " in the canvas became a positive obsession.) For getting this effect of " hollowness " Seurat had recourse to contrasts, the interplay of vertical and horizontal lines, of curves and arabesques. Hence his use of the linear patterns of banderoles and streamers, of parasols and whips, and likewise the diagonals of masts and sticks and chimneys, whose graphic rhythm determines zones of light, while variations of atmosphere provide a sort of flat perspective. Seurat's notorious lack of imagination involved him in much preliminary spadework, evidenced by the abundance of sketches he made for those all-too-few canvases which he produced during the brief ten years of his career. It is interesting to speculate how his art would have evolved had he not died at the age of thirty-two. In these sketches we find something more than an exploration, in pursuance of his theories, of the possibilities of rhythm; there is also sumptuous and superb brushwork, owing nothing to divisionist theory. " Pointillism," never more than an intriguing experiment, seems to have been less a stimulus than an impediment to the free, spontaneous expression to which, had he lived longer, he

G.-P. SEURAT (1859-1891). STUDY FOR LA BAIGNADE, 1883. 6½×10¼″. GEORGES RENAN COLLECTION, PARIS.

ONE OF SEVERAL STUDIES PREPARATORY TO SEURAT'S FIRST LARGE-SCALE COMPOSITION, *LA BAIGNADE*, 1883-1884 (TATE GALLERY, LONDON). THESE RAPID SKETCHES FROM NATURE, STILL SHOWING TRACES OF IMPRESSIONISM, WERE BRUSHED HASTILY ON THE SMALL WOODEN PANELS IN HIS PAINTER'S BOX.

would certainly have given rein. (Though we must recognize that in his case the " dot " is always constructive, never merely analytic.)

The importance of Seurat's work lies in his very personal application of the new methods he had thought up for the constructive lay-out of pictorial space. Cubism, as we shall see, drew freely on these discoveries and inventions and thus, if art-history regards Cubism as the most original way of seeing subsequent to Impressionism, it owes this to some extent to Seurat. In short Seurat might have said, like Cézanne : " I shall remain the primitive of the path I have opened up." No other artist's achievement—except perhaps that of Juan Gris who was to carry Seurat's discoveries a stage farther—better bore out Keyserling's epigram : " In France they make revolutions in order to safeguard tradition."

SEURAT'S THEORY OF ART

The easy competence of Seurat's early sketches proves that he was richly endowed by nature. But young men like to be dogmatic, and indeed it is natural for them to wish to feel that they are backed by solid knowledge — and to air it. Also in the eighteen-eighties Science was very much to the fore and its claims to regulate the future of the world were hotly debated. So we need not be surprised if the young painters of the period took to reading books which bore only indirectly on the practice of their art, and Seurat was attracted to such treatises as N. O. Rood's *The Scientific Theory of Colour,* Charles Henry's *Rapporteur esthétique permettant l'étude et la rectification esthétique de toutes formes,* David Sutter's

I. 36

G.-P. SEURAT (1859-1891). COURBEVOIE BRIDGE, 1886-1887. 18×21¾". COURTAULD INSTITUTE, LONDON.

WHILE STILL PAINTING THE BANKS OF THE SEINE IN THE IMPRESSIONIST MANNER, SEURAT WAS NOW BEGINNING TO USE THAT HIGHLY PERSONAL *POINTILLISTE* TECHNIQUE, WHOSE CLIMAX, OF PERFECT BALANCE AND SHIMMERING INTENSITY, CAME IN 1887.

Phenomena of Sight, Chevreul's *Principles of Harmony and Contrast of Colours,* and Charles Blanc's *Grammaire des Arts et du Dessin.*

The Neo-Impressionists claimed Delacroix for their immediate precursor. Thus in 1880, speaking of Delacroix, Charles Blanc drew attention to his way of " slashing green lines upon pink torsos, which produce exactly the effect of what we now call the optical mixture." But it is always rash to give the credit of a discovery to one artist alone, and many were the great Italians who had resorted to the technique that was now being " scientifically " re-invented.

The outcome of Seurat's investigations was that, with a view to not merely representing light but to making the picture itself a vibrant source of light, he employed what is known as the rainbow palette of pure colours — those of the spectrum — which, though put on in separate dots, blended in the eye, when viewed from the correct distance ; and he also codified another law of optics : that of " simultaneous contrasts." He summed up his theories as follows, in a letter to Maurice Beaubourg :

AESTHETIC. Art is harmony. Harmony implies an analogy of contraries, and also an analogy of similarities of tone, hue and line, disposed in relation to their dominants and under the influence of light, in gay, calm or sad combinations.

The contraries are :

For a tone, a more luminous or pale tone as against a darker.

For the hue, the complementaries ; as when a certain hue of red is opposed to its complementary colour (e. g. red-green ; orange-blue ; yellow-violet).

For the line, lines forming a right angle.

Gaiety of tone is given by the luminous dominant ; of hue, by its warm dominant ; of line, by lines ascending from the horizontal.

Calm of tone is equality of dark and light ; of hue, equality of warm and cool ; of line, the horizontal line.

Sadness of tone is given by the dark dominant ; of hue, by the cold dominant ; of line, by lines descending from the horizontal.

TECHNIQUE. In view of the phenomenon of the duration of a light-impression on the retina.

A synthesis necessarily ensues. The means of expression is the optical mixture of the tones and hues (local colour and that resulting from illumination, by the sun, by an oil-lamp, by gas and so forth) ; that is to say, of light elements and their reactions (shadows), according to the laws of contrast, gradation, and irradiation.

The frame should be in a harmony opposed to that of the tones, hues and lines of the picture.

By common consent Seurat has been designated the originator of Neo-Impressionism. But the patent, so to speak, of his invention is more justly due to Cézanne, who had already

PASSIONATELY FOND OF THE SEA, SEURAT VISITED THE COAST EACH YEAR: GRANDCAMP IN 1885, HONFLEUR IN 1886, PORT-EN-BESSIN IN 1888, LE CROTOY IN 1890, GRAVELINES IN 1889. IN 1888, THE YEAR IN WHICH HE COMPLETED HIS MASTERPIECES, *LA PARADE* AND *LES POSEUSES*, HIS STYLE CRYSTALLIZED IN A CLASSICAL PERFECTION.

G.-P. SEURAT (1859-1891). A SUNDAY AT PORT-EN-BESSIN, 1888.
26×32¼". RIJKSMUSEUM KRÖLLER-MÜLLER, OTTERLO.

said : " I want to make of Impressionism something solid and abiding, like the old masters." And now with a view to consolidating the intuitive discoveries of Impressionism, Seurat set out to reconcile line with colour, the permanent with the fugitive.

It was by a typically modern recourse to science — not quite without precedent, however, when we recall the influence of the XIVth century mathematicians in Italy on linear perspective — that Seurat set about putting Cézanne's dictum into effect. While at the *Ecole des Beaux-Arts* (where his early work bespoke a cult of Ingres and Holbein), this young devotee of draughtsmanship spent his time reading scientific treatises on colour. Naturally he was soon drawn to Impressionism, but for him the great problem was to harness science to the creative impulse.

Meanwhile, in collaboration with Paul Signac, he devoted himself to scientific research-work, familiarizing himself first with Maxwell's experiments, then with Charles Henry's treatises, then with the analyses of light and colour made by the American scientist, N. O. Rood. Illustrative of Prof. Rood's methods is this curious equation (relating to the combination carmine-green) :

$$50\,C + 50\,G = 50\,C + 24\,G + 26\,B \text{ (black)}.$$

(The first element shows the mixture of pigments ; the second its effect in light-rays.)

These investigations from the scientific angle led Seurat, Signac and, with them, Pissarro and, later (in 1887), Van Gogh to formulate the problems of Impressionism and lay down the principles of the course it now must follow for its " consolidation." In a letter to Durand-Ruel, Pissarro set out the programme of what was also called Divisionism. " We must substitute optical mixture for the mixture of pigments. Thus we can break up tones into their constituent elements ; since the optical mixture produces far intenser luminosities than those emitted by pigments mixed in the ordinary way."

Another " law " of Chevreul's, that of the " simultaneous contrast of colours," led them to press their analysis of colour phenomena still farther. Briefly, this " law " lays down that when two objects, of different colours, are placed side by side, neither keeps its own colour, but each acquires a hue resulting from the influence of the colour flanking it.

On the strength of these theories Neo-Impressionism propounded a new method of seeing the world. But the fallacy inherent in this plan for transforming glimpses of the fleeting into something permanent and static led merely to productions that seemed frigid, even petrified. Indeed this venture of Seurat's might figure as a purely personal whimsy, leading nowhere, were it not that his work has qualities of true pictorial, not merely scientific, value, and these, as we shall see, were to make their influence felt.

ONE OF THE STUDIES FOR *THE CIRCUS*, SEURAT'S LAST AND LARGEST COMPOSITION, LEFT UNFINISHED. (LOUVRE, PARIS).

G.-P. SEURAT (1859-1891). STUDY FOR THE CIRCUS, 1891. 21¾×18". LOUVRE, PARIS.

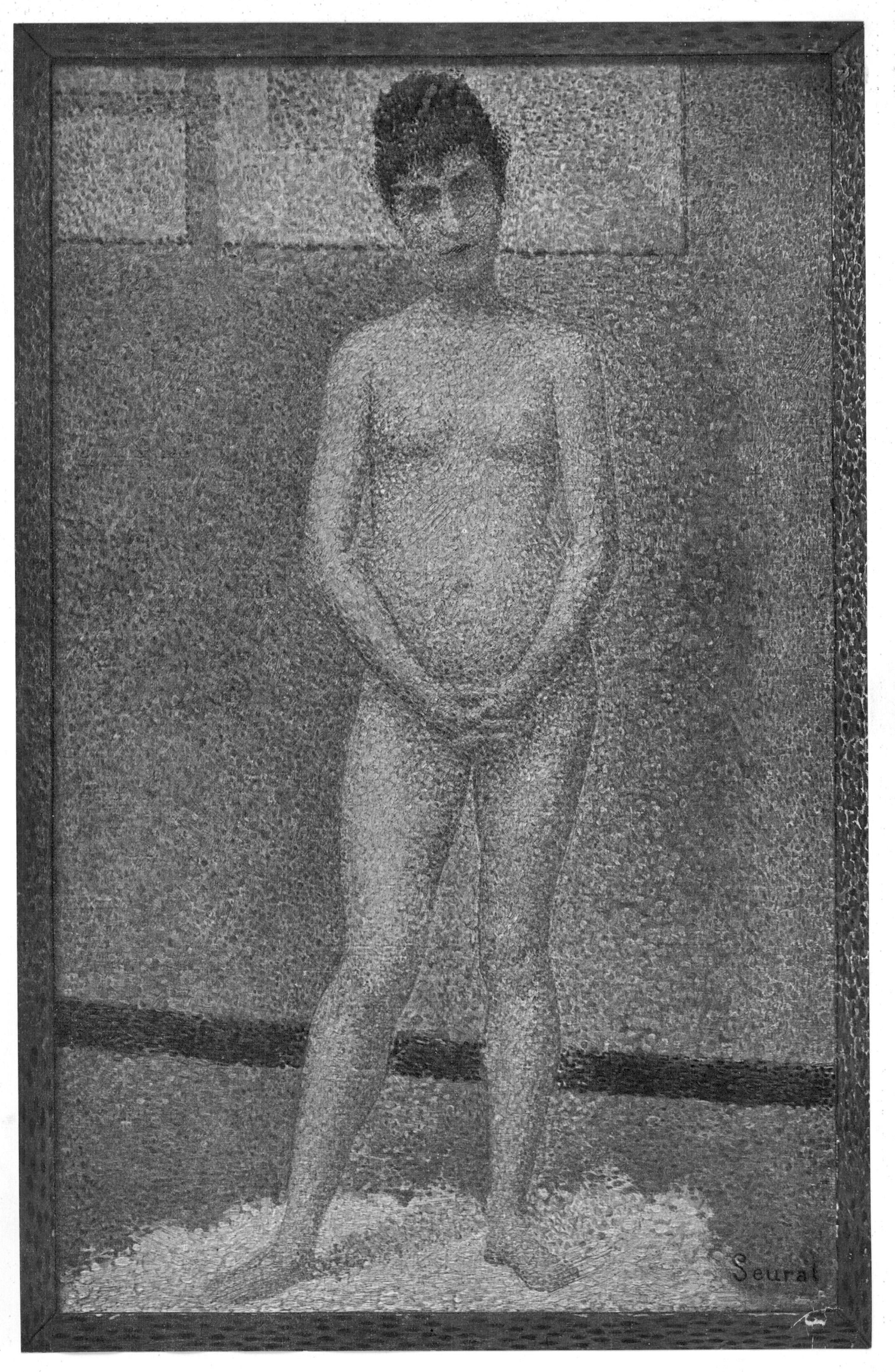

G.-P. SEURAT (1859-1891). POSEUSE, FRONT VIEW, 1887. 10¼×6¾". LOUVRE, PARIS.

SIGNAC

At the time when Seurat, a student at the *Ecole des Beaux-Arts* and still loyal to the principles of classicism, was dutifully copying Ingres and Holbein, Signac was already acquainted with Monet, and the works (in his early manner) which he now was turning out were frankly impressionist. What the two young men had in common was an interest in the problems of colour. To Seurat, who had a scientific turn of mind, fell the strictly analytic work, which covered form as well as colour. Signac, the more impulsive of the two, whose chief interest lay in the practical possibilities of colour, sought above all a means of getting his sensations on to canvas with the maximum intensity. Included in the group which now took form were Angrand, Dubois-Pillet and Cross, as well as Signac and Seurat. They exchanged views — at a café, needless to say ; and it was in the Café d'Orient that Signac expounded Impressionism to his friend. In return Seurat persuaded Signac to read Chevreul's *Contrast of Colours.* Thus their respective temperaments — Signac's all for colour-sensations, Seurat's all for architectural rhythm — struck fire from each other. The rival claims of the permanent and the fleeting were threshed out (as they had been by Monet and Cézanne) and, as might have been foreseen, the durable won the day. Though the two artists joined forces in their research-work, Signac confined his to the investigation of the phenomena of colour, while Seurat concentrated on geometry.

Signac employed the optical mixture exclusively, and in it he found a medium for new colour effects whose tones were never too " strong " for his liking. An accomplished writer, he took it upon himself to publicize the new theory ; he also published an enthusiastic appraisal of Jongkind's art. But he lacked the constructive ability which Seurat's better balanced mind had at its command, and his work misses those architectural qualities which go to " make a picture." What is purest in his art comes out in those luminously simple watercolours in which he gave free rein to his emotion, untrammelled by any scientific preconception.

SIGNAC'S EARLY PHASE SHOWS MONET'S INFLUENCE. IN 1884, WITH SEURAT, HE FOUNDED THE " SOCIÉTÉ DES INDÉPENDANTS AND NOW TOOK UP DIVISIONISM, WHOSE THEORETICIAN AND MOST FAITHFUL EXPONENT HE REMAINED. THIS SEASCAPE OF 1888 HAS STILL MUCH SPONTANEITY ; THE " MECHANIZATION " OF HIS STYLE CAME LATER.

P. SIGNAC (1863-1935). PORTRIEUX, 1888. 17¾×25¼". RIJKSMUSEUM KRÖLLER-MÜLLER, OTTERLO.

I. 40

H.-ED. CROSS (1856-1910). VENICE, PONTE SAN TROVASO, 1873. 24¾×31½".
RIJKSMUSEUM KRÖLLER-MÜLLER, OTTERLO.

THOUGH, LIKE SIGNAC, A DISCIPLE OF SEURAT, CROSS APPLIED POINTILLIST THEORIES LESS RIGIDLY, AND IN THIS RADIANT VIEW OF VENICE, IN WHICH WE HAVE ALREADY A FORETASTE OF FAUVISM, HE GIVES FREE REIN TO HIS EMOTION.

CROSS

Henri-Edmond Cross's real name was Henri Delacroix. For obvious reasons he demurred at using so august a surname ; hence the change. Born at Douai in 1856, he died in 1910 in the South of France, which he had portrayed with such eloquent devotion. He began by painting in dark hues. But he soon joined forces with the Pointillists and showed no less enthusiasm for the magical effects of bright, untrammelled colour.

The work of Cross deserves more interest than is generally accorded it. He was drawn to studying the problems of light and, indeed, as a good disciple of Impressionism, tried to press them to conclusions whose limits he did not foresee at first, the farthest he had in mind being, it seems, Monet's " extremism " in his *Views of the Thames*. His first idea was to carry Pointillism a stage farther. But at bottom he had the classical temperament and was all for constructive lay-out. He was loyal, in short, to the great Italian tradition, and often fell back on scenes taken from mythology. Also the exigencies of Pointillism hampered the natural suppleness of his line, the lyrical flow of his arabesques. He gives the impression of being inclined to set up, as against the quest of pure light, research-work into the secrets of equally pure colour. For he shared Seurat's ambition to give colour alone the function of delimiting surfaces ; without, however, forcing on it the geometrical patterns so dear to his friend. Thus he seems to have anticipated some of the ideas of Fauvism ; indeed Matisse himself has made no secret of his interest in Cross's work.

C. PISSARRO (1830-1903). TÊTE DE PAYSANNE, 1893. 25½×21¼″. PRIVATE COLLECTION, PARIS.

AFTER 1881 PISSARRO APPLIED HIMSELF TO FIGURE STUDIES. HIS TREATMENT NOW TENDED TOWARDS POINTILLISM.

V. VAN GOGH (1853-1890). INTÉRIEUR DE RESTAURANT, PARIS, SUMMER 1887. 17¾×21¼".
RIJKSMUSEUM KRÖLLER-MÜLLER, OTTERLO.

VAN GOGH MET SEURAT IN 1887 AND WAS FOR A WHILE UNDER THE SPELL OF POINTILLISM. "IT'S A MARVELLOUS DISCOVERY," HE WROTE TO HIS BROTHER. "BUT I ALREADY FORESEE THAT NEITHER THIS TECHNIQUE NOR ANY OTHER WILL BECOME A UNIVERSALLY ACCEPTED DOGMA."

GAUGUIN, VAN GOGH, PISSARRO

DIVISIONISTS

Oddly enough three artists whose careers do not suggest that colour sensations were their exclusive, or even their chief interest, displayed much interest in Divisionism. First we have Gauguin who painted a Landscape at Pont-Aven in the technique of the point, or dot; then a Still Life in the same manner, which he laughingly called the "dot-and-carry-one" style.

When, in 1887, Van Gogh visited Seurat, he was much impressed by his big canvases. Indeed he showed considerable enthusiasm for the pointilliste *technique, though this was probably not for its technical qualities, but because it might help him to step up the brilliancy of certain tones needed for the expression of those emotional experiences which bulked so large in his troubled life.*

Likewise Pissarro saw in the divisionist "system" only a set of new formulas and tested them, chiefly, it would seem, with an eye to their technical possibilities. With this in mind he painted a certain number of canvases. But not only did the severely scientific programme of the Pointillists conflict with that free expression of his sensibilities which meant so much to this "poet of the earth," but its formalism cramped the easy movement of his hand and that "colour inspiration" whose spontaneity he was determine to safeguard.

V. VAN GOGH (1853-1890). TÊTE DE PAYSANNE, 1885. 16¼×12½". PRIVATE COLLECTION, ZURICH.

"With red and green I have tried to depict those terrible things, men's passions . . ."

VAN GOGH

A great change was coming over modern painting and with the beginning of the twentieth century there appeared two new movements, both of extreme importance : Fauvism and Expressionism. We may sum up the purport of this change by saying that impressionist sensation was beginning to be replaced by expressionist thought.

The younger men seemed rather at a loss as to the use to make of the legacy of technical devices Impressionism had bequeathed. The pioneers of Neo-Impressionism deliberately " went one better," adding the system of the scientific division of tones to their " juxtaposition." An obviously useful contribution to technique, this extended the resources of Impressionism, but did not open any new or very promising horizons. The truth was that painters were troubling less and less about nature, and tending towards a preciosity, a " Byzantine " cult of pure technique, bordering on mannerism. Thus sensation was in danger of being refined out of existence, and any frank expression of it was coming to seem almost a sign of negligence.

A reaction was inevitable, and it took a drastically contradictory form. Sponsored by Cézanne and Renoir at its early stage, it set up their constructive and architectural conceptions against the vaguenesses of Impressionism. Still, this meant little more than differences of degree. In later phase the differences were fundamental, differences of *kind.*

Sensation being, so to speak, " played out," the artists fell to thinking, and such words as " idea " and " thought " began to replace " impression " and " sensation " in the vocabulary of aesthetics. Once again Courbet's influence was to make itself felt. It will be remembered that he was fond of talking about " thought," even lamenting that he " could find no thought in Raphael." He may have made this remark merely to startle, but one thing is certain — that he called on painting to express ideas. Thus, when he painted *The Stonebreakers,* he was careful to point out the humanitarian notions that had led him to choose this subject.

It was by considerations of this order — as we see in the case of Van Gogh — that painters were now led to switch their interest over from pure painting and technique to what was called " character." Thus Van Gogh observed the sad conditions of the life of the poor, and portrayed these with sympathetic understanding, while Gauguin took a different line, aspiring by means of Symbolism, and by drawing freely on the primitive and archaic, to impart a new significance to art.

If, in Cézanne's words, Monet was " only an eye — but what an eye ! " the Dutchman Van Gogh was only soul — but what a soul ! That of an utterly honest man in quest of an Absolute which he found only in a self-given death. But before reaching this forlorn solution he struggled unremittingly to implement a superhuman dream. And, in the course of the struggle, he assigned to painting an end that was, perhaps, not wholly new, but which he stamped with the mark of his passionate, cruelly frustrated personality.

Impressionism aimed solely at the expression of visual sensations ; Van Gogh's art at the expression of emotional experience. He was fond of Rembrandt, Delacroix, Millet and Daumier. He was all nerves, susceptibility, exaltation, and for him quite trivial happenings had a vast, almost transcendental significance. For a while he worked as a missionary in a mining district, but without success. What he really sought in painting was a sort of self-analysis, but in this too he failed. He asked of art a therapeutic treatment of the smouldering

V. VAN GOGH (1853-1890). STILL LIFE : DRAWING-BOARD WITH ONIONS. $19\frac{3}{4} \times 24\frac{1}{2}$".
ARLES, JANUARY 1889. RIJKSMUSEUM KRÖLLER-MÜLLER, OTTERLO.

THE DATE OF THIS STILL LIFE (WHOSE GRAPHIC ELEMENTS ADUMBRATE SOME ASPECTS OF PICASSO'S ART) CAN BE FIXED BY THAT OF THE MEDICAL YEAR-BOOK ON THE TABLE. IT WAS ONE OF THE FIRST WORKS PAINTED AFTER GAUGUIN'S EVENTFUL STAY AT ARLES.

unrest that never left him ; though it gave temporary alleviation, it could not avert the final, desperate catastrophe.

Unstable, physically unfit, an erotomaniac, a heavy drinker, Van Gogh had all the ills that flesh is heir to. Hence his nerve-racking indecisions as to his true capacities and his vocation. Was he cut out to be a preacher, a painter, or something else — or just nothing at all ? He never solved these problems to his satisfaction. Throughout his life he was the victim of a temperament at the mercy of every passing impulse, uncertain of its ends. Thus his career was one long, almost aimless pilgrimage. His consciousness of his infirmities drew him towards the moral and physical misfits of a social order to which he imagined he belonged. And his lack of self-confidence prevented him from finding within himself the will-power and energy needed to overcome his " inferiority complex." This perhaps is why he sought deliverance in observing the world around him. He, too, was not to paint " as a bird sings." He haunted his fellow-countryman Mauve's studio and took counsel from the Great Masters — in the same spirit as he took up theology courses ; less to find arguments for a faith he lacked than to know the dogmas. Soon he had amassed considerable knowledge ; all but the knowledge of his genius, for never could he get rid of the idea of his own incompetence. In his salutary quest of perfection, his method of reshaping the world had always something primitive, almost brutal about it. His early work is jagged, harsh, overwrought ; he uses dark, heavy pigment, and violent oppositions of colours. Such were Van Gogh's first steps in art.

At this time he was still in Holland. On his father's death he resolved to travel, but, having no programme, merely drifted to the nearest city. This was Antwerp, where he found a quite new atmosphere, and one which led him to go back on many of his old ideas and question the merits of his "reformative" tendencies. For one thing, he discovered Rubens, who vastly amazed him. After a while he moved to Paris, where new discoveries awaited him : Impressionism, Pointillism, Japanese art. And suddenly his palette lightened. He took to using brilliantly pure tones, and painting nudes, sunflowers, *japonaiseries* and such pictures as his *Fourteenth of July*. In a letter he told his brother that he now was painting "in the impressionist style." He was trying to give a new meaning to colour, using it as a derivative of his moods, tranquil or agitated as the case might be. And colour now became not merely a way of escape from his tormented self, but a sort of alcohol, in which he sought to find a counter-irritant. Certain physical effects of colour had been observed ; that blue calms, red excites, and so on. Van Gogh was to press these discoveries to an extreme. Thus figures, landscapes and interiors, often the same ones, are treated by him quite differently according to his physical or mental state at the time of painting. He sees yellow, for instance, not as the product of some mathematical equation (the *pointilliste* view), but as signifying love or friendship. "How lovely yellow is !" he once exclaimed, and, though all his life long he got nothing but rebuffs from women, yellow — love's emblem to his mind — was always his favourite colour. "With red and green I have tried to depict those terrible things,

ONE OF THE LAST AND FINEST PICTURES VAN GOGH PAINTED AT ST-RÉMY BEFORE GOING TO AUVERS. THE "ALPINES" WE SEE HERE SWEPT BY THE MISTRAL FORM PART OF A RANGE OF HILLS BETWEEN THE ARLES PLAIN AND ST-RÉMY.

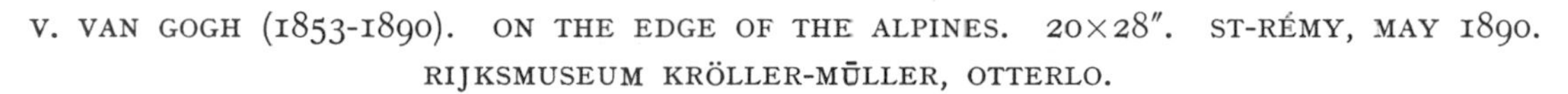

V. VAN GOGH (1853-1890). ON THE EDGE OF THE ALPINES. 20×28". ST-RÉMY, MAY 1890.
RIJKSMUSEUM KRÖLLER-MÜLLER, OTTERLO.

men's passions," was another of his remarks. After painting a café interior, he explained, " I have tried to convey that a café is a place where a man can ruin himself, go crazy, commit a crime." Thus he was always seeking for strongly affective tones corresponding to his emotions, and in the search for " psychological colour " gave extreme attention to the mixing of his pigments — in which, however, chance, of whose good offices Corot so often spoke, played often a considerable part. Thus Van Gogh's conception of painting was essentially a sort of colour symbolism, not without analogies with Christian symbolism, which not only imposed certain attitudes for the characters figuring in religious pictures, but also fixed the colour appropriate to each ; thus blue for the Virgin, violet for martyrs, red for the devil and so forth. " Colour *in itself* expresses something," Van Gogh said. Thus, to body forth his feelings, he did not depend on the subject only, but also on the colour and the form assumed by the colour in the expression of his intensely felt, though more or less repressed emotions.

Around 1888 his health showed some improvement, but this was not to last. In Paris he met Seurat, Pissarro, Signac and Lautrec, and, as ill luck would have it, Gauguin. Doubtless he learned much from Gauguin, but, besides his natural arrogance, Gauguin had all the vanity of the neophyte convinced he has a mission. He made poor Vincent's life unbearable, getting on his nerves to such an extent that one day at Arles, where they then were staying, Van Gogh flung a glass at his head and pursued him with a razor. (Gauguin, we may well surmise, had been " asking for it.") Worse still, Van Gogh cut off one of his own ears. In hospital, thanks to the devoted care of the staff, his mental health improved ; but the shock had been terrible. And yet, in Arles, his troubled mind had found a relative equilibrium ; he had painted starry nights, glowing wheatfields, contented, happy faces *(The Young Peasant, L'Arlésienne, La Berceuse)*, and trees whose swirling movement somehow conjures up ideas of carefree joy and confidence that all is well with the world.

Far from being the sort of neurotic artist who courts such mental crises as a stimulant for his art, Van Gogh dreaded them and always took, if we may put it so, a sane man's view of his insanity. But, despite his efforts, he had another breakdown, and now entered the Saint Rémy Asylum in Provence. Here there was a lull, and now we see his favourite colour, yellow, reappearing triumphantly and more persistently than ever, though invaded here and there by black, green or grey patches that betray anxiety. For, under the surface, unrest persisted ; in a fit of petulance he hurried back to Paris, and then went to Auvers, where Dr. Gachet (of whom he was to make a very fine portrait) looked after him affectionately. But the end was near. At Auvers he painted his *Mairie du 14 Juillet*, in which, though the subject is the gay fourteenth-of-July festivities, he treats it in cold tones. He paints a few more dazzling wheatfields, but though his last canvas coruscates with flaming yellows, hovering above its rippling gold are some ominous patches, the black forms of crows. A few days later he shot himself with a revolver — whose origin has never been traced.

Van Gogh's last picture confirms the pertinacity of his desire to enlist colour in the service of his emotional experiences. It is in this respect that he ranks as a pioneer of Expressionism—less, in his case, the outcome of any technical programme or attitude to art than of a wish to express moods and feelings. And it is doubtless precisely because there was no set theory behind it that Van Gogh's conception of art's function had its lasting influence on the evolution of Modern Painting, an influence which bids fair to continue for some time to come.

In any case it took unmistakable effect upon Fauvism. Van Gogh's assertion that " colour *in itself* expressed something " had opened new horizons, and the " Fauves," who asked nothing better than that colour should be self-sufficient, found in the amazing efficacity of Van Gogh's palette a justification for their abandonment of *nuances* in favour of absolutely pure tones, and a means of conveying the new relationships between coloured planes arising from their conception of the two-dimensional canvas.

DR. GACHET, WHO WAS QUITE A "CHARACTER" AND A FAMILIAR FIGURE AT THE CAFÉ GUERBOIS, WAS ONE OF THE EARLIEST PATRONS AND FRIENDS OF THE IMPRESSIONISTS, WHO OFTEN CAME TO VISIT HIM AT AUVERS. ON LEAVING THE ST-RÉMY ASYLUM IN MAY, 1890, VAN GOGH CAME TO STAY WITH HIM AND PAINTED HIS PORTRAIT; ALSO THAT OF HIS DAUGHTER PLAYING THE PIANO. THE FIRST VERSION IS IN THE FRANKFURT MUSEUM; THE SLIGHTLY DIFFERENT VERSION, WHICH HE GAVE DR. GACHET, HAS BEEN PRESENTED BY HIS CHILDREN TO THE LOUVRE.

V. VAN GOGH (1853-1890). PORTRAIT OF DR. GACHET. AUVERS, JUNE 1890. 26¾×22¼".
LOUVRE, PARIS.

V. VAN GOGH (1853-1890). LA BERCEUSE (Mme ROULIN). ARLES, 1889. 35½×29½". PRIVATE COLLECTION, BASEL.

VAN GOGH PAINTED FIVE SUCCESSIVE VERSIONS OF "LA BERCEUSE," THE MODEL BEING MADAME ROULIN, WIFE OF HIS FRIEND THE LOCAL POSTMAN, WHOSE PORTRAIT HE ALSO PAINTED.

I. 49

P. GAUGUIN (1848-1903). THE VISION AFTER THE SERMON, 1888. 28¾×36¼".
NATIONAL GALLERY OF SCOTLAND EDINBURGH.

ONE OF THE FIRST PAINTINGS MADE BY GAUGUIN AT PONT-AVEN, ON HIS RETURN FROM MARTINIQUE, IN ACCORDANCE WITH THE NEW THEORIES OF "SYNTHESISM" AND "CLOISONNISM." ALBERT AURIER PUBLISHED AN ENTHUSIASTIC DESCRIPTION OF IT IN "LE MERCURE DE FRANCE," FEBRUARY, 1891, USING IT TO ILLUSTRATE HIS FAMOUS DEFINITION OF THE WORK OF ART AS "IDEOLOGICAL, SYMBOLIST, SYNTHETIC, SUBJECTIVE, DECORATIVE."

VAN GOGH AND GAUGUIN

When Gauguin and Van Gogh met in Paris in the autumn of 1886 the two men were greatly struck with each other. In the course of February 1888 Van Gogh left rather hastily for Arles, while Gauguin went to Pont-Aven for the summer. It was now that he painted this wonderful " Vision after the Sermon : Jacob Wrestling with the Angel " *in his new technique (to which he gave the names of Cloisonnism and Synthesism). He asked Van Gogh to come to Brittany, while Van Gogh urged him to move to Arles and to join him in founding a " Studio of the South." The little portraits adorning this correspondence are touching evidence of their liking for each other at this time. Finally Gauguin, always ready for new adventures, packed up and came to Arles on October 20. Somehow they succeeded in living together for two months, though their differences of temperament showed from the start, and the tension between them rose rapidly. On Christmas Day Van Gogh in a fit of madness cut off his own ear; and Gauguin beat a hurried retreat to Paris. But even so there had been time enough for Van Gogh, vastly impressed by Gauguin's intellectual attainments, to modify his style. He painted* L'Arlésienne *after a drawing by Gauguin, and under his influence began the sequence of five pictures known as* La Berceuse *which, while showing traces of the admiration both men had for Japanese prints, have the same decorative rhythm and symbolic harmony as* The Vision.

Pont-Aven

From 1886 to 1890 Pont-Aven, in Brittany, was the favourite resort of a group of artists, who in time came to be known as the Pont-Aven School.

Gauguin went there in 1886, partly, as he said, for reasons of economy, but also because he hoped to find " in this unspoilt land of old-world customs " an atmosphere quite different from that of " our atrociously civilized communities." Here he met his old friend Schuffenecker ; also Emile Bernard, to whom he gave a rather cool reception. Gauguin now seemed to be abandoning the analysis of colour, turning his back on Impressionism, and putting Pissarro, his erstwhile teacher, out of mind. A word that often cropped up in his conversation was " Synthesis." His visit was brief on this occasion ; he soon returned to Paris. During his second stay in Pont-Aven, in 1888, his contacts with other artists were on a wider scale. Several new -isms now came to the fore ; alongside Symbolism there arose Synthesism and Cloisonnism. On this occasion the original trio — Gauguin, Schuffenecker and Bernard — was joined later in the year by Henri Moret, the Dutchman Verkade and Sérusier. By Synthesism was meant " a concise simplification " of the forms expressing the Idea.

But it was Cloisonnism that led to the most heated discussions. Its technique was simple enough — that of binding forms in clean-cut contour-lines. Emile Bernard claimed paternity of the method, but there is no denying that this technique was not, strictly speaking, original ; it had precedents in Japanese prints, in stained-glass windows, and of course in *cloisonné* enamel-work (in which the " cloisons " are left visible) ; not to mention the popular picture-sheets produced at Epinal from the eighteenth century on. This technique found favour with the Pont-Aven group, and Sérusier codified it. It was now that Gauguin painted his *Yellow Christ* and his magnificent *Jacob wrestling with the Angel.* Next year, finding Pont-Aven overcrowded, the group migrated to the near-by village of Le Pouldu, making Marie Henry's inn their headquarters. Here Gauguin made the acquaintance of the Dutch painter Meyer de Haan. The inn parlour was decorated by Gauguin, Henri Moret, Maufra, Meyer de Haan and Sérusier.

There can be no doubt as to the coherency of the theories of the Pont-Aven group. One of these was that the artist should " dare everything," as Gauguin put it. Another, that the traditional views on art borrowed from Greece and Italy should be rejected, and a return made to archaic and hieratic forms, Assyrian or Breton as the case might be. Also that the artist should *suggest* impressions, conveying his " suggestion " by his arrangement of colours, light and shade, and thus produce the effect of music on the pictorial plane ; that outlines should be clean-cut, as in Japaneses prints and stained-glass windows (as described above) ; that flat colour rimmed by contour-lines should suggest a new kind of depth, due to the relative intensity of tones. And all these devices were to be put to the service of that one thing most desirable : the *Symbol.*

P. SERUSIER (1863-1927). LES BRETONNES, 1891.
PRIVATE COLLECTION, PARIS.

I. 50

[...]E DU POULDU, 1890. 28¾×36¼". PAUL FIERENS COLLECTION, BRUSSELS.

[...], GAUGUIN STAYED WITH HIS FRIEND MEYER DE HAAN AT LE POULDU, A HAMLET
[...]ING THIS PROLIFIC PERIOD THAT HIS STYLE ATTAINED COMPLETE MATURITY.

[...]s strike this iron soil, I hear that dull, muffled
[...]nance which I seek for in my painting."

GAUGUIN

[...]in, who was born on June 7, 1848, in Paris, was, to say the [...]n comic opera lines. There figured in it the stock characters [...]ing of Peru, a lady of letters, a jealous lover who shoots her [...]rvitude, a wine-merchant from Bordeaux—and the inevitable

[...] taste of the Latin-American scene, being taken there at the [...]r, brought back to France a few years later). When he was [...], with a tramp's wallet and staff for his sole equipment. In his sixteenth year he took to the sea, as an apprentice in the merchant service, and saw many remote corners of the world. On his return to France he married a Danish lady, by whom he had five children. He became a successful stockbroker, and did well on the *Bourse*, but threw up a good post, and lost all his money; then he was, successively, a commercial traveller, a navvy employed on the Panama Canal (for he had a herculean frame), secretary to a company, a bill-sticker, and finally—after some other avatars—a painter.

He had now found a vocation, unforeseen but fated to be permanent. Still it would not have been like Gauguin not to complicate his new existence. On the usual pretext —that of a craving for evasion, " to escape far, far away, where Nature is at her most exotic," as Mallarmé, the poet, put it—he took sail for the South Sea Islands, on which his choice had fallen, presumably because it would be hard to find a place remoter from France. And after a series of misadventures due to his cantankerous disposition, after creating masterpieces for which almost none of his contemporaries had any use, he died miserably poor and broken in health, neglected and alone.

Such was the picturesque life-story of this singular man. A versatile romancer, a dreamer of exotic dreams, a Bohemian born, with a loathing for every sort of control and an itch for travel, Gauguin had something in him of the knight-errant in quest of an earthly paradise. He held strong ideas of his own and was always ready to indulge in the most scatterbrain exploits ; in short, he was an *enfant terrible* who indulged his natural " contrariness " even on the aesthetic plane, but, above all, and though we cannot imagine how this came about, a painter of genius.

In painting Gauguin found something he had hardly dared to hope for, a means of synthesizing (to use a word he greatly favoured at one period) the multitude of cross-purposes that had hitherto embarrassed him, and welding them together into an harmonious whole. His work, whether the scene be Brittany or the South Seas, is pervaded by colour rhythms whose tone and form alike are imbued with melancholy, deep but never desperate. His happily inspired, wholly unique palette is remarkable for its rich, pervasive harmonies ; though the tones are brilliant, they are muted, recalling—a legitimate analogy since Gauguin himself often associated painting with music—the effect of muted trumpets in jazz bands.

Gauguin became aware of his vocation when in 1871 he made the acquaintance of Schuffenecker, a business colleague, who devoted himself to painting in his leisure hours. It is noteworthy that Gauguin was not a born artist ; he became an artist deliberately. At first he painted as an amateur, and perhaps he would never have gone farther, had he not met Pissarro in 1876. Until now Gauguin had, like all beginners, aimed at realism. He even exhibited in the 1876 Salon, securing admission easily enough. Then came the great slump of 1883. He abandoned his financial career, in which he had done very well for himself, and told his friends, " Now at last I shall paint every day."

He now tried his hand at Impressionism, but soon found that the detailed analysis its juxtaposed touches of colour necessitated cramped his tyle. He blamed Impressionism for centering its research-work on the eye instead of on the secret places of the heart. Indeed he vigorously combated most of the theories of his impressionist friends ; for he required broad surfaces to work on, without lingering over details, much as he needed complete personal freedom and opportunities of travel in far lands. It was perhaps this craving for the remote that made him so keenly interested in Japanese colourprints. Then a new idea waylaid him—he was always having new ideas. Living was cheaper in Brittany, and he now was short of money ; so he migrated (in 1886) to Pont-Aven. Here he met Schuffenecker again, and made Emile Bernard's acquaintance. They spent much time discussing art, and that burning topic of the day, the Symbolist Manifesto, which had just been published and declared that the whole duty of the artist was " to clothe the idea in a perceptible form." Here was a theory after Gauguin's heart ; it justified his replacing the prevailing semi-anecdotal art by the ideology that meant so much to him. Needless to say, he affected to disdain Symbolism, but he stood by its principles none the less. Thus in his South Seas compositions we see him trying " to clothe in a perceptible form " the ideas behind his *Tahitian Eve* and *The Enigma Lurking in the Depths of her Eyes*. Luckily Gauguin's " perceptible forms " were of greater value than his " ideas." However misty, even muddled, were the latter, his methods of expressing them were admirably lucid and precise. Likewise he championed Synthesis, as a counterblast to impressionist analytics ;

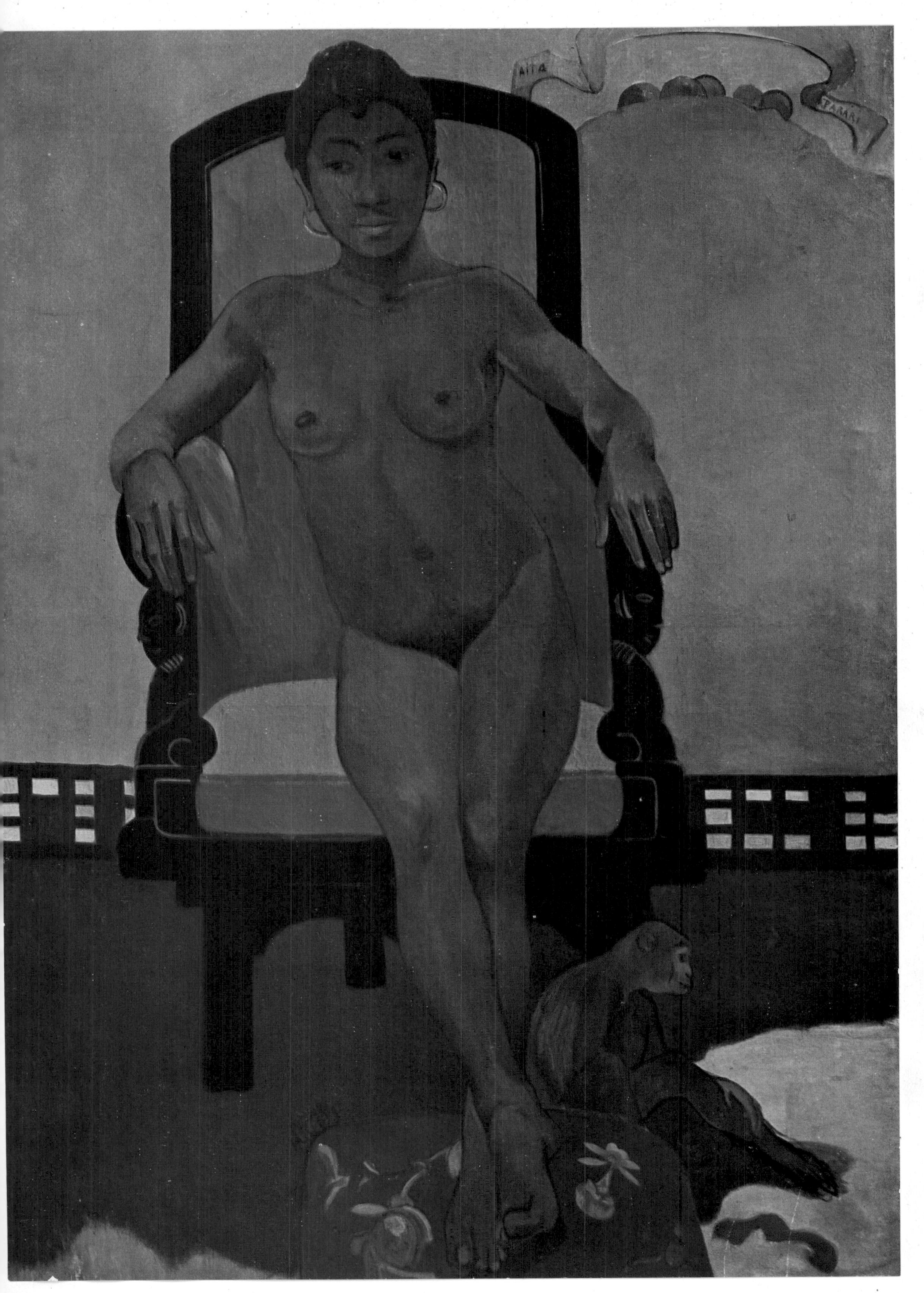

P. GAUGUIN (1848-1903). ANNAH THE JAVANESE, 1893 46×32¾″. PRIVATE COLLECTION, WINTERTHUR.

though this did not prevent him from ridiculing it when he saw fellow-artists making a fetish of its theories. His taste for Japanese art, for stained-glass windows, and even for the gaudy picture-sheets so popular in the last century—all which seemed to fit in with his ideas of Synthesism—led him on to what was known as *Cloisonnism*, which means binding surfaces with heavy contour-lines. It was during this phase that he painted that amazing *Vision after the Sermon*. By now his true personality was asserting itself. "There are noble lines," he said, "and deceptive lines; the straight line gives us infinity, the curve limits creation." Japanese art had taught him much; he now wished to eliminate, to strip his canvas of all but essentials. Form was to be suggested by pure colour; this was now the "Synthesis" he aimed at, and he preconized it with all the zeal of the neophyte, though, as we have already said, his sense of humour came to the fore when he saw it mechanically exploited by disciples who failed to grasp it emotionally. This was Gauguin's most rewarding discovery, the key to his telling simplifications and the fine integrity of his close-knit forms. "Art is an abstraction." He no longer gazes on nature with a view to interpreting it by means of an equivalent; as he tells us, he "thinks" his picture first. (We are reminded of Raphael's *In ipsius mente.*) Of his *Christ in the Garden of Olives* he once said: "It is imbued with an abstract sadness, and sadness is my *forte.*" Another of his remarks was: "What wonderful thoughts one can evoke by form and colour!" For his obsession with "thought" never left him. It was his cult of the Idea that led him to give such titles to his canvases as: "When are you getting married?" "Why are you angry?" "The Spirit of the Dead keeps Vigil" and his famous "Whence come we? What are we? Whither go we?" He had always had a weakness for the "legends" of those cheap picture-sheets—of the "tuppence-coloured" variety—which we have already mentioned; for the captions of illustrated newspapers, the inscriptions that punctuate the Stations of the Cross, ribbon stained-glass windows, and entwine Japanese prints. Fortunately this propensity for "ideas" did not interfere with his discoveries in the field of pure painting, whose great value lies precisely in the fact that they derive from the Unconscious—to which, as it so happened, Odilon Redon was now proclaiming his indebtedness. Much has been made of his cult of the exotic, but this was due above all to his constant desire to be on the move, seeking—he knew not what. The dreams he dreamt in Brittany became realities in the South Seas, indeed his Tahitian technique conformed to that fine remark he made in earlier days: "Whenever my clogs strike this iron soil of Brittany, I hear that dull, muffled yet mighty resonance which I seek for in my painting."

Packed with suggestion, his art constantly aspired towards a pictorial equivalent of emotional experience. The influence he was to have on the "Nabis" group, on Sérusier (who was to act as spokesman of Gauguin's aesthetic theories), on Bonnard, Vuillard, Vallotton and Maurice Denis, was due to his feeling for the decorative—which they proceeded to stylize—and for the part that colour could be made to play, keyed up to its highest intensity. "How do you see this tree?" he once asked a friend. "It's green, you say? Well then put down green—the richest green on your palette." On the other hand Gauguin had much affection for Ingres and Delacroix, and indeed declared that there was nothing that drawing could not do. But "line is colour," he explained, and added: "Beware of complementary colours; you'll never get a harmony out of them, only a clash of tones." Two decades later Fauvism and Cubism took over his technique of using planes of flat colour set within dark outlines and his expressive contours—but only after purging his aesthetic theories of all ideological considerations.

Gauguin's boldness served as an example. "I wished," he wrote to his friend de Monfreid, "to vindicate the artist's right to dare everything." For that "right" he personally paid dear. His strange, adventurous career came to a melancholy end in the Marquesas Islands, where he died in April, 1903, his limbs covered with eczema, under somewhat mysterious conditions. Suspicions were aroused by an empty medicine-bottle found beside him. He had made many enemies, some of them influential, by his denunciations of civilization and its hypocrisies, which had caused him so much suffering.

P. GAUGUIN (1848-1903). LES PAROLES DU DIABLE, 1892. 37×23½". HARRIMAN COLLECTION, NEW YORK.

IN MAORI: *PARAU NO TE VARUA INO*. EVIDENTLY GAUGUIN HAD MUCH AFFECTION FOR THIS PICTURE; AT HIS 1895 AUCTOIN SALE HE BOUGHT IT IN FOR FIVE HUNDRED FRANCS. SEVERAL SKETCHES AND STUDIES PRECEDED IT: HIS FIRST IDEA FOR THE PICTURE, A LEAD PENCIL DRAWING, IS IN THE LOUVRE; THE FINAL PASTEL "WOMAN OF TAHITI" IN THE BASEL MUSEUM IS ALSO A STUDY FOR THIS PICTURE.

1891-1900

1891 Van Gogh Retrospective Exhibition at the Salon des Indépendants. Death of Seurat. Gauguin leaves for Tahiti.
Foundation of La Revue Blanche by the Natanson brothers.
Steinlen in the **Gil Blas** illustrated magazine.
Gatherings of symbolist poets at the **Café Voltaire.** Aurier's Manifesto in the "Mercure de France."
Bonnard shows for the first time at the Indépendants. Lautrec's first **poster** for the Moulin-Rouge.
The "Théâtre d'Ombres" (shadow plays) at the **Chat Noir.** First exhibition at Le Barc de Boutteville's.

1892 Joint exhibition by Renoir and Pissarro at Durand-Ruel's.
Lautrec's first **colour lithographs.** Posters for the **Divan Japonais** and **Les Ambassadeurs.**
Twice-yearly exhibitions at Le Barc de Boutteville's, until 1897.
Seurat Retrospective Exhibition at **La Revue Blanche.** Salon de la Rose-Croix.
Small monochrome paintings on cardboard by Bonnard, Vuillard, Vallotton.

1893 Lugné-Poë founds his **Théâtre de l'Œuvre; set and programmes** by Vuillard and his friends.
Lautrec exhibition, boulevard Montmartre. Degas exhibits landscapes in pastel at Durand-Ruel's.
Bonnard at 65, rue de Douai. Lithographs. Illustrations for Claude Terrasse's **Solfège.**
Opening of the **Vollard Gallery.** Matisse and Rouault in Gustave Moreau's studio.

1894 Uproar regarding the Caillebotte bequest to the Luxembourg Museum.
Vuillard's first murals. Publication of **Le Rire** and **L'Ymagier** (R. de Gourmont, Jarry).
Gauguin's receptions in his studio in the rue Vercingétorix. Portrait of **Annah la Javanaise.**
Odilon Redon Exhibition at Durand-Ruel's.

1895 Cézanne Exhibition at Vollard Gallery (November-December: over 100 canvases).
First public **motion-picture shows** given by the Lumière brothers in basement of the Grand Café.
Lautrec visits London. Sets for La Goulue's booth at the **Foire du Trône.**
At the Salon, Tiffany shows stained-glass windows after designs by Vuillard, Lautrec, Bonnard, Sérusier, Vallotton.
Volard publishes **Quelques aspects de la Vie de Paris.** Lithographs by Lautrec, Bonnard, Vallotton.
Second Gauguin auction sale at the Hôtel Drouot. Gauguin goes to Tahiti for the second time.

1896 At Durand-Ruel's, Bonnard's first one-man show (49 paintings, posters, lithographs).
Lautrec travels in Spain. **Ubu-Roi** performed at the Théâtre de l'Œuvre.
Théâtre des Pantins. Matisse's first appearance at the Salon de la Nationale.
Deaths of Verlaine and E. de Goncourt. Marcel Proust publishes **Les Plaisirs et les Jours.**
Libre Esthétique. Exhibition at Brussels.

1897 Lautrec visits London, Holland. **Portrait of Berthe Bady** (Albi Museum).
Exhibitions of Impressionist Painters at London and Stockholm.
La Revue Blanche publishes Gauguin's manuscript: **Noa-Noa.**
In Tahiti Gauguin paints vast triptych: **Whence come we? What are we? Whither go we?** (Boston Museum).
The **Théâtre Antoine** in the Salle des Menus Plaisirs. **Loïe Fuller** at the Folies-Bergère

1898 Mellerio publishes **La Lithographie originale en couleurs.**
Bonnard illustrates Peter Nansen's **Marie**; Lautrec, Jules Renard's **Histoires naturelles.**
The Art Theatre founded at Moscow; the **Sarah Bernhardt** Theatre in Paris.
Toulouse-Lautrec Exhibition in London. Death of Stéphane Mallarmé.

1899 Cézanne sells Le Jas de Bouffon and retires to Aix. Renoir "discovers" Cagnes.
Nabis give Group Exhibition at Durand-Ruel's as a **Homage to Odilon Redon.**
Second Cézanne Exhibition at Vollard's. Chocquet auction sale at the Hôtel Drouot.
Matisse, Derain, Jean Puy, Laprade meet at the **Académie Carrière.**
Signac publishes his Study: "D'Eugène Delacroix au Néo-Impressionisme."
Special issue of the Belgian review "La Plume" devoted to the Belgian painter, James Ensor. Death of Sisley.

1900 **World's Fair. Exposition Centennale** of French Art at the Champ-de-Mars.
Félix Fénéon organizes Retrospective Seurat Exhibition at "La Revue Blanche."
Bonnard illustrates **Parallèlement** for Vollard (109 colour lithographs).
Picasso's first stay in Paris. Meets Berthe Weil.

1901 Death of Toulouse-Lautrec at the Château de Malromé (September 9).

Symbolism

Jean Moréas declared, in the " Manifesto " which he published in the *Figaro* (September 18, 1886), that Symbolism was the only mode of expression " capable of logically conveying the contemporary tendencies of the creative spirit in art." Here the word " creative " (as indeed the term " Symbolism ") was for the first time frankly used in its full modern application. Amongst the literary reviews, *La Plume*, *Le Mercure de France* and *La Pléiade* championed the new theory. But it was Albert Aurier who for the first time, in 1891, with his article " Symbolism in Painting " (in the *Mercure de France*) pointed out its possible application to pictorial art and he acclaimed Gauguin leader of the Symbolist art movement. The aim of this school was " to clothe the idea in a form perceptible to the senses." Nature was to be observed " by way of the dream," and all primitive, archaic and exotic forms of art into which symbolic allusions could be read, were to be turned to account. The work of art was to be " ideational, symbolical, synthetic, subjective, decorative." Paul Sérusier now became the painter-theoretician of the new school. In 1891 was opened the first exhibition of Impressionist and Symbolist Painters, at the Le Barc de Boutteville Gallery. In it figured amongst others the names of Anquetin, Bernard, Bonnard, Denis, Lepère, Filiger, Ranson, Roussel, Schuffenecker, Sérusier, Toulouse-Lautrec, Vuillard, Cross, Luce, Gauguin, Willette, Signac, Zuloaga, and even that of Manet — artists, in fact, of greatly differing tendencies.

"I body forth imaginary beings built in termes of material logic."

REDON

Redon was born in 1840, at Bordeaux. Thus there was only a year's difference between him and Monet, Renoir, Cézanne and Sisley, but he never shared in the impressionist venture, even declaring that " painting is not mere representation of three-dimensional forms, but human beauty adorned with the prestige of thought." Thus once more the word " thought " appears in painting. But Redon gives it a meaning very different from that which Courbet or Gauguin gave it ; for him it means the poetic afflatus. And it was with a long tradition, implicit in the work of Hieronymus Bosch, Arcimboldo, Dürer, Hogarth, Goya, Blake, Füssli and de Grandville that Redon linked up his theories ; a tradition that he set out to renew and amplify, and which half a century later Surrealism was to carry on.

In the solitude of his provincial home, young Redon (like so many youngsters) discovered that, if you look long enough, you find quaint little forms and scenes in lace curtains, in wallpaper, on misted windows, in tangled clouds. We must picture a small boy, precocious and living in a dream-world of his own, having few of the traits of childhood, but already many of the mental kinks of grown-ups. For him the least object, like Blake's " grain of sand," is a microcosm of a world whose secrets are his alone. Thus, when he grows to manhood, he gives a new significance to every pebble, every blade of grass. To our wondering eyes he discloses a strange cosmogony, but one of such precision that we are persuaded of its reality. All his life Redon was more in contact with poets than with painters ; he was a close friend of Mallarmé, Valéry and Francis Jammes. He wrote much, always with discernment. In his dream of clothing the idea with form, according to the symbolist prescription, and above all of opening magic casements by grace of the poet's vision, he tried as it were to psychoanalyse animal, vegetable and even mineral entities, so as to

O. REDON (1840-1916). THE SPHINX (AFTER 1900). 23½×19¾".
HAHNLOSER COLLECTION, WINTERTHUR.

make them yield their secrets ; and these he utilized for building up his private universe. He makes no secret of the source of his inspiration. " All is done by docile submission to the uprush of the Unconscious." His sole concern was to discover that element of the magical or fabulous which lies at the heart of all things seen, their secret, creative essence, and to express it. Thus that miracle by which the little acorn becomes a mighty oak quickened his sense of childlike wonder. Indeed all life was like a fairy-tale to him, a fairy-tale whose truth he ever sought to demonstrate. Compact of imagination, his art stood to reality as does an oriental tale to a modern novel. When, in his sixtieth year, he called in colour to help him to express his vision, he endowed it with a special significance, lifting it above the plane of reality by glints of sharp, metallic tones, like electric sparks. When he paints a girl or a flower, the girl is almost a flower, the flower a girl. And the other living things he depicts, butterflies or queer, monstrous beings, have an oddly petrified look, as though held in the mysterious silence of a glass globe through which we glimpse them ; almost the eerie immobility of waxworks.

When thought intrudes on painting there is always a danger that the latter will be given a literary turn, and tend towards the illustration. But, in the case of Redon, is it painting that " illustrates " the poetry or *vice versa* ? It would seem that his art owes all to imagination, and " image " is implicit in that word " imagination." In fact Redon's " thought " found in painting an appropriate medium, its native tongue. And the great artist makes this good not only by the exquisite precision and the vitality of his drawing, and its accomplished style, but by the use of a palette, sometimes brilliant, sometimes all in subtle nuances, in which the sober dignity and the subdued sheen of the colours have the mysterious grandeur of medieval frescos.

O. REDON (1840-1916). THE CYCLOPS (AFTER 1900). 25¼×20".
RIJKSMUSEUM KRÖLLER-MÜLLER, OTTERLO.

J. ENSOR (1860-1949). THE GARDEN OF LOVE, 1891. 29½×39½". Dr TRÜSSEL COLLECTION, BERN.

HERE WE SEE ENSOR'S FANTASY IN PLAYFUL MOOD; ITS OTHER, LESS CAREFREE ASPECT, IMPINGING ON EXPRESSIONISM, WILL BE CONSIDERED IN THE SECOND PART OF THIS WORK.

"To the land of Mockbelieve and quivering unrest I set sail in my dream-ship beflagged with ink-scrawled flames,"

ENSOR

As a rule Expressionists are gloomy people who rarely smile, and only with an effort. Ensor, however, is a genial Expressionist; even of death he makes a jest. His art reminds us of those sumptuous Still Lifes painted by his Flemish forerunners, in which upon a table piled with good fare, one sees a skull (hence the name *vanitas* for a picture of this kind).

For Ensor painting is not the handmaid of any utopian vision. He uses it for gently scolding a world whose imperfections he discerns, but of which he never can quite despair. While Redon invents a private and peculiar wonderland, Ensor is always under the spell of his own childhood, which, fortunately perhaps, has for him no spurious "glamour." No doubt it was peopled by the most attractive fairies, but there were also spiders, ogres, even macabre stuffed Chinese. In short the fairyland of which he has the freedom is highly realistic. And his robust health has seen him cheerfully through a life that was by no means "roses all the way," up to the comfortable age of ninety.

Following another Flemish tradition, he tricks out his satires with a whimsy deriving more from Hieronymus Bosch, from Huys and Breughel (in the *Proverbs*) than from caricaturists such as Hogarth, Rowlandson or Gilray. Naturally the idea of death often visits our near-centenarian, but he merely snaps his fingers at the visitant. He bedecks skeletons with masks, wings and gaudy finery ; makes them strike quaint, undignified attitudes. The truth is, he has no fear of death ; rather, Death fears him and seems to overlook him, despite the picture of a skeleton he made entitled " *Myself in 1960*." But he is not obsessed with death ; his art has also a happy, carefree side. Thus in his *Garden of Love* and his celebrated *Entrance of Christ into Brussels*, we see on all sides merry, smiling faces, fantastically radiant like those in some jovial old picture-book. He has also a curious reserve, leading him often to hide the features of his characters under inexpressive masks. These manikin-like entities, living a wholly fictitious life, tend to make his works seem a phantasmagoria of nacreous shells, phosphorescent fishes, and shining, puffed-out faces, in which his mischievous handling of colour has its fling, indulging a youthful exuberance of tonalities with a zest that carries all before it.

But there is one theme by which Ensor is frankly overawed—forgetting Belgian *Zwanze*, and for once feeling no wish to smile—and this is when he paints the sea. He was born within sight of the sea, and has lived beside it, never forsaking it even for a day in the ninety years of his life. It is indeed his vital element. Even when writing of it in prose, he uses a poet's pen. " Wondrous sea of Ostend, all in pearls and opals, Virgin sea that I love—alas, that the soiling, sacrilegious immundicity of painting should dare to sully your divine lineaments and to besmear your garments woven of rainbow glints and silken white ! " In thus writing Ensor, the ironist, has for once laid irony aside.

THIS WORK ILLUSTRATES MUNCH'S EARLY MANNER WHILE HE WAS STILL UNDER THE INFLUENCE OF FRENCH NEO-IMPRESSIONISM AND SYMBOLISM. HE FIGURES AGAIN IN OUR CHAPTER ON EXPRESSIONISM, TO WHICH SCHOOL HE ESSENTIALLY BELONGS. HE STUDIED OFF AND ON IN PARIS, ESPECIALLY BETWEEN 1889-1890 AND 1895-1897. LAUTREC, SEURAT, VAN GOGH AND GAUGUIN WERE THE PAINTERS HE MOST ADMIRED, AND HE WAS MUCH INTERESTED IN LITHOGRAPHY AND WOOD ENGRAVING.

ED. MUNCH (1863-1944). LANDSCAPE BY NIGHT, 1900. 47¼×31¼". KUNSTHAUS, ZURICH.

LITERARY AND ARTISTIC LIFE IN PARIS FROM 1884 TO 1900

If we wish to understand the art of Lautrec and that of the great painters during the last decades of the nineteenth century, we need to have some idea of the atmosphere of Paris at the time, the night life in Montmartre, the ever closer connection between literary and art movements, the great strides made in the technique of illustration, the increasing number of reviews, cabarets, theatres and shows of every imaginable kind, the part played by colour lithographs, woodcuts, posters, illustrated books, the first appearance of the cinema — in short the complete change in the décor *of Parisian life, and the new way of seeing the world that this involved.*

REVIEWS AND MAGAZINES

A great many small reviews and periodicals made their appearance from 1885 onwards, and did much to disseminate the avant-garde *theories of the day. Thus in 1886 there appeared successively* La Pléiade *(March 1),* Le Décadent *(April 10), and* La Vogue *(April 11), the last named edited by Léo d'Orfer, then from May 13, by Gustave Kahn, assisted by Fénéon, who published Rimbaud's* Illuminations, *Verlaine's* Poètes Maudits *and Fénéon's study of Seurat and the Neo-Impressionists. Other magazines launched in this year were* Le Symboliste *(G. Kahn, Moréas, Paul Adam), the 'new series' of the* Revue Indépendante *which proclaimed as its ideal* "the union of all the arts in a common effort to refashion modern life," *and G. Lecomte's* La Cravache. *In 1889 came* Le Moderniste, *sponsored by Albert Aurier, Gauguin's exponent and Symbolism's chief theoretician; and, lastly, Léon Deschamps'* La PLUME, *destined to remain until 1904 (as Ernest Raynaud put it) "the most faithful mirror of contemporary aesthetic life." The last-named periodical organized at its office (in the rue Bonaparte) a permanent exhibition of painters in sympathy with the aims of the review. The 'Salon des Cent' published at modest prices colour posters, lithographs, reproductions of works in the museums, and devoted special issues not only to poets (Verlaine and Moréas) but also to painters, amongst them Redon and Ensor. January 1890 saw the first issue of the* Mercure de France, *whose programme was to give "a complete panorama of the new movement in literature and art." In October, 1891, the famous* Revue Blanche *was launched by the Natanson brothers; it brought together all whose names were coming to the fore in literature and art, and championed notably Lautrec and the 'Nabis'. In 1894 came Arsène Alexandre's* Le Rire *and Jarry's and Rémy de Gourmont's* L'Ymagier *which, with masterpieces of ancient* imagerie, *included Gauguin's woodcuts. All these reviews were illustrated by painters, organized exhibitions and devoted much of their space to art movements, while their premises were used for making contacts and the exchange of views on art. Turning to the dailies and weeklies, we must not overlook* Le Gil Blas Illustré *(with Steinlen's drawings) and the* Figaro *(with Forain's).*

THE THEATRES

This period was remarkable for the number of 'art theatres' that now sprang up, and not only were the best symbolist and foreign plays performed in them but, for the first time, young painters were regularly commissioned to design scenery, costumes and programmes.

In 1887 Antoine's Théâtre Libre *started its run of uncompromisingly realistic plays. In 1890 Paul Fort founded the* Théâtre d'Art, *seconded by Mallarmé, Verlaine, Verhaeren and Maeterlinck, and Fort recruited Sérusier and Gauguin as designers. A benefit performance for the latter was given on the eve of his sailing for Tahiti. In May, 1893, Lugné-Poë founded the* Théâtre de l'Oeuvre, *enthusiastically backed by his friends Vuillard, Maurice Denis and Ranson, who took an active part in the production and employed the new developments in colour lithography and painting in tempera for the sets and programmes. The* Oeuvre *opened with a production of Ibsen's* Rosmersholm, *with sets by Vuillard, who was, according to Lugné-Poë, "the most interested in the stage and the best art adviser" of the group. The most memorable performance was that of* Ubu Roi *on December 10, 1896. Lugné-Poë also employed foreign artists, Burne-Jones and Munch, the latter of whom designed the programme of* Peer Gynt. *Nor must we forget the* Théâtre des Pantins *launched in 1897 with Bonnard's puppets, and the famous* Théâtre du Grand-Guignol.

THE CIRCUS, FAIRS, DANCE-HALLS

From the days of Renoir's Clown Musician *and* Jeunes Filles du Cirque *(1868), and Degas'* Miss Lola *(1879), scenes of circus life had never lost their appeal for painters. And Toulouse-Lautrec, Seurat, Bonnard and Forain as well as many minor artists continued to explore this rich field of visual adventure.*

Parisians had then the choice of four establishments of this order : the Hippodrome, the Cirque Médrano (which still exists), the Cirque Fernando (now the Cirque d'Hiver) and the Nouveau Cirque (no longer in existence), built in 1866 on the site of the Bal Valentino in the Faubourg Saint-Honoré. The exploits of acrobats, lion-tamers, clowns and circus-riders, no less than the striking colour effects of a vast yellow arena ringed round by red-plush tiers of seats in the crude glare of gaslight (the lighting arrangements were still somewhat primitive) fascinated the painters, who found in the circus a host of promising subjects, and often struck up friendships with the performers. Before becoming mother of Utrillo and herself a great painter, Suzanne Valadon was a circus acrobat. Loïe Fuller, Footit and Chocolat, and M. Loyal also inspired the artists to some celebrated works.

The periodical Fairs at Neuilly and le Trône, with their merry-go-rounds and their booths — two panels for the exterior of La Goulue's were painted by Lautrec — likewise supplied artists with many exciting subjects. Nor must we forget the popular dance-halls, such as the Moulin-Rouge, Bullier, and the Moulin de la Galette, which contributed to give this period of Paris life its memorable gaiety and glamour.

MONTMARTRE

In the early days of Impressionism Montmartre was still almost a country village. From 1886 onwards (at the time when Lautrec decided to live there and get its 'atmosphere' on to canvas) it became more and more the centre of Paris night-life and, by the same token, the resort of artists, writers, and 'Bohemians' in general. There was a spate of shows and entertainments on the famous Butte, and though its somewhat feverish jollity often seemed artificial, this was in keeping with the rhythm of the period. This was also the heyday of the Café-Concert, the music-hall and the ' cabaret artistique ' ; two such cabarets, especially, made Parisian history, Rodolphe de Salis' Chat Noir *(with its shadow-plays) and Aristide Bruant's* Le Mirliton.

SPORT

Artists cast an observant eye on the beginnings of the craze for ' le Sport ' — which meant athletic contests of all kinds, tennis, foot-races and especially bicycle-racing (round about 1885). The long-distance cycle-races, such as that from Paris to Brest (in which figured such champions as Terront and Corre) as well as track-racing (with Zimmermann, the American), furnished artists with striking themes, in which the bunched-up attitudes of the racing cyclists struck a new note. In January, 1885, the Galerie Petit ran an exhibition on the theme ' Sport in Art.' In 1895 Tristan Bernard, sporting editor of La Revue Blanche, *spent most of his time at the Buffalo cycling track, where Lautrec often joined him.*

LITHOGRAPHY, POSTERS, ILLUSTRATED BOOKS

Fin de Siècle *art is characterized by its decorative trend and its exploitation of techniques ' on the side.' Thus etching, neglected by all the Impressionists except Pissarro, came into high favour after 1890, Gauguin and Munch revived the woodcut, and the lithograph especially became popular with artists and public. Print-shops opened everywhere in Paris, Munich and Vienna, the centenary of lithography was celebrated in 1895, and specialist periodicals began to appear : in 1895* L'Estampe Originale ; L'Estampe Moderne *and* L'Estampe et l'Affiche *in 1897. The coming of colour lithography led to a new treatment of the illustrated book ; the first venture was that of Maurice Denis, who illustrated Gide's* Voyage d'Urien *in 1893, and the first real success, Bonnard's illustrated* Parallèlement, *appeared in 1900. These led the way to the triumph of poster art, perhaps the most significant form of expression of this period. It was, in fact, a symbol of the correlation between such diverse arts as book-illustration, the art of the theatre and that of the music-hall, to the new developments of which it drew constant attention. The first colour poster was Cheret's, for the Bal Valentino, in 1869 ; then came Bonnard's France-Champagne posters in 1889 ; then Lautrec's posters for the Moulin-Rouge, beginning in 1891. The historical importance of the posters is great not only because Lautrec put the best of his genius into it, but also because it formed the most direct link between art and life under all its aspects, completely changed the look of the streets, and effectively conditioned the visual responses of the public to the new trend of art.*

I. 58

E. DEGAS (1834-1917). NU ACCROUPI DE DOS, C. 1890-1895. 7×5½".
LOUVRE, PARIS.

"What would Degas say to it?"

Around 1895 the art of Toulouse-Lautrec was at its zenith; and the "Nabis" group, which included Bonnard and Vuillard, was coming to the fore. All three were barely thirty; Degas was sixty. His influence had all its old prestige. He cut the figure of a pundit, but the ideal pundit; one who teaches nothing and suggests everything. He was still extolling themes drawn from everyday life and including quite ordinary objects. And he still insisted on the paramountcy of drawing in the exact analysis of form. As for colour, he had now come to recognize its merits, by dint of raising it to a pitch of unreality which was presently to lead Bonnard to the notion of "pure painting."

Thus his work, bespeaking a restless, ever vigilant intelligençe, that inspired a healthy deference, not to say awe amongst his juniors, had a highly salutary effect on them.

Indeed we can well believe that even the very greatest of his successors, including our contemporaries, have often asked themselves when trying to appraise a just completed work: "What would Degas say to it?"

"Were I not a painter, I'd wish to be a doctor, a surgeon . . .
I have aimed at rendering the true, not the ideal."

TOULOUSE-LAUTREC

Like Raphael, Toulouse-Lautrec died at the age of thirty-seven. His life had been embittered by physical infirmity, and his health shattered by heavy drinking. A few days before his death he was heard to murmur: "And life's a fine thing, they say!"

In the wistful irony of this remark we have the key to all his work. His keen intelligence prompted him to laugh, if a little wryly, at an existence which, despite successes in the field of art, was full of sadness; but intelligence is more an irritant than an anodyne. And his marvellous powers of observation, his brilliant summings-up of forms and faces — never failing in the smiling tolerance that comes of good breeding — confess the disillusionment of a *grand seigneur* confronted by life's seamier aspects.

Born in 1864 at Albi, Henri de Toulouse-Lautrec came of an old and renowned family, that of the Counts of Toulouse. A delicate child — this was due, perhaps, to the fact that he came of a very old stock weakened by inbreeding —, he had two bad falls when he was fourteen, breaking first one thigh and then the other. This checked the natural growth of his limbs and gave him a grotesque, top-heavy stature, his legs remaining too short for his body. His whole career was influenced by this disablement; he was deterred from indulging in the normal recreations of a country gentleman, riding, hunting, dancing and the like. His father lost interest in the boy, but happily his mother did her best to make life easy for

H. DE TOULOUSE-LAUTREC (1864-1901). JANE AVRIL DANSANT, C. 1892. 33½×17¾". LOUVRE, PARIS.

I. 59

I. 60

H. DE TOULOUSE-LAUTREC (1864-1901). LA GOULUE AND VALENTIN-LE-DÉSOSSÉ, 1890. 24×19¾″.
HAHNLOSER COLLECTION, WINTERTHUR.

LA GOULUE AND HER PARTNER, THE "RUBBER-LEGGED" VALENTIN, FAMOUS FLOOR DANCERS AT THE "MOULIN" HAVE BEEN IMMORTALIZED BY LAUTREC IN A SERIES OF PAINTINGS. THIS COMES FROM ONE OF THE PANELS DECORATING LA GOULUE'S BOOTH AT THE "LE TRONE" FAIR IN 1895.

him. Unable to play an active part, and condemned to being a looker-on throughout his adolescence, he used his eyes to good effect and sharpened his wits on what he saw. And with something of a child's delight in "making pictures" for his own delectation, he made sketches in which we already find a feeling for essentials, of a competence and intensity which he was never to surpass.

The horses he could not ride, the animals he could not hunt, the birds whose airy freedom taunted the relative immobility to which he was condemned — these furnished themes that whiled away the long hours he perforce spent seated in his chair. Thus his whole activity centered on what was for him, to begin with, only a pastime, something to

LA GOULUE ENTERING THE MOULIN ROUGE BETWEEN HER SISTER AND A DANCER. IT WAS FOR THE MOULIN ROUGE THAT, IN 1891, LAUTREC MADE HIS FIRST POSTER, WHICH ATTRACTED MUCH ATTENTION. IN SEPTEMBER 1892 A CHANGE OF MANAGEMENT WAS FOLLOWED BY A SPECTACULAR REOPENING, WITH ALL LAUTREC'S FAVOURITE STAR-PERFORMERS. HE PAINTED EIGHT CONSECUTIVE PICTURES IN THE SETTING OF THE MOULIN ROUGE, OF WHICH THIS RANKS AS ONE OF HIS GREATEST WORKS.

H. DE TOULOUSE-LAUTREC (1864-1901). AU MOULIN-ROUGE, 1892. 31½×23½". PRIVATE COLLECTION, PARIS.

make him forget his troubles ; indeed he drew without a thought of " art," like a man idly tracing arabesques on a café table. Struck by his talent, his parents had him take lessons from an artist friend of the family by the name of Princeteau, who specialized in hunting and racing scenes. Next, he entered the Ecole des Beaux-Arts and studied under Bonnat and Cormon. Needless to say, he soon gave up the Ecole, and took to haunting Montmartre, then the centre of all art activities in Paris. He was now aged twenty. Under the joint influences of Manet, Degas, Van Gogh and Japanese art, the mere amateur blossomed out into an artist taking his *métier* with high seriousness. But, still mindful of the numbing effect of the teaching of the Ecole, he would not let his spontaneity be trammelled by rules, and found even Degas, whom he greatly admired, too much of a theory-monger for his taste. Already he was thinking less of the picture to be painted than of the observation to express. Montmartre, in short, was merely a hunting-ground, and his interest in its quaint denizens was not that of a chronicler of *mores* ; it presented a diversity of oddities, just what he needed to whet his imagination.

It was chiefly scenes of movement that attracted him : dancing, games, the circus. Above all he had a predilection for decoration — which calls for large surfaces. Hence his early enthusiasm for the poster ; it provided ample space to work on and called for rapid execution. And in the field of poster art, his vital freely flowing drawing has given us masterpieces of the *genre*. Thus he was led on to create those big decorative compositions in which his joy in space is seconded by the splendid freedom of his line. The large panels he made for La Goulue's booth are of this order and the soberness of the colour, the architectural solidity of the composition, assimilate these works to frescos that " hold the wall together " with a wholly classical effectiveness. Here, too, he reveals his supreme gift of rendering movement, on whose expression his mind was always bent.

But he was also one of the greatest French portrait-painters. His almost painful sensibility is that of a Van Gogh — but a Van Gogh with a difference. He, too, is quick to mark the signs of moral and physical degradation on faces, but unlike Van Gogh he does not think of pitying or reforming these unfortunates. Rather, he exorcises his own grievances by painting them, without cruelty and with but a tinge of bitterness. Their features, given a twist as it were of laughter or distress by the jerky, incisive drawing, bespeak the painter's amazing powers of analysis ; these portraits have something of the quality of neat impromptus, flashes of mordant wit. But Toulouse-Lautrec never presses his comments to the point of caricature ; he is strictly accurate, if passionately accurate. For he no more claims to depict manners and morals then does a landscape-painter to teach horticulture. His portraits are summings-up and, in the same way as he simplifies line, he fines down teh expression of emotion to essentials.

He did not take pleasure in vice, he submitted to it, nor did he try to " evangelize " it — in the dubious manner of a Rops for instance. He merely observed, and recorded what he saw. When he portrayed with harsh realism the woman of the street, this was not so much to stress her features or to make the portrait lifelike as to make it *live*. And if he chose prostitutes as models, this was because he had a romantic notion that their world was purer, more innocent, than that of blameless domesticity, which, for good reason, held little interest for him. But in his dealings with vice he always kept a well-bred distance. At bottom he laughed at it, even perhaps too promptly, for fear he should be moved to weep.

To colour he usually gave an ornamental rôle, being careful to avoid any sort of stridency ; as indeed is proved by his painting on cardboard, an absorbent. He had no great liking for colours which called for meticulous handling, long stretches at the easel, or numerous sittings. He usually inserts the colour within the drawing, though on occasion he, too, " draws with the brush," and equals Manet in a virtuosity he never troubled to exploit.

What is inimitable in Toulouse-Lautrec is that knack of instantaneously registering movement manifest in those sketches in which he " captures " life and expression with a few decisive lines, thanks to that curious sleight of hand innate and peculiar to himself — which elicited from his teacher, Bonnat, the incredible remark : " Your drawing's simply atrocious ! "

H. DE TOULOUSE-LAUTREC (1864-1901). FEMME ROUSSE ASSISE SUR UN DIVAN, 1897. 16½×12½". PRIVATE COLLECTION, WINTERTHUR.

IN 1897 LAUTREC PAINTED STUDIES OF WOMEN DRESSING, NUDES (WITH THIS SAME MODEL), GLIMPSES OF WOMEN'S INTIMATE LIFE, ALL CHARMINGLY SUB-ACID AND SOPHISTICATED. HE NOW ABANDONED POSTER ART WITH ITS FLAT PLANES AND ABRUPT TRANSITIONS, FOR THE SOFTER, SUPPLER TECHNIQUE OF LITHOGRAPHY, AND EFFECTS OF ALMOST POINTILLIST VIBRANCY. ABSORBED BY THE CARDBOARD, THE FORCEFUL BRUSHSTROKES LOOK LIKE LONG STREAKS OF PASTEL.

H. DE TOULOUSE-LAUTREC (1864-1901). L'ANGLAISE DU "STAR" DU HAVRE. 16¼×12½". MUSÉE, ALBI.

ON LEAVING THE SANATORIUM (JULY, 1899) TO WHICH HE HAD BEEN TAKEN, LAUTREC WENT TO LE HAVRE WITH HIS FRIEND PAUL VIAUD. HE FREQUENTED THE ENGLISH CAFÉ-CONCERTS ON THE QUAYS, WHICH WERE STAFFED BY ENGLISH GIRLS. LAUTREC BECAME SO ENTHUSIASTIC ABOUT THIS BARMAID AT THE "STAR" THAT HE PROMPTLY SENT TO PARIS FOR HIS PAINTING GEAR AND MADE THIS SUPERB PORTRAIT OF HER.

With a description of the " Nabis " movement, of the art of Bonnard and of that of Vuillard we conclude our survey of the beginnings of Modern Painting in the nineteenth century.

Bonnard called himself an Impressionist ; he was perhaps the last of the Impressionists. But whereas the earlier Impressionists never boldly tackled the problem of the autonomy of colour, Bonnard considerably advanced its claims by the liberties he took with nature in general, with the human body and especially the individual object ; liberties which were destined to take full effect only in the twentieth century. Bonnard's art may be regarded as a half-way house between Modern Painting in its initial phase (from Courbet's day to his) and our contemporary art, inaugurated chiefly, it would seem, by Matisse.

And now we usher in the long series of colour-plates illustrating the course of twentieth-century art with reproductions of its most characteristic works.

THE NABIS

For all art movements a time inevitably comes when the members of the group part company, each following the lead of his own temperament. As a matter of fact the young men of the " Nabis " group showed an unusual cohesion, and its effects were exceptionally lasting.

In the mid-nineties great confusion reigned in the world of painters. In a work entitled " The Idealist Movement in Art " (1896) André Mellerio sought to reconcile the various seemingly conflicting tendencies of the time and to show that, appearances notwithstanding, they pointed in the same direction. Thus he lumped together — somewhat arbitrarily — Seurat, Signac, Luce, Angrand, Lucien Pissarro, Van Rysselberghe, Schuffenecker, Lautrec, Ibels, Anquetin, Guillaumin, Maufra, Verkade, Maurice Denis, Emile Bernard, Filiger, Sérusier, Vuillard, Roussel, Vallotton, Ranson, Bonnard and others. Mellerio assigned the members of this impressive galaxy to five sub-groups : Neo-Impressionists, Synthesists, Mystics, Neo-Traditionalists, and the portentously named " Chromo-luminarists." The whole duty of the modern painter (according to Mellerio) was to let the Idea dictate the form and to achieve expression by means of *signs*. But if it was a matter of bodying forth impressions, could not this result quite well be secured by purely pictorial methods ? Which was what the " Nabis " hoped to do.

This name " Nabis " — taken from the Hebrew, and signifying prophets or *illuminati* — was given them by Cazalis, the poet. Amongst the adherents to the newly formed group were Sérusier, Maurice Denis, Ranson, Vuillard, Roussel, Ibels, Bonnard, Piot, Verkade, Vallotton and Maillol. Maurice Denis organized group dinners at the *Os à Moelle* restaurant and though arguments ran fast and furious, high good humour reigned at these reunions. Another rallying centre was the *Revue Blanche* office. Thadée Natanson, its editor, has left an account of these gatherings, in which he was struck by Sérusier's " excitability," by Vallotton's sharp tongue, and Roussel's " bold flights of fancy." Bonnard, he noticed, " loved to contradict everyone else," while Vuillard displayed " a most acute intelligence."

Needless to say *littérateurs* swarmed at the *Revue Blanche* office, but the " Nabis " fought shy of literary incursions into painting. They had not forgotten the regrettable articles written by men like Zola, Huysmans, and so many others, proving, it seemed, that novelists, and even poets, were impervious to the lyrical appeal of painting pure and simple. Thus they listened with only half an ear to Maurice Denis when he expounded theories which he stated with much lucidity, but which led him into a tangle of contradictions whence he needed all his sleight of mind to extricate himself. They were interested only in the interplay of forms and colours, not in theories.

In fact, for them the symbolist adventure was ancient history. Worse, it tended to restore the disciplines of the Ecole des Beaux-Arts under an insidious form. Bonnard was determined to safeguard that precious impulse towards freedom which was enlarging his vision of the world of things ; while Vuillard found in his own sensibility all he needed for giving his work constructive form. Even the names they gave their works were calculated to annoy their symbolist friends. Thus Bonnard was responsible for : " The Old Lady with her Hens," " The Cup of Coffee," " The Cat," " The Wine Merchant's " ; and Vuillard for " The Jar of Gherkins," " Still Life with Cabbages," " Glass and Onions," " The Wild Rabbit." Obviously there was nothing here for " Ideists." Meanwhile possibilities of painting on cardboard were explored ; the painters mixed turpentine with their pigment and this, combined with the absorbent quality of the cardboard, gave wonderfully " mat " effects. Another device of theirs was to leave the cardboard bare in places ; and another to apply cool tones upon an undercoat of warm. In short the " Nabis " relied on technique alone for the interpretation of their impressions ; we have here a new Impressionism, at once wider in its implications and more " intimate." It registered one step farther on the path towards the complete autonomy of the purely pictorial.

MAURICE DENIS

The "Nabis" group found their spokesman in Maurice Denis (1870-1943), a very able writer to whom we are indebted for some enlightening disquisitions on art. Denis had a gift for putting into words the theories and aspirations of the new school. In one memorable and often quoted phrase he summed up the guiding principle of all contemporary art. "We must never forget that any painting — before being a warhorse, a nude woman, an anecdote or whatnot — is essentially a flat surface covered with colours arranged in a certain order." This enjoinder was (and still is) vigorously attacked by champions of the type of art whose chief merit lies in the expression of character and which forbids painting to look elsewhere for its inspiration. Again, Maurice Denis wrote, after seeing one of Gauguin's works : "Thus we learn that all art is a transposition, the impassioned counterpart of an experienced sensation." Denis always insisted on the absolute necessity for the *organization* of the picture, on the lines laid down by Seurat. In this respect his pronouncements have had much effect on the painting of to-day. As a painter, Denis began by conforming to the symbolist programme, in, for example, his *Menuet de la Princesse Maleine* and his young girls in flowing dresses, whose arabesques were adopted by what was called the "Modern Style." After a stay in Italy (to which we owe his delightful *Souvenirs*), won by the graces of Florence and Siena, he bade painters follow in the footsteps of the Primitives, whose spontaneity, as he said, "smelt sweetly of life." But he was against the academic conception of Italian art.

Under the influence of a Dominican, Père Janvier, Denis gave his art a religious trend and in 1919 he founded, with Georges Desvallières, the "Studios of Sacred Art," with a view to the revival of religious painting.

Schooled in all the technical devices of the *métier*, his art was somewhat overlaid by his erudition, which handicapped him in exercising the spontaneity which none the less he warmly advocated.

ROUSSEL

A schoolfellow of Vuillard at the Lycée Condorcet, and subsequently his brother-in-law, Ker-Xavier Roussel practised, like all the "Nabis," the small scattered strokes favoured by Monet and Renoir. The strict precision of the Japanese line did not attract him, nor was he interested in scenes of private life.

What he liked was the open air, and the *motifs* drawn from mythology that he delighted in served him for polyphonic effects in which bold and subtle contrasts could be intermingled. No sedulous observer of nature, he took the greatest liberties with literal reality. He employed the "mat" tones dear to the "Nabis" and favoured the use of cardboard and tempera, since they gave him those fresco tints which so well accorded with his decorative instinct.

K.-X. ROUSSEL (1867-1944). RURAL SCENE. C. 1903. 6¾×6″.

VALLOTTON

Born in Switzerland, at Lausanne, Félix Vallotton went to Paris when he was twenty-five and studied at the Académie Julian. His early efforts were under stern control, his teacher being Jules Lefèbvre who had made himself a great name with his *Truth Arising from the Well*, an erstwhile glory of the Luxembourg Museum and now relegated, unwanted and unseen, to the attics. Young Vallotton, to begin with, was all for his master's uncompromising academicism. The change came in the early 'nineties when he met the " Nabis " and, burning his old idols, developed an enthusiasm for decoration, poster-art and lithography.

The spontaneity of his work of this period surprises, when we recall the bleak precision of his later art. At this stage he painted seaside and street scenes and his ebullient technique found all it needed for its exercise in the most everyday objects — hats, shoes, dogs and cats —, which he depicted with much liveliness and wit. The dynamic effervescence of this relatively brief phase makes a curious contrast with the static compositions of his later manner.

It was with his adoption of a new, highly personal aesthetic that Vallotton's true temperament emerged. Henceforth he painted nudes and portraits that aim above all at the expression of character, and always with a cruelly precise technique whose studied coldness, often carried to an excess that disconcerts us, suggests the presence of some repressed anxiety or fixed idea. Vallotton's drawing is now reduced to bare essentials, but he seems to practise this austerity less with a view to giving his line any specific quality than with a deliberate intent to discard every trace of the superfluous ; one suspects that this was a counterblast to the happy spontaneity of his friends Vuillard and Bonnard, which he lacked — and envied. " The smooth perfection of the egg " delighted him, so he said. And his cult of the " object " became a veritable obsession ; in fact he seems to find in it a means of eliminating, annihilating, his own personality with a cold and calculated vehemence. Thus his figures have a frozen immobility, a truth truer than life and oddly disquieting for the observer. We are reminded of the queer, haunted expression of the waxworks in the Musée Grévin or Madame Tussaud's ; or that of the holy figures, under domes of glass, in Jesuit churches.

We find in Vallotton's later work what looks like a new objectivity. Indeed the *Neue Sachlichkeit* movement may well have been inspired by the intriguing, hermetic but highly suggestive art of Félix Vallotton.

F. VALLOTTON (1865-1925). THE STREET, 1895. 10½×13¾".

"One begins a portrait without knowing the model; when one has finished it, one knows the model, but the portrait is no longer lifelike."

VUILLARD

Edouard Vuillard was born at Puiseaux (in the Saône-et-Loire) on November 11, 1868. He was educated first at the Ecole Rocroy, then at the Lycée Condorcet. Several of his school-friends were destined to become famous ; amongst them being two painters, Maurice Denis and K.-X. Roussel, his brother-in-law to be. He lost his father in 1884, when he was only sixteen. His mother lavished on him a tender devotion, and as long as she lived he never left her side ; she was, in fact, the great love of his life.

His youth was spent in the charmed circle of the home ; and it was this early atmosphere of happy intimacy that gave his life the wonderful serenity which none of his biographers has failed to note. " Your house is like your face," a poet wrote, and when we look at photographs or portraits of Vuillard, we glimpse a diffidence that is not due to any lack of courage, a discreetly questioning regard, a little unsure perhaps, but smiling, untouched by any tragic sense of life. No artist's work better resembles its creator than does Vuillard's. He never tried to explore regions beyond his ken, or to overstep his natural frontiers in quest of adventures which seemed to him uncalled-for. That longing to " escape " which has haunted the lives of so many artists was never his. True to impulses which had never played him false, he always respected those of others ; none showed a friendlier understanding than he of the experiments of the younger generation.

Thanks to the rich intensity of his palette and the exquisite taste governing its choice, no less than to the structural solidity of his compo-

VUILLARD'S WORKS OF 1897-1898 ARE AMONGST HIS GREATEST. TURNING AWAY FROM SYSTEMATIZED DISTORTIONS AND THE LURE OF " MODERNISM," HE NOW GIVES CAREFUL THOUGHT TO THE LAY-OUT, AND HIS COLOUR PATCHES ARE SOLIDLY BUILT INTO THE COMPOSITION.

E.VUILLARD (1868-1940). LA TOILETTE, C. 1898. 9¾×6½". PRIVATE COLLECTION, PARIS.

I. 66

sition, Vuillard enjoyed a privilege rare indeed, and one which many of those who lacked these qualities may well have envied — the privilege of having won the admiration of all the painters of his day, whatever their personal aesthetic viewpoints and whatever their individual merits. The reasons for this eminence are various, but chief amongst them is the classical and wholly admirable humility of a man of unquestioned genius towards an art which was never put to the service of personal ambition or self-display.

In Vuillard's art was a unity, a singleness of purpose, hard to come by at a time when so many and such different art movements were tugging in opposite directions. Symbolism, for instance, whose influence on painting was so vacillating and short-lived, appealed for the most part to artists who found a remedy for the lacunae of their instinct in the strict application of ready-made aesthetic theories. But, though Vuillard's art has been assigned to this school, his sensibility ranged far beyond it. The same was true of Verlaine, with whom Vuillard had much affinity, despite differences of temperament too obvious to need mention. Then, again, Japanese art must have delighted Vuillard, with its simplicity, its novel lay-out, its cunning arabesques ; but it is no less certain that this art had nothing new to teach him. All its specific qualities — and many others — were already his, and the most he found in them was a confirmation of the similar intentions to which his instinct had already given rise. Verlaine's name has just been mentioned ; a line from his *Chansons grises* might be a summing up of Vuillard's art.

" Où l'indécis au précis se joint."

A precise indecision ! Whereas in Bonnard's more spectacular vision, indecision is allowed to exercise all its compelling yet so fragile charm, Vuillard, while remaining thoroughly impressionist, puts into practice — quite instinctively — Cézanne's famous injunction, to make Impressionism " something solid and abiding." Despite certain similarities of tone, like those we find between the Picassos and the Braques of the analytic period of Cubism, due as much to the sureness of taste common to both artists as to the fact that both painted often on a highly absorbent substance, cardboard, there is an essential difference between the techniques no less than between the aesthetic viewpoints of Bonnard and of Vuillard.

Vuillard had zealously espoused the teachings of the Pont-Aven School. Led on by his friends Denis and Roussel, he was launched into the fray, even joined in the dinners in the Passage Brady, and did posters, programmes and panels, painted either in oils, or oftener with the then fashionable tempera, on canvas or cardboard, for the " Oeuvre " theatre. Vuillard's " Intimism " found an outlet in the pursuit of simplification ; he stripped his work of all but essentials, using bold, highly expressive yet sober and invariably constructive lines. His feeling for precision, which was to make him the most accomplished of the " Nabis " group, was coming into evidence. The element of " indecision " in his work is indicated in the stylization of his tones. He uses a very thin pigment, the tones are firmly indicated but without emphasis ; they are essentially variations on neutral tints, and are painted " flat " ; on whites and browns especially, recalling monastic tonalities, the garb of Dominican or Benedictine friars. On the occasions when he indulges in bright hues he mutes these, as it were, giving them deep sonorities far more emotive than his friends' rather excessive use of the " pedal." In fact his work brings to our mind a murmurous, spell-binding chamber music ; all the more compelling for its serene restraint. If ever there was an art for professionals, it is Vuillard's ; and few are the artists who have not been fascinated by it.

Nevertheless it is inimitable. Like Renoir, Vuillard has had no disciples, doubtless because his art derives from no theory, but is the mirror of a highly gifted personality. In his highest achievements, lying as they do between the decorative fantasy of his early days and the naturalistic academicism of 1920, Vuillard found the perfect balance — indeed in his qualities there are no defects. And the reason for this is that, in his tireless experiments with the basic stuff, the *matière* of art, he steered a middle course between Bonnard's fluent exuberance, and the stiffness Degas often shows in the lay-out of his compositions.

E. VUILLARD (1868-1940). INTERIOR, 1898. 19¾×16¼″. PRIVATE COLLECTION, PARIS.

THIS IS ONE OF VUILLARD'S MOST DISCUSSED WORKS; NOTEWORTHY IS THE ALMOST TOTAL ABSENCE OF MODELLING. BUILT IN RECTANGULAR PLANES (THUS ANTICIPATING CUBISM), IT HAS THE CLASSICAL INTERPLAY OF VERTICALS AND HORIZONTALS. THE COLOUR HARMONY, IN WHICH "EARTHY" TONES ARE LIGHTLY ACCENTED WITH PATCHES OF PINKS AND PEARL-GREYS, IS CHARACTERISTIC OF VUILLARD.

E. VUILLARD (1868-1940). OLD LADY EXAMINING HER NEEDLEWORK, 1893. 11½×10½". PRIVATE COLLECTION, PARIS.

ONE OF VUILLARD'S MASTERPIECES. THE SUBTLETY OF THE TONES AND THE REFINEMENT OF THE COMPOSITION RECALL A VERMEER, BUT A VERMEER MORE SPONTANEOUS, MORE "ALIVE."

Hard things have been said about his "lapses" during the period when he mixed in "society." Equally unjustly he has been reproached with living in an ivory tower. It would be truer to say that Vuillard's art stood aside from the main stream because its place was outside Time. Indeed it is studied by contemporary artists much as they study a masterpiece of high antiquity in order to detect the secret of its permanence. In the long progress of art there are often breathing-spaces, and perhaps Vuillard stands for one of these. Indeed it well may be that Vuillard will have played in Modern Painting the part that a Corot played in Romanticism.

E. VUILLARD (1868-1940). THE RED BEDROOM. 15¼×12¼". PRIVATE COLLECTION, ZURICH.

E. VUILLARD (1868-1940). PORTRAIT OF CIPA GODEBSKI, C. 1897. 26½×20½". PRIVATE COLLECTION, PARIS.

"At bottom I am an Impressionist," he said to Matisse...

BONNARD

Pierre Bonnard's art marks the starting-point of the epoch of Modern Painting properly so called. Or, if we wish to have a more precise date, we may synchronize its beginning with that famous aphorism of Maurice Denis, which so well summed up the aspirations of all art-movements from his day to ours. " Remember that a painting — before being a warhorse, a naked woman, an anecdote or whatnot — is essentially a flat surface covered with colours arranged in a certain order." This was published on August 23, 1890, in the review *Art et Critique* and signed " Pierre Louis " (Denis' pseudonym). All Pierre Bonnard's work bears out this *dictum* but, in putting it into practice, he adapted it to the moods of a very personal sensibility, and, as we can see, allowed himself great latitude in the application of its last word, " order."

Pierre Bonnard was born on October 13, 1867, at Fontenay-aux-Roses. The charming name of this Parisian suburb, conjuring up as it does visions of flowers and colourful retreats, was apt for the birthplace of a great painter whose art is all in delicate nuances, fine shades of feeling. And, since we have touched on nomenclature, we may follow with the names of some of Bonnard's pictures, which give an excellent conspectus of the artist's favourite themes : *The Little Fauns, Daphnis and Chloe, The Cabhorse, Paradise, At the Moulin Rouge, The Laundry Girl, The Doffed Chemise, The Three Graces, The Panorama, The Dining-Room, The Cock and Hen.* In this little anthology, as it were, of his work we find a pleasing variety : almost sentimental tenderness and sensuality, ironic wit and innocence, a feeling for the intimate and a sensitive response to the sights of the world around him — in short, an all-inclusive vision.

As is well known, many of our great artists made heavy weather of their careers ; Bonnard's life, though it had its moments of sadness, was relatively plain sailing. He did well at school (in classics) and obtained his school certificate without difficulty ; on his father's advice he then studied for an administrative post in the *Enregistrement.* Having failed in the examination, he entered the office of a Deputy Attorney with a view to obtaining, later, a magisterial post. Then, one day, having extracted a drawing from one of the big office files (which served him more as a hiding-place for such things than as a source of instruction), he succeeded in selling it for a hundred francs. It was a study for a poster advertizing a brand of champagne. This was enough to make him promptly throw up his law studies, and he may well have echoed Gauguin's cry of liberation : " Now at last I shall paint every day ! " (1889).

The work of the great exile of Tahiti has always influenced our youthful artists, and Bonnard was no exception. One of Gauguin's sayings, " There are only two kinds of artists — the imitators and the revolutionaries " was an obvious enjoinder to young artists to choose freedom. His advice was, however, difficult to follow ; Gauguin himself had opened up so many and such various new paths whose names were not, like " Impressionism," foisted on them by ironical critics, but were chosen by the painters themselves, that (since youth is always eager to be in the *avant-garde*) the young artists were hard put to it to choose their way. There were Cloisonnism, Symbolism, Synthesism and Ideism to choose from or combine — pending the advent of " Neo-Traditionalism " which was to unite under Sérusier's aegis Bonnard, Vuillard, Roussel, Ranson and Vallotton. Meanwhile, to be in the fashion, the group gave themselves a name, the " Nabis " — a Hebrew word meaning " prophets."

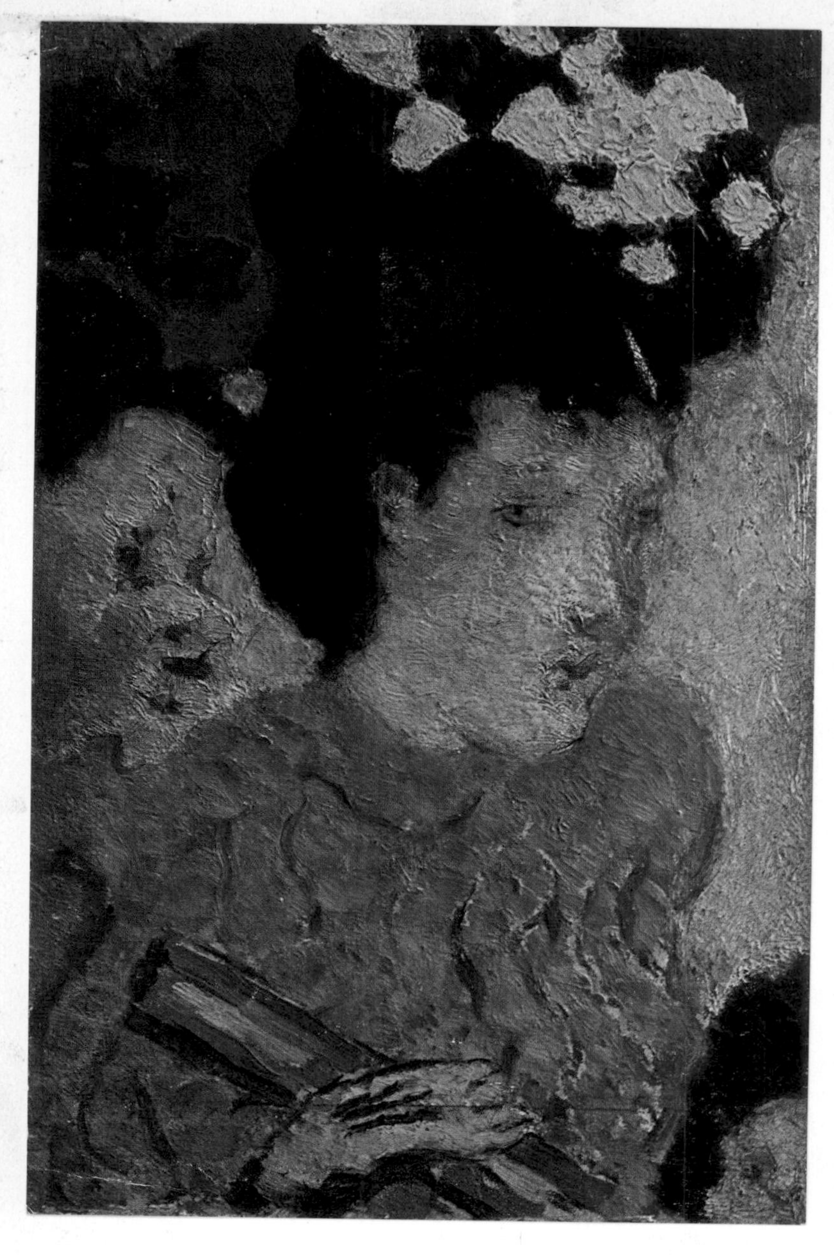

P. BONNARD (1867-1947). WOMAN'S HEAD, C. 1892.
10½×7". PRIVATE COLLECTION, WINTERTHUR.

IT WAS PROBABLY THIS EXQUISITELY HARMONIOUS COLOUR-SCHEME THAT LED MAURICE DENIS TO REMARK ON BONNARD'S "FELICITOUS HANDLING OF DARK TONES AND GREYS."

Bonnard had already met Vuillard at the Académie Julian; likewise Vallotton, Ibels, Ranson, and Sérusier who held the post of student-in-charge at Julian's. Sérusier ruled his fellow students with a rod of iron; he was much looked up to because he had known Gauguin intimately, and he propagated the Master's theories to good effect. He also discoursed on Plotinus, Pythagoras, the "Gold Section," the "Holy Proportion" and similar esoteric topics, duly impressing his hearers, especially Maurice Denis, and perhaps young Bonnard, too. Needless to say, Bonnard entered the Ecole des Beaux-Arts; but he stayed there a year only. After competing unsuccessfully for the Prix de Rome with his *Triumph of Mordecai* (which his masters persisted in regarding as a bad joke), he had no further use for the Academy. (This was in 1888.) Henceforth, possessing a technique that he had no need to learn, since, like all great artists, he had it in the blood, he set to shaping the course of his aesthetic on lines of his own choice. During his period of military service (1890-1891) he painted *The Parade* in which we find already a superb mastery of his medium, equal, perhaps, to that of the greatest works of his maturity.

But, by way of Gauguin, it was Japanese art that most influenced Bonnard. After carefully studying Japanese colourprints, he tested for himself the efficacy of flat planes, modelling reduced to a minimum, composition in two dimensions, lines intersecting in such a way as to give the impression of a new kind of depth. The "Japanese Nabi" (as his friends came to call him) also experimented in the employment of drawing alone for condensing form — in a somewhat decorative manner. He used flat tones and because he painted on cardboard his colours were low-keyed; also he mixed a good deal of turpentine in his pigment. He was always trying to attain that "dull, muffled yet mighty resonance" which Gauguin had sought and found. For the most part, however, in his early phase, Bonnard concentrated on drawing, poster-designing, and lithography; on black-and-white and the arabesque. In any case his palette was very subdued, in accordance with the anti-impressionist trend of the time, which he, too, followed, and he made much use of blacks and greys. In short, pending the day when Bonnard was to let his natural impulses take charge, colour with him was kept very much in the background. For there is a sort of pedantry in youth; fresh from the Schools, a young man often deliberately calls his temperament to heel.

Around 1890 there began a lasting friendship between Bonnard, Vuillard, Denis, Roussel and Lugné-Poë, founder-to-be of the famous Théâtre de l'Oeuvre. Most of them had been fellow-students at the Lycée Condorcet. In the following year the Natanson

BONNARD'S SISTER, ANDRÉE, MARRIED CLAUDE TERRASSE, THE COMPOSER, AND THEY HAD SEVERAL CHILDREN. ONE OF BONNARD'S MASTERPIECES, THIS CANVAS BOLDLY DEVELOPS THE JAPANESE TECHNIQUE OF COMPOSITION BY PLANES. IT HAS SOMETHING OF THE FRESCO AND OF THE DECORATIVE AMPLITUDE OF THE ARTIST'S NEXT PHASE. IT ALSO MARKS ANOTHER STEP TOWARDS THE LIBERATION OF PAINTING FROM REPRESENTATIONAL SERVICE WHICH CULMINATED IN THE XXth CENTURY.

P. BONNARD (1867-1947). THE TERRASSE FAMILY, 1892. 12¼×10¼". MOLYNEUX COLLECTION, PARIS.

P. BONNARD (1867-1947). THE CIRCUS, C. 1900. 21¼×25½". PRIVATE COLLECTION, PARIS.

CIRCUS LIFE FASCINATED MANY GREAT ARTISTS—RENOIR, DEGAS, SEURAT, LAUTREC AND, LATER, PICASSO; BONNARD, WHO LIVED IN MONTMARTRE ROUND ABOUT 1900 WAS NO EXCEPTION. BUT WITH HIM THE CIRCUS IS NOT AN OCCASION FOR DRAUGHTSMANSHIP BUT FOR PAINTING IN ITS PUREST SENSE AND HIS "PATCHWORK" TECHNIQUE NOW BECOMES MORE LUMINOUS, WARMER, STILL MORE VIBRANT WITH LIFE.

brothers launched the *Revue Blanche,* that famous periodical which did so much to promote the new movement in literature and art that took form in the 'nineties. It provided a forum for discussions of all that pertained to art, and in these Sérusier, Vallotton and Roussel made great names for themselves.

Literature was brilliantly represented in the review by Henri de Régnier, Félix Fénéon, Alfred Jarry, Tristan Bernard, Pierre Louys and other leading lights of the younger generation. This movement had a very distinctive unity of tone ; it was hostile to the noisy and bombastic, indeed to any over-emphasis (however sincere the feeling behind it), and it stood for a gentle tolerance, for nuances, for observation and invention tempered by the grace of wit and an amiability never lapsing into the mawkish.

The truth was (and in fact he made no secret of it) that Bonnard was a natural Impressionist, and for this reason symbolist or " ideist " theories could never hold him long. He was quite unmoved by Albert Aurier's solemn announcement that art was " the representative materialization of what is loftiest and divinest in the world — in other words, the Idea." All he asked of painting was for it to interpret the impressions given him by what he saw ; and all his life was one long, observant, fascinated contemplation of the infinite variety of things. Thus, once he had escaped from the literary atmosphere of the *Revue Blanche,* he rid his palette of the constraints imposed by theories alien to his temperament, and gave free rein to that creative joy in light and colour which enabled him to transform the humblest domestic object into something rare and wonderful, aglow with rainbow hues. And now he had set his fancy free to roam, he indulged his sensations in, as it were, a round-the-world voyage, which, however, he did not terminate like Gauguin in some South Sea island ; he brought them back to their starting-point — that finely adjusted sensibility which he never allowed to founder on the reef of virtuosity, or a mannerism. Thus, guided by his natural impulses and his fine sensitivity he indulged happily in the boldest, most surprising dissonances, those " grace-notes " of which he alone had the secret, and those persistent —

WE FIND HERE A BOLDNESS OF COMPOSITION UNATTAINED BY DEGAS OR BY LAUTREC. THE OVAL OF THE TABLE PRESSES FORWARD FROM THE CANVAS WHOSE RECTANGLE SEEMS TO HAVE BEEN THRUST ASIDE. THE PRODIGIOUS VITALITY OF THIS COMPOSITION LIES IN THE FACT THAT IT SEEMS LESS A PICTURE THAN THE RECORD OF A SUDDENLY GLIMPSED SCENE IN MOVEMENT.

P. BONNARD (1867-1947). THE CHECKERED TABLECLOTH (MADAME MARTHE BONNARD AND HER DOG " DINGO "), 1910-1911. 32¾×33½". HAHNLOSER COLLECTION, WINTERTHUR.

P. BONNARD (1867-1947). NUDE WITH LAMP, 1912. 29½×29½". HAHNLOSER COLLECTION, WINTERTHUR.

TOWARDS 1912 BONNARD'S ATTITUDE TOWARDS THE WOMAN'S BODY CHANGED ; INSTEAD OF REGARDING IT AS A PLASTIC ELEMENT TO BE WORKED INTO THE ATMOSPHERE OF THE PICTURE, HE STUDIES IT FOR ITSELF, ANALYSES AND DRAWS IT CAREFULLY, MAKING HIS EXACTITUDE OF LINE CONTRIBUTE TO THE EXALTATION OF THE COLOUR.

but how delightful ! — " blunders " with which critics often reproached him. When he painted, the colours seemed to pour from his hand, like the many-hued ribbons from a conjuror's sleeve. And suddenly we see as it were a new Space emerging, created by the warmest, strongest colour-schemes, but an accommodating Space, providing scope for happy divagations. It is easy to see why Bonnard was not cut out for the career in a government office to which his father had destined him. He had no head for figures or formalities. Any sort of precision would have gone against the grain of one who loved to linger on the way to admire a passing cloud, the glimmer of a street-lamp, the quivering of a leaf or even a blade of grass, the flutter of a woman's dress. One pictures him gazing fixedly at the object, his eyes wide with fascinated wonder, until he forgets all about it, letting his thought drift on ; then, later, when he is standing in front of his canvas, the image floats up again into his consciousness, by virtue of some law of the persistence of visual impressions. In rendering sensations Bonnard went farther than all the Impressionists, including Cézanne and Renoir. With Bonnard painting reached a pitch of abstraction never yet obtained in the quest of "pure painting." He painted — to use Monet's simile — "as a bird sings," but in his case it was like the nightingale which never quite recaptures its first refrain, and indulges in seeming-endless variations until its voice dies out amongst the trees. Thus it was with Bonnard's great mural compositions; they do not always "hold the wall together" according to the rules of decorative art, but seem magically to extend it to infinity,

TO STRIKE A BALANCE BETWEEN IMPULSE AND INTELLECT IS ALWAYS A CRUCIAL PROBLEM FOR THE PAINTER. HERE BONNARD BEGAN BY COMPOSING AND DRAWING; THE COLOUR CAME AFTER AND WAS MADE TO TALLY WITH THE LAY-OUT. BUT BONNARD LETS THE SAIL DISCLOSE THE SKY'S IMMENSITY; THE VAST DECORATIVE COMPOSITIONS IN WHICH HE WAS TO GIVE HIS GENIUS FOR DELICATELY NUANCED BEAUTY, ITS FULL SCOPE, ARE NEAR AT HAND.

P. BONNARD (1867-1947). AT SEA: THE HAHNLOSER FAMILY, 1924-1925. 38½×40½".
HAHNLOSER COLLECTION, WINTERTHUR.

I. 77

P. BONNARD (1867-1947). FRUIT, 1920. 13¾×12½". PRIVATE COLLECTION, ZURICH.

HERE, SUCH IS THE BOLDNESS OF THE TONES THAT THEY ARE ALWAYS ON THE BRINK OF CLASHING, BUT SERENELY THE BALANCED DRAWING AVERTS THIS DANGER. IT IS "DRAWN" IN THE SENSE BONNARD GAVE THE WORD WHEN HE SAID: "TO REPRESENT ON A FLAT SURFACE VOLUMES AND OBJECTS LOCATED IN SPACE, THIS IS THE PROBLEM OF DRAWING."

like the skies in Tiepolo's cupolas. Bonnard used to say that his art lay midway between Intimism and Decoration.

Defenders of Academicism have thought to belittle certain tendencies of modern art by saying it is merely decorative. They employ the word "decoration" in its invidious sense, meaning what is added wantonly by way of ornament to catch and please the eye, in other words, something superfluous, adding no real significance to a work of art. Actually, however, great painters have never fought shy of using the word " decoration " ; nor have they ever wished to exclude decoration from their art, as something reprehensible. For Bonnard the

P. BONNARD (1867-1947). LE POT PROVENÇAL, 1930. 29½×24½". HAHNLOSER COLLECTION, WINTERTHUR.

P. BONNARD (1867-1947). THE YELLOW SHAWL, 1933. 49¼×37½". PRIVATE COLLECTION, PARIS.

problem was not that of embellishing a wall, but that of organizing it pictorially as a surface to be covered, an architectural fact to be implemented. This, in fact, was the classical approach. When speaking of Intimism and Decoration, Bonnard was defining two forms of creative art : that of the easel-painter intent on expressing emotional experience, whose concentration within a restricted space intensifies its potency ; and that of the fresco-painter, whose vision calls for large surfaces over which the imagination can range without spatial restriction.

Bonnard's art inaugurated the period of Modern Painting. It contains intimations of Fauvism, in that it enables visual sensations to express themselves with a hitherto undreamed-of intensity. Perhaps Bonnard was the true creator of that romantic cult of pure colour, which, while provoking the inevitable reprisals from embattled classicism, led painting towards a fuller emancipation from the tyranny of the object.

HERE WE SEE BONNARD'S ART IN ALL ITS FAR-FLUNG SPLENDOUR ; HIS COLOUR SEEMS TO SING IN UNISON WITH THE LANDSCAPE, AND IN RAPTUROUS FREEDOM HE LAVISHES ON HIS CANVAS THE WEALTH OF A PALETTE INCOMPARABLY RICH AND LUMINOUS.

P. BONNARD (1867-1947). LE CANNET, 1940-1941. 22½×13¼". PRIVATE COLLECTION, PARIS.

P. BONNARD (1867-1947). FRUIT, 1946. THE ARTIST'S LAST PICTURE.
22¼ × 13¾". GALERIE MAEGHT COLLECTION, PARIS.

BIOGRAPHICAL AND BIBLIOGRAPHICAL SUMMARIES
INDEX OF NAMES

BIOGRAPHICAL AND BIBLIOGRAPHICAL SUMMARIES

BIOGRAPHIES. The chronological biographies record the chief and, above all, the most significant events in the lives of the artists, giving frequent glimpses of the great painters' private lives. They are not only portraits of the artists, but also summaries of facts enabling the reader to appraise the men and their works from both the historical and the aesthetic point of view.

BIBLIOGRAPHY. The bibliographical notes give lists of the written matter available to the student desirous of prosecuting farther his researches: the writings and correspondence of the artists themselves, the books they illustrated, monographs and studies of their works, and, lastly, catalogues and lists of the chief exhibitions, with the date and locality of each.

BAZILLE, Frédéric (1841-1870)

1841 Born at Montpellier, December 6th; of a middle-class, protestant family. His father, a wine-grower on a large scale, became senator for the Hérault Department on 1879. His mother was Marguerite Vialars. The family was friendly with the famous connoisseur, Bruyas, who made him acquainted with modern painting, Courbet and Delacroix, at an early age. He took some drawing lessons from a modeller, Baussan. Began studying medicine at Montpellier; was allowed by his parents to go to Paris to finish his studies, giving his spare time to painting.

1862 Enters Gleyre's studio in November; meets Monet, Renoir, Sisley. This meeting has a decisive effect on his career. He lived in close friendship with Renoir and Monet during his brief life as an artist, sharing his studio with one or the other, and for a while with both at once. Better off than his friends, he gives them material aid; Monet, always in financial straits, is most persistent in his demands.

1863 Easter holidays with Monet at Chailly-en-Bière, in Fontainebleau Forest. Sees much of Baudelaire's friend Commandant Lejosne.

1864 Honfleur, with Monet, Boudin, Jongkind.

1865 Sits for two figures in *Le Déjeuner sur l'Herbe*, Monet's open-air composition, and himself paints his *Lisière de Forêt* and *L'Ambulance Improvisée*. From January 15, 1865, to February 4, 1866, lives with Monet, 6 rue de Furstenberg, in the house in which Delacroix died. At Méric he paints the portrait of his cousin Thérèse des Hours, *La Robe Rose* (Louvre).

1867 Lives with Renoir in the rue Visconti. Buys Monet's *Women in the Garden*, for which he pays by monthly instalments. Spends summer at Aigues-Mortes.

1868 Exhibits *La Réunion de Famille* at the Salon.

1869 Takes studio in the rue de la Condamine (Louvre, Plate p. 20). Becomes an habitué of the Café Guerbois. Very friendly with E. Maître, Stevens, and Fantin-Latour who includes him amongst Manet's admirers in his group portrait: *The Artist's Studio* (Louvre).

1870 Exhibits two canvases at the Salon: *Bathers* and *Flowers*. Mobilized in a Zouave regiment, goes to Philippeville with his unit; comes back to France and is killed in the battle of Beaune-la-Rolande (November 28).

BIBLIOGRAPHY

G. Poulain, *Bazille et ses amis*, Paris, 1932 (partial catalogue); G. Charensol, *L'Amour de l'Art*, January, 1927; G. Poulain, *La Renaissance*, April, 1927; E. Scheyer, *The Art Quarterly*, 1942; M. Sarraute, Paris, 1948 (thesis at the Ecole du Louvre).

Exhibitions.

Salon d'Automne 1910 (23 exhibits. Prefaced by L. Werth); Retrospective Exhibitions at Montpellier in 1927 and 1941; Association des Etudiants Protestants, Paris, 1935.

BONNARD, Pierre (1867-1947)

1867 Born October 13 at Fontenay-aux-Roses near Paris. His father, head of an office in the War Ministry, hailed from the Dauphiné province; his mother, Elise Mertzdorff, was an Alsatian.

1877-85 Had a classical education, at which he did well, at the Vannes Lycée and Louis-le-Grand.

1885-88 Under pressure from his father, studies law.

1888 Ecole des Beaux-Arts. Fails to obtain Prix de Rome. The work he submitted was "not serious enough." Studied at the Académie Julian, where he met Denis, Vuillard, Ranson, Sérusier. In October Sérusier comes back from Pont-Aven with Gauguin's "talisman." Influence of Japanese prints and Chinese art.

1889 A decisive year. Gauguin's art, on view at the Volpini exhibition, is a revelation. A group is formed: the "Nabis." Bonnard makes a poster, *France-Champagne*, preceding Lautrec's posters (1891), which he sells for a hundred francs. Gives up his law studies; decides to be a painter.

1890 Military Service at Bourgoin. *The Parade* (Private collection, Switzerland). His sister Andrée marries his friend Claude Terrasse, the composer. Shares a studio, 28, rue Pigalle, Montmartre, with Vuillard, Maurice Denis and Lugné-Poë.

1891 Exhibits 9 pictures at Salon des Indépendants, which are praised by G. Geffroy, the critic. The Natanson Brothers launch *La Revue Blanche*, in which he at once collaborates. The "Nabis" have their first exhibition in Le Barc de Boutteville's Gallery.

1892 Again exhibits in Salon des Indépendants (March-April) and at Le Barc de Boutteville's (November). Small stylized black and grey panels, much admired by R. Marx and Aurier. *Tête de Femme* (Plate, p. 102), *Corsage à carreaux* (Ch. Terrasse Coll., Fontainebleau). At Père Tanguy's shop studies Cézanne's canvases. Strikes up friendship with Odilon Redon.

1893 Has a studio 63, rue de Douai. Colour-lithographs for *La Revue Blanche* and *L'Escarmouche*. Lugné-Poë founds Le Théâtre de l'Oeuvre; Bonnard helps with the sets and costumes. Meets Vollard, who is now opening his gallery.

1895 Vollard publishes *Quelques aspects de la Vie de Paris*, with 12 lithographs by Bonnard. Tiffany exhibits at the Salon a set of stained-glass windows, one of which, *Maternity*, is from a design by Bonnard. Bonnard sometimes accompanies Lautrec in his nocturnal jaunts in Montmartre.

1896 Bonnard's first exhibition, in Durand-Ruel's gallery, is discussed at length by G. Geffroy and T. Natanson. Collaborates with Terrasse at the *Théâtre des Pantins*.

1897 Group exhibition at Vollard's. Lithographs shown at *La Libre Esthétique*, Brussels.

1898 Bonnard illustrates *Marie*, a novel by Peter Nansen; his first illustrated book. In the spring begins the illustration of Verlaine's *Parallèlement*, commissioned by Vollard; the sketches are intermingled with the printed matter — the first indication of a form the modern illustrated book was often to take.

1899 Large-scale group exhibition at Durand-Ruel's as a 'homage' to Odilon Redon. Bonnard enters into a contact with Bernheim-Jeune gallery, and continues to frequent the *Revue Blanche* group. Very friendly with Felix Fénéon.

1900 From 1890 to 1900 shares his time between Paris and the family home in Dauphiné. From 1900 onwards alternates his stays between Paris and the neighbourhood; rents a little country house at Montval; often visits Denis at St. Germain-en-Laye and Roussel at l'Etang-la-Ville.

1901 Exhibits a large triptych at Salon des Indépendants.

1902 Vollard publishes *Daphnis et Chloé* with Bonnard's illustrations.

1903 Exhibits at the first Salon d'Automne; *Bourgeois Afternoon*.

1904 Illustrates Jules Renard's *Histoires Naturelles*. One-man show at Bernheim's: intimate scenes, women dressing.

1905 Two pictures at Salon des Indépendants, five at Salon d'Automne, admired by André Gide. Spends his summers at Villennes or Vernouillet, sometimes at Cotteville in Normandy.

1907-10 Travels in Belgium, Holland, England, Italy, Spain, Tunisia.

1912 Buys a small house at Vernonnet near Vernon; *Ma Roulotte*. From now on till 1938 he divides his time between the Seine Valley and the South (Grasse, St.-Tropez, Le Cannet). Declines Legion of Honour decoration. Has studio in Paris, 22, rue Tourlaque. His palette has grown brighter, as a result of the Provençal atmosphere. Large decorative panels.

1913 Travels in Holland and, with Vuillard, in England.

1914-18 Lives at St. Germain-en-Laye.

1918 Spends the summer at Uriage. Has a studio in Paris, 56, rue Molitor.

1923 Death of Claude Terrasse.

1925 Buys a small house at Le Cannet, near Cannes. Watercolours. His Paris residence: 48, boulevard des Batignolles.

1926 Goes to the United States.

1930-32 Arcachon. Winters at Le Cannet.

1930-38 Spends summers at Deauville and Trouville. Seascapes.

1940 Deaths of Madame Bonnard and Vuillard. Bonnard retires permanently to his country home at Le Cannet (a brief stay in Paris, in 1945). His lyrical emotion rises to a last, vivid intensity. His final achievement is a decorative religious work: *Saint Francois de Sales Visiting the Sick*, an altar picture for the church at Assy in Haute-Savoie.

1947 Dies, January 23, at Le Cannet.

BIBLIOGRAPHY

Writings by the Artist.

Correspondence, Paris, 1944; Interviews and observations collected in *L'Art et l'Affiche*, 1898; *Verve*, August ,1947; *Arts de France*, 1947.

Monographs and Appraisals.

T. Natanson, *Revue Blanche*, 1896; L. Cousturier, *L'Art décoratif*, 1912; F. Fosca, Paris, 1919; G. Coquiot, Paris, 1922; L. Werth, Paris, 1923; C. Roger-Marx, Paris, 1924 and 1931; C. Terrasse, Paris, 1927 (with catalogue of graphic work by J. Floury); A. Fontainas, Paris, 1928; G. Besson, Paris, 1934; J. de Laprade, Paris, 1944; A. Lhote, Paris, 1944; T. Natanson, Gischia, L. Werth, G. Diehl, Paris,1945; P. Courthion, Lausanne, 1945; J. Leymarie, *L'Amour de l'Art*, 1946; F. Jourdain, Geneva, 1946; G. Besson, *Arts de France*, 1946; G. Jedlicka, Zurich, 1947; J. Beer, Paris ,1947; J. Rewald, New York, 1948; Special Number of *Le Point*, 1943; *Formes et Couleurs*, 1944; *Verve*, 1947.

Illustrated books.

Peter Nansen, *Marie*, Paris, 1898 (Ed. La Revue Blanche); Paul Verlaine, *Parallèlement*, Paris, 1900 (109 lith., 9 eng.), Vollard; *Daphnis et Chloé*, Paris, 1902 (109 lith.), Vollard; O. Mirbeau, *La 628-E8*, Fasquelle, Paris 1908; A. Gide, *Le Prométhée mal enchaîné*, N. R. F., Paris (30 drawings); C. Anet, *Notes sur l'Amour*, Crès, Paris (14 woodcuts); O. Mirbeau, *Dingo*, Vollard, Paris, 1924 (55 etchings); *Les Histoires du Petit Renaud*, N. R. F., Paris, 1926 (50 drawings in colour); A. Vollard, *Sainte Monique*, Vollard, Paris, 1930; C. Roger-Marx, *Simili*, Sans-Pareil, Paris, 1930; P. Bonnard, *Correspondances*, Verve, Paris, 1944.

Exhibitions.

1896, Galerie Durand-Ruel, Paris (49 paintings, lithographs); Gal. Bernheim-Jeune, Paris, 1904; 1909, February (36 paint.); 1910, March (34 paint.); 1911, May-June (21 paint.); 1912, June-July; 1913, May-June (21 paint.); 1917, Oct.-Nov. (11 paint.); 1924, April, Gal. Druet, Paris, Retrospective 1891-1922; 1924, June-July; 1926, May-June (24 paint.); 1926, Nov.-Dec., Gal. Bernheim-Jeune, Paris (20 paint.); 1928, April, De Hancke & Co., New York (40 paint. Introduced by C. Anet); 1932, May 29-July 3, Zurich, Kunsthalle, Bonnard-Vuillard; 1934, March, Wildenstein Gallery, New York (44 paint.); 1941 and 1943, Galerie Pétridès, Paris; 1942, March, Weyhe Gal., New York; 1946, June-July, Gal. Bernheim, Paris (34 paint.); 1946, Dec.-1947, Jan., Bignou Gal., New York (15 paint.); 1947, Hommage du Salon d'Automne et du Salon des Indépendants; 1947, May, Ny

Carlsberg Glyptotek, Copenhagen (69 items); 1947, Oct.-Dec., Orangerie, Paris (197 items. Prefaced by C. Terrasse); 1948, Museum of Modern Art, New York (147 items); 1949, June-July, Kunsthaus, Zurich (250 items. Prefaced by J. Leymarie, Introduction by W. Wartmann).

CÉZANNE, Paul (1839-1906)

1839 Born at Aix-en-Provence, 23, rue de l'Opéra, Jan. 19. The family hailed from a village named 'Cézanne' (Cesena) on the Italian side of Mont Genèvre, but was of French stock. His father Louis-Auguste Cézanne, a hat-maker, married in 1844 one of his work-girls, Honorine Aubert, by whom he had already had two children, Paul and Marie (born on July 4, 1841) who was always tenderly devoted to her brother.

1844 Attended dameschool in the rue des Epinaux, until 1849.

1847 His father took over the Banque Barges then in liquidation and launched it as a new concern, the Banque Cézanne et Cabassol. Located at 24, rue des Cordeliers, then 14, rue Boulegon, at Aix.

1849 Day-boarder at the Ecole St.-Joseph.

1852 Boarder at the Collège Bourbon (now Lycée Mignet) until 1856; day-boy from 1856 to 1858. Thorough classical education, backed by religious teaching. Amongst his schoolfriends were Baptistin Baille and notably Emile Zola with whom he remained very intimate until their quarrel in 1886.

1856 Works under Gibert at the Aix School of Drawing. Second prize in 1858. Also studies music; much enthusiasm for Wagner. Fond of country walks with Baille and Zola.

1859 Takes degree in Letters (classified 'moderately good'). Begins the correspondence with Zola who is now at the Lycée Louis-le-Grand, Paris. His wish is to go to Paris to study painting, but his father insists on his entering the Law School at Aix. This year, Cézanne *père*, whose bank is prospering, buys a country house near Aix, "Le Jas de Bouffan," where young Cézanne spends the summer and instals a studio.

1860 He tries to persuade his father to let him devote himself to painting, and his mother and sister Marie back him up in this. Besides Zola and Baille, with whom he subsequently loses touch, his friends at this time are a sculptor Philippe Solari (his faithful friend until his death), who did his bust in 1904, Numa Coste who was to become a journalist, Emperaire a painter, and Valabrègue an art-critic. Is now influenced by Loubon and the paintings in the Caravaggio manner in the Aix Museum.

1861 April. His father yields at last and goes with him to Paris. He lodges rue des Feuillantines, attends the Suisse Academy, where he meets Guillaumin and Pissarro, the latter of whom greatly influences him. Visits the Louvre and Salon. In September, after a setback at the Ecole des Beaux-Arts, has a fit of homesickness, goes back to Aix and takes a post in his father's bank, though he still attends drawing classes in the evening. He now dies murals at Le Jas de Bouffan: *The Four Seasons*, *Interior* (Museum of Modern Art, Moscow), inspired by illustrations in a fashion paper.

1862 Nov.-1864, July. Second stay in Paris. Works at the Suisse Academy; becomes very friendly with Pissarro, Guillaumin, Oller, Guillemet, Bazille, Monet, Sisley, Renoir. With Zola visits the 1883 Salon des Refusés. He still admires above all Delacroix and Courbet. Embarks on a series of intensely romantic works, executed in dark, dramatic, 'lurid' (as he calls them) tones — a manner which is to persist until 1872.

1864 Again loses heart and returns ro Aix. From 1864 to 1870 shares his time between Paris and Aix. The pictures he sends in to the Salon are invariably rejected. At Aix from July 1864, to beginning 1865.

1865-67 Takes lodgings in the rue de l'Est in Paris, then at 22, rue Beautreillis. Spends the end of the year and the beginning of '66 in Provence. In July, 1866, goes to Dennecourt with Baille, Solari, Valabrègue and Zola. Back at Aix from Aug., 1866 to Jan., 1867. Rejected at the 1866 Salon, protests to the Director of Fine Arts. Introduced to Manet who admires his Still Lifes. Does portraits of *Valabrègue* (Coll. Pellerin, Paris), *Emperaire* (Coll. Lecomte, Paris), and of *The Artist's Father Reading L'Evénement* (Coll. Lecomte, Paris), the newspaper which published Zola's first articles on Manet.

1867-69 Long stays in the South. When at Paris constantly moving; rue de Chevreuse, rue de Vaugirard, rue Notre-Dame-des-Champs. Baroque compositions with erotic tendencies: *The Rape* (J. Maynard Keynes Collection, London), *The Orgy* (Coll. Lecomte, Paris), *The Temptation of St. Anthony*.

1870 During the war lies low at L'Estaque, near Marseilles, where he lives with Hortense Fiquet, a young model met in Paris.

1871 After the Commune returns to Paris and lives in the same house as Solari, 5, rue de Chevreuse.

1872 Birth of his son Paul (Jan. 4). Now living in the rue de Jussieu; in the spring goes to St. Ouen-L'Aumône; then visits Pissarro at Pontoise.

1873 Settles down at Auvers-sur-Oise, near Dr. Gachet. Paints *The Hanged Man's House* (Louvre. Plate, p. 35) and several landscapes showing Pissarro's influence. Meets Père Tanguy.

1874 Takes part in the First Impressionist Exhibition, thanks to Pissarro's good offices, and despite the opposition of the other exhibitors. His canvases, *Paysage à Auvers*, *The Hanged Man's House*, and *A Modern Olympia* (Coll. Dr. Gachet) were those most derided by the public. A short stay at Aix.

1875 Now living at 120, rue de Vaugirard; later, Quai d'Anjou. Meets Chocquet.

1876 Spends summer at L'Estaque. Refuses to join in the Second Group Exhibition.

1877 Works at Pontoise, Auvers. Shows 17 canvases at Third Group Exhibition (Still Lifes and Rueil landscapes), but the public is still hostile.

1878 Retires to L'Estaque; spends some months with his mother, now seriously ill. Trouble with his father about his way of living. Zola aids him financially. Cuts loose from Impressionism.

1879 Again rejected at the Salon, despite Guillemet's intervention. From May, 1879, to February, 1880, spends a quiet year with his family at Melun, often visiting Zola at Médan.

1880 Living at 32, rue de l'Ouest, Paris, from Feb. 1880 to May 1881. Makes Huysmans' acquaintance. Spends summer with Zola at Médan.

1881 With Pissarro at Pontoise, May to Oct. Short stay at Aix in November.

1882 Renoir visits him at L'Estaque. Accepted at the Salon as 'Guillemet's pupil.' In Paris February to September. Settles at Le Jas de Bouffan.

1883 Works in neighbourhood of Aix and at L'Estaque. Then roams Provence with Monticelli. In Dec. visited by Renoir and Monet.

1884 A mysterious love-affair which ends unhappily. June and July stays with Renoir at La Roche-Guyon. Returns in August to the South, where he stays until 1988. Works chiefly at Gardanne, a small town perched on a hilltop near Aix. The 'classical' element in his style is growing more and more pronounced.

1886 Marries Hortense Fiquet (April); breaks with Zola, who in his novel *L'Œuvre* modelled one of the characters, an unsuccessful painter, on Cézanne. On Oct. 23 his father dies, leaving him a comfortably large estate.

1887 Exhibits with the 'XX' Group at Brussels.

1888 Stays in Paris. Country rambles in the Ile-de-France.

1889 Entertains Renoir at Le Jas de Bouffan. Exhibits at the 'Décennale' (World's Fair) thanks to Choquet's insistence.

1891 A pleasure trip to Switzerland and in the Jura region. First attack of diabetes.

1892 Stays at Fontainebleau. To this extremely fertile phase of his career belong the 5 versions of *The Card-Players*, the series of *Baigneuses*, and that of the *Montagne Sainte-Victoire*.

1894 Spends autumn at Giverny in the home of Monet, who introduces him to Rodin, Clemenceau, Gustave Geffroy.

1895 First exhibition at Ambroise Vollard's. His work is cold-shouldered by the public, but thought much of by artists and some connoisseurs. *Portrait of Gustave Geffroy* (Coll. Lecomte, Paris) and *The Boy in a Red Waistcoat* (Plate, p. 48).

1896 In Paris Jan. to June, 1896. At Aix June to Sept. 1896. During this period he 'takes a cure' at Vichy and makes a short stay beside the Lake of Annecy. Makes the acquaintance of the young poet Joachim Gasquet who becomes his warm admirer.

1897-98 Often worlks at Montbriant on the estate of his brother-in-law, Conil. Here he paints some fine views of the Valley of the Arc overhung by Montagne Sainte-Victoire; he also paints at Le Tholonet in a room fitted out as a studio at the *Château-Noir*. He also rents a *cabanon* (shanty) at the Bibemus quarry, above the Aix barrage.
Oct. 15 his mother dies. Visits Paris.

1899 Sells Le Jas de Bouffan and settles in a small flat at 23, rue Boulegon at Aix, with a devoted housekeeper, Mme Brémond. Exhibits three canvases at the Indépendants.

1900 Figures at the Centennial Exhibition; his fame is steadily increasing, abroad as well as in France. The Nationalgalerie, Berlin, purchases one of his pictures. Maurice Denis paints his *Hommage à Cézanne* (Musée d'Art Moderne, Paris), showing Bonnard, Denis Redon, Roussel, Sérusier and Vuillard grouped round the Aix Master.

1901 Exhibits at *La Libre Esthétique*, Brussels, and at the Indépendants. Buys some land on the Les Lauves road north of Aix and has a studio built on it.

1902 The death of Zola, Sept. 29, despite their rupture, is a great blow to him. Mirbeau tries to secure his nomination to the *Legion d'Honneur*, but fails.

1904 Stays some weeks at Paris and Fontainebleau. An entire room at the Salon d'Automne devoted to his work. This is his year of triumph. Young admirers come to Aix to pay their respects; provincials such as Léo Larguier, Joachim Gasquet, Charles Camoin, and Parisians, Edmond Jaloux, Roussel, Maurice Denis, Emile Bernard.

1905 He exhibits again at the Salon d'Automne and the Indépendants. Finishes the *Grandes Baigneuses* on which he had worked seven years.

1906 On Oct. 15, caught in a rainstorm while painting in the open his *Cabanon de Jourdan* (Plate, p. 50), he collapsed on the roadside. A passing laundry cart picked him up, and he was taken home. He died on Oct. 22.

BIBLIOGRAPHY

1. *Correspondence.*

Letters, edited by J. Rewald, Paris, 1937; London, 1941.

2. *Catalogues.*

L. Venturi, *Cézanne, son art, son œuvre*, Paris 1936, 2 Vol. Indispensable. 1634 Items (805 paintings), 1619 illustrations. Preceded by an excellent critical study. Exhaustive bibliography (561 items). New and enlarged edition in preparation.

3. *Reminiscences.*

A. Vollard, Paris, 1914; J. Gasquet, Paris, 1921; E. Bernard, Paris, 1921; G. Rivière, Paris, 1923; L. Larguier, *Le Dimanche avec Paul Cézanne*, Paris, 1925; E. Jaloux, *Souvenirs, L'Amour de l'Art*, 1920; *Souvenirs*, C. Camoin & M. Laforgue, *L'Amour de l'Art*, 1921.

4. *Monographs and Appraisals.*

J. Meier-Graefe, Munich, 1910; J. Rivière, Paris, 1910; E. Faure, Paris, 1910; G. Severini, in l'*Esprit Nouveau*, Nov., Dec., 1921; J. Meier-Graefe, *Cézanne und sein Kreis*, Munich, 1922; T. Klingsor, Paris, 1923; A. Salmon, Paris ,1923; R. Fry, *Cézanne, A Study of his Development*, New York, London, 1927; E. d'Ors, Paris ,1930; G. Mack, *Paul Cézanne*, New York, London, 1935; M. Raynal, Paris, 1936; J. Rewald, *Cézanne et Zola*, Paris, 1936; R. Huyghe, Paris, 1936; F. Novotny, Vienna, 1938; A. C. Barnes &

V. de Mazia, *The Art of Cézanne*, New York, 1939; G. Jedlicka, Zurich, 1939; J. Rewald, *Cézanne, sa vie, son œuvre, son amitié pour Zola*, Paris ,1939; L. Venturi, *P. Cézanne, Water-colours*, London, 1943; R. M. Rilke, *Lettres sur Cézanne*, Paris, 1944; E. A. Jewell, New York, 1944; P. M. Auzas, Paris, 1945; E. Loran, *Cézanne's Composition*, Los Angeles, 1946; B. Dorival, Paris, 1948; A. Lhote, Lausanne, 1949; Special numbers of *L'Amour de l'Art*, 1920 and 1936; of *La Renaissance* and *L'Art Sacré*, 1936.

5. *Exhibitions.*

1895, Nov.-Dec., Gal. Vollard, Paris (100 exh.); Salon d'Automne, 1904 (33 exh.), 1905 (10), 1906 (10), 1907 (58); Gal. Bernheim-Jeune, Paris, 1807, 17-29 June (79 water-col.), 1910, 10-22 Jan. (68 exh.), 1914, 6-17 Jan. (30 oils), 1926, June (58 oils, 99 water-col.); 1934, Nov. 10-Dec. 19, Pennsylvania Museum of Art, Philadelphia; 1936, Orangerie, Paris (184 Items. Cat. by C. Sterling, Pref. by P. Jamot); 1936, Aug. 30-Oct. 12, Kunsthalle Basle (173 Items); 1936, Nov.-Dec., Gal. Bignou, New York (30); 1937, Sept.-Oct., Museum of Art, San Francisco; 1939, Centenary Exhibitions: P. Rosenberg, Paris, Feb. 21-Apr. 1 (35. Pref. by Tabarant); Rosenberg & Helft, London, Apr.; Bernheim-Jeune, Paris, May 15-June 13; Wildenstein, London, June-July (46 oils, 30 water-col., 20 drawings) and New York; Marie Harriman, London, Nov.-Dec.; Lyons Museum (42 oils, 17 water-col., 15 drawings); 1940, Bignou Gal., London; 1947, Gal. de France, Paris: *L'Influence de Cézanne*, Preface by A. Lhote; 1947, Apr., Wildenstein Gal., New York (88 pictures loaned by U. S. A. Collections).

COURBET, Gustave (1819-1877)

1819 Born June 10 at Ornans (Doubs); came of a family of big Comtois wine-growers. His father Régis Courbet, stemming from a long line of landowners, was an idealist, something of a dreamer and inventor of an improved harrow and of a five-wheeled coach. His mother, Sylvie Oudot, came from the well-to-do middle-class; a sensitive, tactful and reserved woman. Three younger sisters, Zélie, a musician, who died young, Zoé and Juliette. His grandfather, Jean-Antoine Oudot, a Republican and admirer of Voltaire, had a great influence on him.

1831 Indifferent studies at the small seminary of Ornans. He is interested only in drawing and in country excursions, and strikes up a friendship with the Franc-Comtois poet Max Buchon. As a subject for a French essay, he was given, aptly enough, Bonald's dictum: "The artist is the interpreter of his own nature."

1837 His father want to make an engineer of him, and sends him as a boarder to the Collège Royal at Besançon. Neglects his studies but attends the drawing classes of Flajoulot, a painter in the 'David' manner. His first pictures and the lithographs illustrating Max Buchon's poems date from this time. He prevails upon his father to send him to Paris, under the pretext of studying law.

1842 Puts up in a hotel, then in December rents a studio in rue de la Harpe. Works hard, receives advice from Hesse and Bonvin, visits the Louvre (the Rembrandt rooms and the Spanish Gallery). Makes copies, landscapes, genre-pictures *(Loth and his Daughters)*, portraits. Studies the nude at the 'Suisse' Academy, spends some days at Fontainebleau and comes back with views of the forest.

1844 Exhibits at the Salon his *Courbet au chien noir* (Petit-Palais, Paris), the only picture accepted out of the five he had sent in, and the first of those self-portraits in which his pictorial 'narcissism' works wonders.

1845 *Les Amants dans la campagne* (Lyons Museum). He writes: "Within five years I must make my name in Paris."

1846 *L'homme à la pipe* (Montpellier Museum). Travels in Holland where he admires Rembrandt, then goes to England.

1848 Settles down 32, rue d'Hautefeuille; exhibits his *Walpurgis Night* (painted in 1840), praised by Champfleury.

1849 *L'après-dîner à Ornans* obtains a second medal at the Salon; this picture was brought for the Luxembourg, then sent to the Lille Museum. Drawn towards social realism by the revolution, he paints the *Stonebreakers* (Dresden Pinacothek). Gatherings at his studio and at the Brasserie Andler; grows intimate with Champfleury, Proudhon, Baudelaire, Bainville, Murger, Schanne.

1850 First success at the Salon with a contribution of eight pictures among which the *Stonebreakers* and *Burial at Ornans* (Louvre). Exhibitions at Besançon and Dijon. At Louveciennes, makes the acquaintance of Corot in Francis Wey's house.

1851 Travels in Belgium and to Munich.

1852 At the Salon exhibits the *Demoiselles de Village* (Metropolitan Museum, New York), a portrait of his three sisters in their native countryside; it is bought by the Duke de Morny.

1853 *Les Lutteurs, La Fileuse endormie, Les Baigneurs*, startle the Salon by their realism; these last two pictures are bought by Bruyas, who becomes patron and protector of our painter. Courbet makes his friends' portraits. *Proudhon et sa famille* (Petit-Palais, Paris), *Champfleury, Bruyas, Baudelaire* (Montpellier Museum. Plate, p. 3).

1854 Exhibits at Frankfurt-am-Mein. Stays at Montpellier as Bruyas' guest and paints for him *La Rencontre*; back to Ornans, passing through Switzerland. Pays a visit to Max Buchon. His stay in the South has made his palette lighter and brighter.

1855 Courbet sends 14 pictures to the World's Fair (11 accepted) and in June has a one-man show of 41 pictures, the *Pavillon du Réalisme*, including the two famous compositions which were refused at the official Salon: *The Burial* and the *Atelier* (Louvre). These two exhibitions caused a stir and brought his art into notice.

1856 Travels to Ghent, back to Ornans through Germany. At the Salon, *Les Demoiselles des bords de la Seine* (Petit-Palais, Paris).

1858-59 Stays in Germany where he paints hunting scenes: *Le Cerf forcé* (Montpellier), *Combat de cerfs* (Louvre), and one of his masterpieces: *La Dame de Francfort* (Zurich Museum).

1859 Back in Ornans, then in Paris, where he often goes to the Brasserie des Martyrs, and meets young Claude Monet.

1860 A great success at the Salon. Travels to Honfleur where he 'discovers' Boudin. Speaks at the Congress of Arts at Antwerp. Influences Belgian and German painting. In Dec. opens a School of Painting at the request of pupils of the Beaux-Arts, among whom is Fantin-Latour, and chooses a bull for their first model.

1862 Stays in Saintonge with Castagnary, at Baudry's house. Finds Corot there and with him paints landscapes and flowers.

1865 Season at Trouville. Paints 35 pictures among which the *Belle Irlandaise* (William Rockhill Nelson Gallery), and a series of seascapes. Monet and Whistler become his pupils.

1866 At Deauville in Sept., at the Count de Choiseul's.

1867 Another one-man show at the Rond-Point de l'Alma, opposite Manet's (110 pictures). Stays at Saint-Aubin-sur-Mer.

1869 Etretat. Numerous seascapes among which *La Vague* (Louvre). Travels in Germany where he meets with great success. Returns to Ornans through Switzerland. Refuses the Légion d'honneur.

1871 The Commune. President of the Artists' Commission. Implicated in the affair of the dismantling of the Vendôme column. Arrested June 7, sentenced to six months' imprisonment at Ste. Pélagie, where he paints his admirable Still Lifes of flowers and fruit. His mother dies.

1872 Undergoes an operation in Neuilly hospital, in January. Set free. Back to Ornans in May. Officially excluded from the Salon.

1873 Exhibition in Vienna. Success brings him orders; he asks his pupils, Pata, Morel, Ordinaire, to help him. Threatened by the re-opening of the Vendôme Column proceedings, escapes to Switzerland in July and settles down at La Tour-de-Peilz, near Vevey. His friends try to have him exonerated, but encounter the hostility of Meissonier and the Institute.

1877 In May, sentenced to pay 300,000 francs to the State. His estate is confiscated and sold. His health grows worse. Dies Dec. 30. Buried in La Tour-de-Peilz.

1919 June 10. Centenary of his birth. His ashes are brought back to his native village, Ornans.

BIBLIOGRAPHY

The lbasic work is that of G. Riat, *Gustave Courbet, peintre*, Paris, 1906. The chief monographs and studies: Camille Lemonnier, Paris, 1878. Gros-Kost, *Courbet, souvenirs intimes*, Paris, 1880. B. Lazare, *Courbet et son influence à l'étranger*, Paris, 1911. Castagnary, *Fragments d'un livre sur Courbet*, Gazette des Beaux-Arts, 1911-1912. Théodore Duret, Paris, 1918. Julius Meier-Graefe, Munich, 1921. A. Fontainas, Paris 1921., G. de Chirico, Rome, 1925. Ch. Léger, Paris, 1929. P. Courthion, Paris, 1931. K. Berger, *Courbet in his Century*, G. B. A. 1943. H. Naef, Bern, 1947. P. Courthion, *Courbet raconté par lui-même et par ses amis*, Geneva, 1948. R. Huyghe, G. Bazin, H. Adhemar, *L'Atelier de Courbet*, Paris, n. d.

Exhibitions.

1855, Exh. and Sale of 41 pictures and 4 drawings, 7, avenue Montaigne, Champs-Elysées (Préface by G. Courbet); 1867, Exh. at the Rond-Point du Pont de l'Alma (110 pictures, 3 drawings, 2 sculp.); 1882 May, retrosp. exh. at the Ecole Nationale des Beaux-Arts (193 nos, Cat. and Pref. by Castagnary); Salon d'Automne 1906-1909, March 22.-Apr. 9, Bernheim-Jeune Gal. Paris (32 pict.); Dec. 1917-Jan. 1918, Bernheim-Jeune Gal. Paris (Notice, Th. Duret); 1909 Apr. 7-May 18, Metropol. Museum, New York, Centenary Exhib. (40 nos.); 1929 May-June, Palais des Beaux-Arts de la Ville de Paris (Pref. by Gronkowski, 131 nos.); 1930 Sept. 28-Oct. 26, Wertheim Gal. Berlin (Pref. Ch. Léger); March 15 1935-March 30 1936, Kunsthaus, Zurich (131 nos); 1937, May 4-29 P. Rosenberg Gal. Paris (18 nos.); 1938 May 3-29th, The Baltimore Museum of Art (25 nos.); 1938 May 10-June 11, Resenberg and Helft, London (19 nos.); 1948, Dec., Wildenstein Gal., New York (43 pict.); 1949, June, A. Daber Gal. Paris, Exh. for the 130th anniversary of his birth (18 pictures).

CROSS, Henri Edmond (1856-1910)

1856 Born at Douai, May 20. His mother was of English origin.

1874 At Ecole des Beaux-Arts, Lille.

1876 At Bonvin's studio, Paris. At Bonvin's suggestion adopts the English translation of his family name (Delacroix) as pseudonym.

1881 Exhibits at Salon for the first time. Like his teacher's, his painting is dark, realistic. Gradually discovers Impressionism.

1884 Exhibits at Salon des Indépendants his *Coin de Jardin à Monaco*, and regularly exhibits there until 1891. Becomes intimate with Seurat and Signac, and takes up Pointillism.

1891 Suffering from chronic rheumatism, settles in the South, at Cabassou on the Estérel region. Pure colour, the light of Provence.

1904 Travels in Italy; Venice, *Ponte San Trovaso* (Plate, p. 59), then Tuscany and Umbria.

1908 Another visit to Italy. Friendship with Maurice Denis. Combines classical structural lay-out with exuberant colour; his art greatly influences the early phase of Matisse and Fauvism. Many water-colours. Mythological scenes.

1910 Dies at St-Clair, near Le Lavandou. "To look at life, to have sensations and to set them in order — that, I think, is enough for our joys, and for our torments, here below."

BIBLIOGRAPHY

Writings by the Artist.

Cross's notebooks were published by F. Fenéon in *Le Bulletin de la Vie Artistique*,

Vols. I-VII, May-Oct., 1922. Hitherto unpublished fragments of correspondence are quoted by J. Rewald in his monograph on *Seurat*, Paris, 1948.

Appraisals.

L. Cousturier, *Art* et *Décoration*, 1907; *l'Art Décoratif*, 1913; E. Verhaeren, *Sensations* Paris, 1927.

Exhibitions.

Gal. Durand-Ruel, Paris, 1899; Gal. Keller & Reiner, Berlin, 1901; Gal. Druet, Paris, March 21-April 8, 1904; Gal. Bernheim-Jeune, Paris, April, 1907 (Pref. by M. Denis); Oct. 17-Nov. 5, 1910; Feb. 24-March 7, 1913; 1923; Gal. Druet, Paris, March 21-April 8, 1926 (Pref. by E. Verhaeren); Gal. Druet, Paris, 1927; April 10-30, 1937 (119 items. Pref. by M. Denis).

DEGAS, Edgar (1834-1917)

1834 Born at 8, rue St. Georges, Paris ,July 19. Eldest of a wealthy and cultured family. His father ,Pierre Auguste, born in Italy, was a bank manager; his mother, Célestine Musson, daughter of a Creole of New Orleans.

1845 At school at the Lycée Louis-le-Grand; struck up a friendship with Henri Rouart, his schoolfellow.

1847 Death of his mother.

1852 Leaves school with a certificate of merit for drawing. Lives at 4, rue Mondovi, converts one room into a studio; it has a view on the Tuileries and Place de la Concorde. His father, an enthusiast for art and for Italian music, is a friend of the collectors, Lacaze and Marcille, of the Valpinçons and Gregorio Soutzo; the last-named teaches young Degas etching.

1853 Begins studying law, but soon gives it up. Spends much time in the Cabinet des Estampes and the Louvre. His preferences are for Raphael, the Italian Primitives, Holbein and Clouet.

1854 Goes to Naples.

1855 On April 8 enters Ecole des Beaux-Arts, in Louis Lamotte's class; under the influence of master Flandrin acquires the 'Ingres' manner. Fellow classmates are Fantin-Latour, Delaunay, Bonnat. Visits Montpellier, Sète, Nîmes. He would like "to combine Mantegna's intelligence and tenderness with the gusto and opulence of colour of Veronese."

1856-57 Visits Naples and Rome, where he meets his friends Delaunay and Bonnat, Bizet the composer, Gustave Moreau, Edmond About; makes a long stay with his aunt Bellelli at Florence: *The Old Italian Woman* (Chester Beatty Coll., London), *The Roman Beggar Woman* (Coll. Durand-Ruel, Paris). Makes many studies and copies in the museums; an etching 'Degas in a Soft Hat.'

1858 At Rome. Travels in Umbria. Stays again with his aunt in Florence, from Aug. 1858 to April 1859, begins his *Portrait, of the Bellelli Family*, finished in Paris (Louvre). A big composition which reveals his insight into character.

1860 On his return from Italy, under the influence of Ingres he is strongly drawn towards historical painting and does a series of legendary and mythological scenes, for which he makes some admirable crayon studies. *Young Spartans Exercising* (Tate Gallery, London). Stays with the Valpinçons at Le Mesnil-Hubert, a racing and horse-breeding centre, near the Le Pin stud-farm.

1861 *Semiramis Founding a Town* (Louvre). First studies and drawings of men on horseback. Becomes friendly with Duranty, champion of Realism, and with Manet.

1862 *Gentleman-riders' Race: Before the Start* (Louvre).

1864 First pastels. Portraits of Manet.

1865 Last historical composition: *Les Malheurs de la Ville d'Orléans* (Louvre). In this year paints *The Lady with the Chrysanthemums* (Metropolitan Museum, New York) in which he inaugurates (under the influence of Japanese art, which Bracquemond had made known to Parisians in 1856) that "off-centre" lay-out which he is frequently to practise henceforward.

1865-70 Some fifty portraits, the most famous of which is his *Tête de jeune Femme* (1867, Louvre), whose linear density and psychological insight are remarkable. "The great thing," he writes, "is to make the head expressive of the modern feeling towards life; one should make people's portraits in everyday, typical attitudes. Beauty should mean no more than a certain type of face." His picture of the *Orchestra of the Paris Opera* (Louvre, and see Plate, p. 10), a characteristic *tour de force*, witnesses to his growing interest in the theatre and the ballet, which are now to be his favourite subjects.

1869 Travels in Italy. Seascapes at Boulogne, Trouville, St. Valéry.

1870 Gunner in a Battery commanded by Henri Rouart.

1871 During the Commune stays with the Valpinçons. Paints ballets-dancers. Begins being anxious about his sight.

1872 Meets Durand-Ruel. Works at the Opera. In the autumn goes with his brother to New Orleans, where he paints *The Cotton Office* (Pau Museum).

1873 March. Returns to Paris at 77, rue Blanche; December. Travels in Italy.

1874 E. de Goncourt visits him and admires his work. Takes an active part in organizing the First Impressionist Exhibition, at which he shows ten pictures. One, his *Examen de Danse*, is bought by Faure for 5000 francs.

1874-77 Takes part in the Second and Third Group Exhibitions. Dancing and racing subjects; also realistic scenes: *The Pedicure* (Louvre), *The Laundresses*, *L'Absinthe* (Louvre), *The Ambassadors* (Lyons Museum). Frequents the Café de la Nouvelle-Athènes.

1880 Travels in Spain. Etchings with Mary Vassatt and Pissarro.

1881 Exhibits his first work of sculpture at the Salon, a wax statuette of a *Dancer*. Pastels.

1884 At Le Mesnil-Hubert with the Valpinçons. Also at Dieppe.

1885 In August visits Le Havre and Dieppe, where his interview with Gauguin takes place. His eyesight is giving him more and more trouble and during this period he gives up *genre* subjects and anecdotal realism, and aims exclusively at rendering plastic form and rhythms. He specializes in nudes and dancers, and his new manner shows a much simplified execution—broader, tenser, thick-textured, slashed with contrasting tones. He indulges now in technical experiments, mixing turpentine with his paint, using tempera, and dried pastel, in successive layers.

1886 In January at Naples. Exhibits a "series of nude women, bathing, washing, drying themselves, dressing their hair or having it dressed for them."

1888 At Cauterets in August and September.

1889 Travels with Boldini in Spain; also in Morocco.

1893 Exhibits a series of pastel landscapes at Durand-Ruel's.

1896 In August at Le Mont Dore.

1897 Goes to Montauban to see the Ingres collection there.

1898 He stays with his friend Braqueval the painter, at Saint-Valéry-sur-Somme. Little is known of his last years. Unmarried, misanthropic, Degas lived a very secluded life, seeing only a few friends, such as Bartholomé the sculptor, Daniel Halévy, and Henri Rouart in whose country house at La Queue-en-Brie he sometimes stayed. From 1890 onwards he built up a remarkable collection of pictures, in which Ingres (20 pictures) and Delacroix (13 pictures) had pride of place. He was also one of the first to buy Gauguin's works. He had become almost completely blind, he had tried his hand at all the technical methods then known, but the years brought no peace to his restless spirit. As a last resort he took to employing charcoal, touched up with pastel, and to modelling wax figures.

1912 His lifelong friend Rouart died in this year. In this year, too, the house in which he had lived for twenty years and to which he was much attached was pulled down.

1917 He died in Paris on September 27.

BIBLIOGRAPHY

Writings by the Artist.

Lettres de Degas, publiées et annotées par M. Guérin, Paris, 1931 (new ed., 1945). P. A. Lemoisne, Les Carnets de Degas au Cabinet des Estampes; *Gazette des Beaux-Arts, 1921.*

Catalogues.

P. A. Lemoisne, *Degas et son Œuvre.* 4 Vol. Paris, 1946. Indispensable. L. Delteil, *Le Peintre-Graveur Illustré*, v. IX, Paris, 1919. J. Rewald, *Degas, Works in Sculpture*, New York, 1944. *Degas, Sculptures Inédites*, Geneva, 1949.

Reminiscences.

A. Michel, 'Degas et son Modèle,' *Mercure de France*, Feb., 1919; W. Sickert, 'Degas,' *Burlington Magazine*, Nov., 1917; G. Moore, 'Memories of Degas,' *Burlington Magazine*, Jan.-Feb., 1918; A. Vollard, Paris, 1924; G. Jeanniot, 'Souvenirs sur Degas,' *La Revue Universelle*, Oct.-Nov., 1933; E. Rouart, 'Degas,' *Le Point*, Feb., 1937; G. Rivière, 'M. Degas,' Paris, 1935.

Monographs and Appraisals.

G. Geffroy, *L'Art dans les deux Mondes*, Dec. 20, 1890; M. Liebermann, Berlin, 1899; A. Lemoisne, Paris, 1912; P. Lafond, Paris, 2 Vol., 1918-19; H. Hertz, Paris, 1920; J. Meier-Graefe, Munich, 1930; J. H. Rivière, *Les Dessins de Degas*, 1922-23; P. Jamot, Paris, 1924; J. B. Manson, London, 1927; Special number of *L'Amour de l'Art*, July, 1931 (R. Huyghe & G. Bazin); Paul Valéry, *Degas, Danse, Dessin*, Paris, 1938; D. Rouart, *Degas à la Recherche de sa Technique*, Paris, 1945; J. Leymarie, *Les Degas du Louvre*, Paris, 1948; J. Lassaigne, Paris, 1948; D. Rouart, *Monotypes*, Paris, 1948; W. Hausenstein, Bern, 1948.

Exhibitions.

1893, Gal. Durand-Ruel (pastels); 1924, April 12-May 2, Gal. G. Petit (Cat. by M. Guérin, Introd. by D. Halévy); 1931, Orangerie, Paris; '*Degas portraitiste et sculpteur*' (Cat. C. Sterling; pref. P. Jamot); 1931, Fogg Art Museum; 1936, Pennsylvania Museum of Art, Philadelphia (Cat. H. P. McIlhenny, Pref. P. J. Sacks, Introd. Miss A. Mongan); 1937, March-April, Orangerie, Paris (Pref. P. Jamot, Cat. J. Bouchot-Saupique & M. Delaroche-Vernet. 247 Items); 1939, June, Gal. A. Weil, Paris, 'Degas peintre du Mouvement' (Pref. C. Roger-Marx); 1947, Feb. 5-March 9, Cleveland Museum of Art (86 Items).

DENIS, Maurice (1870-1943)

1870 Born at Grandville, Nov. 25. His father was an employee on the Ouest railway, his mother Hortense Adde, a milliner. Taken when three months old to St-Germain-en-Laye, where he lived for the rest of his life. A brilliant pupil first at the Pension Villon, then at the Lycée Condorcet. Taught drawing by a Brazilian artist, Balla.

1888 Académie Julian. Converted to the Pont-Aven theories of aesthetics by Sérusier.

1890 Exhibits a pastel, *The Choir-boy*, at the Salon; publishes an article on art in *Art et Critique*.

1891 Joins in the 'Nabis' exhibition at Le Barc de Bouteville's gallery. Nicknamed "the Nabi of beautiful icons."

1893 Helps in designing sets and costumes for Lugné-Poë's *Théâtre de l'Œuvre.*

1895 First journey to Italy; he now reverts to the classical, humanist art-tradition. Tuscany and Umbria.

1897 Second journey to Italy; André Gide takes him to Rome.

1903 Goes with Sérusier to the Beuron Monastery, by way of Strasburg, Nuremberg, Munich.

1905 Travels in Spain with Mithouard. Avila.

1906 'Pilgrimage,' with Roussel and Emile Bernard, to Aix, to pay respects to Cézanne. He has already painted his *Hommage à Cézanne* (Musée d'Art Moderne, Paris).

1908 Teaches, with Sérusier, at the Académie Ranson.

1907-08 Stays in Italy which speed up his tendencies towards 'Neo-Classicism.' He now travels widely; to Moscow (1909), Dominica (1913),

Switzerland (1914), Siena (1921), Algeria and Tunisia (1921), the United States and Canada (1927)' Rome (1928), and in 1924 goes on pilgrimage to the Holy Land, to Greece and Italy.

1919 With Desvallières founds the 'Studios of Sacred Art' for the revival of religious painting. His work alternates between 'intimist' easel-pictures and big decorative works, religious and other: the Chapelle Ste Croix at Le Vésinet (1899), Théâtre des Champs-Elysées (1912), cupola of the Petit-Palais (1924-25), the Saint Louis Church at Vincennes (1927), the Lycée Claude Bernard (1938), the League of Nations building, Geneva (1939).

1943 Dies in a motor-car accident, Nov. 3.

BIBLIOGRAPHY

An able writer and critic, Maurice Denis published a number of books and articles which attracted much attention: articles in *Art et Critique*, 1890; in *L'Occident*, 1907 and 1908; *Théories*, Paris, 1913; *Nouvelles Théories*, Paris, 1921; *Charmes et Leçons de l'Italie*, Paris, 1913; *Histoire de l'Art Religieux*, Paris, 1939; *Sérusier, sa Vie, son Œuvre*, Paris, 1942.

Monographs and Appraisals.

G. Geffroy, *La Vie Artistique*, 1891; P. Jamot, *Gazette des Beaux-Arts*, 1911; P. Alfassa, *Mercure de France*, 1912; J. L. Vaudoyer, *Art et Décoration*, 1913; L. Cousturier, *Art Décoratif*, 1913; M. Lafargue, *L'Amour de l'Art*, 1924; F. Fosca, Paris, 1924; M. Brillant, Paris, 1929; *L'Art Sacré*, Special No., Dec., 1937; G. Barazetti, Paris, 1945; P. Jamot, Paris, 1946.

Illustrated Books.

A. Gide, *Le Voyage d'Urien* (20 Lith. in colour), Paris, 1893. *L'Imitation de Jésus-Christ* (216 woodcuts), Vollard, Paris, 1903. Dante, *Vita Nuova*, Paris ,1907. P. Verlaine, *Sagesse* (72 colour woodcuts), Vollard, Paris, 1911. *I. Fioretti*, Paris, 1913. P. Claudel, *Sainte Thérèse*, Paris, 1916. A. de Vigny, *Eloa*, Paris, 1917. F. Thompson, *Poèmes*, Paris, 1942.

Exhibitions.

Gal. Druet, Paris, 1904, 1908, 1911, 1918, 1921, 1927; 1924, Apr. 11-May 11, Retrospective Exhibition, Pavillon de Marsan (150 Items. Pref. A. Peraté); 1941, May 23 - June 15, Gal. Louis Carné, Paris; 1945-46, Travelling Exhibition of the State Museums: 'Maurice Denis, his Masters, his Friends, his Pupils' (Pref. by B. Dorival).

GAUGUIN, PAUL (1848-1903)

1848 Born June 7; his father, Clovis Gauguin, was a journalist from Orléans employed on *Le National*, his mother, Aline Chazal, daughter of Flora Tristan, a famous propagandist and Saint-Simonian doctrinaire, of Peruvian blood.

1851 After the *coup d'Etat* the family sailed for Peru. His father died on the journey. Stayed four years at Lima.

1855 Returned to Orléans. Schooling at the Petit Séminaire.

1865 Entered the merchant-service, as a navigating cadet (like Manet and Baudelaire). Sailed from Le Havre to Rio several times on the *Luzitano*.

1868 Served on the cruiser *Jérôme-Napoléon*.

1871 On leave, April 23. Gives up the sea, and by the good offices of his guardian Gustave Arosa enters Bertin's stockbroking business in the rue Laffitte, where he makes friends with a colleague, Emile Schuffenecker. Does very well in business.

1873 Nov. 22, marries a Danish girl from a middle-class family, Mette Sophia Gad. Starts drawing.

1874 Paints as an amateur. Builds up a collection of impressionist pictures (Manet, Cézanne, Pissarro, Renoir, Monet, Sisley).

1876 Has a picture, *Viroflay Landscape*, accepted at the Salon. Meets Pissarro.

1879 Stays with Pissarro at Pontoise during the holidays.

1880 Leaves his residence in rue des Tourneaux, and rents a studio, 8, rue Carcel. Takes part in the Fifth Impressionist Exh. (7 paintings, 1 bust).

1881 Sixth Impressionist Exh. Huysmans describes his landscapes as "diluted Pissarro" but is loud in his praise of a nude study (now on loan at the Ny Carlsberg Glyptotek, Copenhagen).

1882 Seventh Impressionist Exh. Huysmans finds he "shows no progress."

1883 Crucial year. Gauguin throws up his post at Bertin's. "Now I shall paint every day." Works with Pissarro at Osny.

1884 For economy's sake lives at Rouen from March to October. Early in November goes with his wife and children to Denmark. His exhibition there closed by order of the Academy.

1885 Jan. 14, in a letter to Schuffenecker expounds his theories about art. Quarrels with his wife's family, and makes himself unpopular with the Danes. Fails to arrange for an exhibition and in June, leaving his wife, returns to Paris with his son Clovis. Extreme poverty. Works as a billsticker. Lives first in Impasse Frémin; moves Oct. 13 to rue Cail. Ill in hospital.

1886 May 15-June 15. Eighth and Last Impressionist Exh. Fénéon says, "M. Gauguin's tones are very near each other; hence the soft harmonies we find in his work."

First Stay at Pont-Aven (June-Nov., 1886). Paris.
June. Gauguin boards out his son at Antony and for the first time goes to Brittany, staying at the Pension Gloanec, Pont-Aven (Finistère). First contact with Emile Bernard in August; neither has much to say to the other. In Nov. returns to Paris; meets Van Gogh in Montmartre.

1887 Stays in Paris until April. According to Daniel de Montfreid, quoted by C. Chassé (*Gauguin et le Groupe de Pont-Aven*, Paris 1921), "Gauguin's first stay in Brittany, previous to his journey to Martinique, was a period that left no noticeable mark on his art." But from 1886 to 1891 and between his two trips to Tahiti, Gauguin revisited yearly this primitive land which had cast its spell on him. "When my clogs strike this iron soil," he said," I hear the dull, muffled, mighty resonance I seek for in my painting."

Martinique (April-December, 1887)

April 10. With Charles Laval Gauguin embarks at Saint Nazaire for Panama, then Martinique, whence they return in December, prostrated by dysentery and fever. "I'm bringing back a dozen canvases, four with figures much superior to anything I did at Pont-Aven." (*Letters*, p. 116, 1946.)

Paris—Pont-Aven (December, 1887-October, 1888)

1887 Dec. Back in France, Gauguin puts up with Schuffenecker, 29, rue Boulard.

1888 Second stay at Pont-Aven, until October. Second and, this time, fruitful meeting with Bernard, in August. Beginnings of Cloisonnism and Synthesism. *The Vision after the Sermon* (National Gallery of Scotland, Edinburgh. Plate, p. 69). First one-man show at Boussod & Valadon's, by the good offices of Theo van Gogh, Vincent's brother.

Arles (October-December, 1888)

Oct. 20. Gauguin goes to Arles with a view to founding with Van Gogh the "Studio of the South." Funds are supplied to the two men by Theo ; they reciprocally influence each other. They visit the Montpellier Museum. Gauguin makes his *Portrait of Vincent Painting Sunflowers* (on loan to Municipal Museum, Amsterdam). But the two men were very different and got on each other's nerves, with tragic results.
Dec. 23. In a fit of madness Vincent cuts off his own ear. Gauguin hurries back to Paris.

Paris (End December, 1888-April, 1889)

On his return to Paris Gauguin again stays with Schuffenecker until he secures a studio (25, avenue Montsouris).

1889 World's Fair. Gauguin enthusiastic over Japanese art. Exhibition of the Impressionist and Synthesist Group at the Café Volpini, Place du Champ-de-Mars. The public laugh it out of court, but the young 'Nabis' — Sérusier, Maurice Denis, Bonnard — are much impressed.

Pont-Aven—Le Pouldu (April, 1889-November, 1890)

Gauguin's third stay in Brittany, the longest and most decisive, broken by short stays in Paris at the beginning of 1890.
April. Spends the summer at the Pension Gloanec, frequently exploring the surrounding country.
October. Irritated by the tourists and colony of artists infesting Pont-Aven, Gauguin moves to a small inn owned by Marie Henry (known as Marie Poupée) at Le Pouldu. Some of his cronies follow: Seguin, Filiger and, notably, the Dutchman Meyer de Haan. It is in the primitive setting of Le Pouldu, with its Breton 'Calvaries,' that Gauguin's personality takes definite form and he fully achieves his new 'vision,' at once simplifying and synthetic. The Visitors' Book at the inn shows that he stayed there from Oct. 2 to Nov. 7, 1890. *The Yellow Christ* (Albright Art Gallery, Buffalo), *Landscape at Le Pouldu* (Paul Fierens, Brussels. Plate, p. 71).

Paris (December, 1890-April, 1891)

1890 End December, returns to Paris. Homeless he again stays with Schuffenecker, who is now living at No. 12, rue Durand-Claye ; then in a hotel in the rue Delambre.

1896 Associates with the symbolist writers who meet once a week at the Café Voltaire. Etching of Mallarmé. Copies Manet's *Olympia*. Leads a poverty-stricken, Bohemian life in Montparnasse. Resolves to go to Tahiti.
Feb. 23. Fist sale of 30 pictures at the Drouot auction-rooms (catalogue prefaced by Mirbeau), to collect funds for his journey.
March 23. Farewell banquet in his honour at the Café Voltaire, presided over by Mallarmé.
April 4. Sails for Tahiti.

First stay in Tahiti (June, 1891-July, 1893)

June 8, lands at Papeete. Disappointed by the European colony at the capital, he acquires a hut amongst the natives in the Mataeia region some 25 miles south of Papeete. *Ia Orana Maria* (Lewisohn Coll., New York).

1892 Works hard despite ill-health. *Ta Matete* (Basel Museum). *Parau no te Varua Ino* (Harriman Coll.).

1893 But no money is coming in and, at the end of his tether, a sick man, Gauguin is compelled to return to Europe. Tries again to organize an exhibition at Copenhagen.
Aug. 3. Arrives at Marseilles.

Paris—Brittany (August, 1893-February, 1895)

Goes to Orléans ; inheritance from his uncle Isidore.
Rents a studio, 4, rue Vercingétorix, where he lives with *Annah la Javanaise*, whose portrait he paints (Private Coll., Winterthur. Plate, p. 73). Gives picturesque weekly parties at the studio.
Nov. 4. Opening day of his exhibition at Durand-Ruel's, organized at Degas' suggestion (Preface by C. Morice). No financial success, it has much influence on Bonnard, Vuillard and the other 'Nabis.'

1894 Jan. Travels to Bruges (Memling), then to Copenhagen (last meeting with his wife).
April-Dec. At Pont-Aven and Le Pouldu with Annah, who involves him in a brawl with drunken sailors in which he breaks his ankle.
Dec. Returns to Paris. Annah has vanished, after looting his studio.

1895 Disgusted with life in Paris, he decides to return to Tahiti.
Febr. 18. Second auction-sale, catalogue prefaced by a letter from Strindberg. Sale a complete failure.
March. Sails for Tahiti.

Second stay in Tahiti (July, 1895-Sept., 1901)

July. Lands in Tahiti. Finds Papeete still more Europeanized and goes to the west coast, the Punaoia district, where he has a large and relatively palatial hut on native lines built for himself.

1896 Oct. His health is breaking up and he suffers horribly from his sense of being alone, an outcast. "I am so utterly discouraged and demoralized that I cannot conceive of anything worse in store for me."
However, in November, he is feeling better. "I am recovering and, thanks to this, have got through a lot of work."

1897 Death of his daughter Aline. Stops writing to his wife. In hospital. A year of masterpieces : *Nevermore* (Courtauld Institute,

London), *Te Rerioa* (Id.), *Les Trois Tahitiens* (A. Maitland Coll., Edinburgh), *Whence Come We ?* (Boston Museum).

1898 Attempted suicide. Takes work in the local Public Works office. *Le Cheval Blanc* (Louvre).

1899 In trouble with local authorities. Publishes satirical broadsheets : *Les Guêpes* and *Le Sourire.*

1900 April. " I am mustering all the energy that's left to me and, fond as I am of my house, I shall try to get rid of it and sell off everything with as little loss as possible. Then I shall move to one of the Marquesas, where living's cheap and easy."
Aug. " Am leaving for the Marquesas. At last ! " (*Letters to de Monfreid,* pp. 310, 321).

Dominica (Aug., 1901-*May,* 1903*).*

1901 November. Long letter to de Monfreid in which he describes his new home, which he calls *La Maison du Jouir* and the conditions under which he works. " Here poetry springs from the soil, unsummoned, and all one needs to body it forth is to let one's mind go dreaming as one paints."

1902 March. " Though my health is bad as ever, I have started working steadily again ; you can't imagine the peacefulness of my life, all alone amongst the leafage ! " *Contes Barbares* (Folkwang Museum, Essen).
Aug. His heart is giving him trouble and eczema has broken out on his limbs, causing him intense suffering. He knows that he is mortally ill, and his one idea is to return to France for treatment. His friend de Monfreid dissuades him.

1903 March. Contentions with the Local Government, the Bishop, and the police (for championing the natives). Unjustly sentenced to three months' imprisonment and fine of 1000 francs (March 31). Unable to appeal, lacking funds for the journey to Tahiti.
April. Last letter to de Monfreid ends : " all these worries are *killing me.*"
May 8. About 11 a.m. death of Gauguin.

BIBLIOGRAPHY

1. *Writings and Correspondence.*
Noa-Noa, 1891-93 (Paris, 1924). *Cahier pour Aline,* 1893, manuscript. *Les Guêpes, Le Sourire, L'Indépendant de Tahiti,* 1899-1900 newspapers with articles by G. *Racontars d'un Rapin,* 1902, manuscript. *Avant et Après,* 1902 (Paris, 1923). *Lettres à G. D. de Monfreid* preceded by ' Hommage à Gauguin ' by V. Segalen, Paris, 1919 and 1930 (new ed. printing). *Lettres à A. Fontainas,* Paris, 1921. *Letters to A. Vollard and A. Fontainas,* ed. by J. Rewald, San Francisco, 1943. *Lettres à sa femme et à ses amis,* publ. by M. Malingue, Paris, 1946.

2. *Catalogues.*
M. Guérin, *L'Œuvre Gravé de Paul Gauguin,* Paris, 1927 (2 Vols.). General catalogue in preparation. Centenary Exh. at the Orangerie, Paris, July-Nov., 1949 ; descriptive notices, with bibl. and unpublished documents, by J. Leymarie, and Introd. by R. Huyghe.

3. *Monographs and Appraisals.*
J. de Rotonchamp : *Paul Gauguin,* Paris, 1906 (new ed. 1925) ; basic. See also C. Morice, Paris, 1919, C. Chassé, *Gauguin et le Groupe de Pont-Aven,* Paris, 1921. J. Dorsenne, *La Vie Sentimentale de P. Gauguin,* Paris, 1927. W. Barth, Basel, 1929. W. S. Maugham, *The Moon and Sixpence* (fictionalized biogr.), London and New York. A. Alexandre, *P. Gauguin, sa Vie et le Sens de son Œuvre,* Paris, 1930. R. Cogniat, *La Vie ardente de P. Gauguin,* Paris, 1936. Pola Gauguin, *Paul Gauguin, mon Père,* Paris, 1938. J. Rewald, Paris and London, 1938. E. Bernard, *Souvenirs inédits sur Gauguin,* Lorient, 1941. A. de Witt, *Vita e Arte di Gauguin,* Milan, 1946. Malingue, *Gauguin, le Peintre et son Œuvre,* Paris, 1948. J. Taralon, Paris, 1949. Important review articles : O. Mirbeau, *L'Echo de Paris,* Feb. 16, 1891. G. A Aurier, *Le Mercure de France,* March, 1891. *Revue Encyclopédique,* April, 1892. E. Bernard, *Mercure de F.,* June, 1895, Dec., 1903 ; Dec., 1908. A. Seguin, *L'Occident,* March, April, May, 1903. V. Segalen, *Mercure de F.,* June, 1904. M. Denis, *Mercure de F.,* Jan., 1904 ; *Occident,* May, 1910. G. de Chirico, *Convegno,* Milan, March, 1920. L. Venturi, *L'Arte,* March, 1934. C. Chassé, *L'Amour de l'Art,* Apr., 1938. A. M. Berryer, *Bull. des Musées d'Art et d'Histoire,* Jan., 1944, Brussels. D. Sutton, *Burlington Magazine,* April, Nov., 1949. Special number of *Mercure de France,* Oct., 1903 ; of *L'Art et les Artistes,* Nov., 1925 ; of *Ver y Estimar,* Buenos-Ayres, Nov., 1948. M. Raynal, Geneva, 1949.

Exhibitions.

1888, Gal. Boussod & Valadon, Paris ; 1893, Gal. Durand-Ruel, Paris (49 paintings, 2 sculp. Pref. by C. Morice) ; 1903, Gal. Vollard, Paris ; 1906, Salon d'Automne (227 Nos. Pref. by C. Morice) ; 1907 (March, April), Gal. Mitkke, Vienna ; 1910, Gal. Thannhauser, Dresden and Munich ; 1917, March 7-31, Gal. Nunés & Fiquet, Paris (39 Nos. Pref. by L. Vauxcelles) ; 1919, Oct. 10-30, Gal. Barbazanges, Paris ; 1923, April 16-May 11, Gal. Dru, Paris (68 Nos. Pref. D. de Monfreid) ; 1926, Copenhagen, Oslo ; 1926, Dec., Assoc. Paris-Amérique Latine, Paris (135 Nos. Coll. F. Durio) ; 1928, Jan.-Feb., Luxembourg, Paris : *Gauguin Sculpt. et Graveur* (107 Nos.) ; 1928, July, Aug., Kunsthalle, Basel (254 Nos. Pref. and Cat. by W. Barth) ; 1928, Biennale, Venice, Retrospective Exh. (42 Nos.) ; 1928, Gal. Thannhauser, Berlin (230 Nos. Pref. and Cat. by W. Barth) ; 1931, May 26-June 14, Gal. de la Pléiade, Paris : *Exp. de Gauguin, Œuvre Gravé* (Introd. and Cat. by Henri Petiet) ; 1936, March, April, Wildenstein Gal., New York ; 1936, May 1-21, Fogg Art Museum, Cambridge, Massachusetts ; May, June, Mus. of Art, Baltimore (Pref. by H. Focillon) ; Sept. 5-Oct. 4, Mus. of Art, San Francisco (139 Nos. Pref. and Cat. by G. L. McCann Morley) ; Nov., Gal. des Beaux-Arts, Paris (Pref. by H. Focillon, Cat. by R. Cogniat) ; 1942, May 15-June 13, Gal. Marcel Guiot, Paris (Watercolours, monotypes, drawings. Pref. and Cat. by Marcel Guérin) ; 1946, April 3-May 4, Wildenstein Gal., New York (91 Nos. Pref. by S. Maugham) ; 1948, May, June, Retrospective Exh. for Centenary of Gauguin's birth, Ny Carlsberg Glyptotek, Copenhagen (129 Nos. Pref. and Cat. by Haavard Rostrup) ; 1949, July-Oct., Centenary Exh., Orangerie, Paris (117 Nos. Introd. by R. Huyghe, Cat. by J. Leymarie).

JONGKIND, Johann Barthold (1819-1891)

1819 Born June 3rd, at Latrop, in the province of Over-Yssel, Holland, the eighth son of a clergyman, who had ten children. As a young man, lawyer's clerk.

1836 His father dies. Attends lectures at the School of Drawing, The Hague. Becomes pupil of the landscape-painter, Schelfhout.

1843 His teacher gets him a 'Royal Pension' of 200 florins. Does watercolours from life.

1845 Meets Isabey, then settles in Paris, Place Pigalle (1846). Visits the studio of Isabey; then those of Picot and Dupuis. Acquainted with Ciceri and A. de Dreux.

1848 Travels in Holland. One of his pictures is accepted by the Salon *(Port de Mer)*. Already leading a vagabond life.

1850-52 Travels in Normandy, Brittany. At the Salon obtains a third medal. Drink, debauchery, continual poverty.

1853 The Royal Pension is discontinued. He lives in the rue Breda. Acquainted with Stevens, Troyon, Courbet; his pictures do not sell well, prices range from 7 to 200 francs. At the Hôtel des Ventes, 117 watercolours bring in 497 francs.

1856-60 Returns to Holland; badly received, he regrets leaving France; goes back to Paris. Takes his evening meals with Courbet, and resumes his irregular life. Returns again to Rotterdam where he remains till 1860; his physical and moral condition worsens. Appeals to his Parisian friends, who organize a sale on his behalf: Bonvin, Braquemond, Corot, Chaplin, Diaz, Harpignies, C. Jacques, Isabey, Cals. The last-named brings him back to Paris.

1860 Monet writes to Boudin: "The only good seascape-painter we have, Jongkind, is dead for art, he's raving mad!" Jongkind meets Mme Fesser, a compatriot, who devotes her life to saving him; "An angel of devotion," says E. de Goncourt, "though with her thick moustache she looks more like a *vivandière* of the Old Guard."

1861 Lives for a while in the rue de Chevreuse, then on the road again: Nevers, Le Havre, Honfleur, etc.

1862 At Le Havre, with Boudin and Monet.

1863 Exhibits at the *Salon des Refusés*. At Honfleur in 1864 and 1865.

1865-70 Success comes, bringing orders for pictures. In spite of Mme Fesser's solicitude, his health remains very poor; nevertheless he goes on travelling: Antwerp, Rotterdam, Dordrecht, Brussels, Chartres, Nantes. In 1870, arrested as a spy, then released. Returns to Paris during the Commune.

1871-78 Connoisseurs flock to him. "People come," he says, "from England, from America, even from Russia to buy my pictures."

1878 Settles down at La Côte Saint-André, near Grenoble, where he remains till his death, except for a journey to Provence in 1880 and short trips to Paris.

1879-83 His health grows worse, he suffers from mental disorders, hemorrhage, dizziness. A sale made after the death of his patron Bascle brings in 193,950 francs.

1884-90 Persecution mania. His physical state worse than ever. Refuses to take his friends' advice and "go slow." Visit of Henri Rochefort. First paralytic stroke.

1891 He is taken to St. Rambert's Asylum, St. Egrève, near Grenoble. Dies suddenly on Feb. 9th., Mme Fesser, whose devoted care enabled him to reach his 72nd year, died on Nov. 23rd, of the same year.

BIBLIOGRAPHY

Moreau-Nélaton, Paris, 1918. P. Colin, Paris, 1921. P. Signac, Paris, 1927.

Exhibitions.

1814, Fenoglio Gal. Grenoble: (107 Items. Pref. by A. Farcy); 1935, May 1-15, Paris, Hôtel du Figaro; 1936, Nov. 16-30, Paris, G. Stein Gal. (Pref. C. Roger-Marx); 1941, Oct.-Dec., Museum of Grenoble, 50th Anniversary Exhibition (271 oils and watercolours); 1942, May-June, J. Dubourg Gal. Paris; 1948, July-Sept. Communal Museum. The Hague; and 1949, Orangerie, Paris (227 Items. Pref. C. Roger-Marx).

MANET, Edouard (1832-1883)

1832 Jan. 23, born at 5, rue Bonaparte (then the rue des Petits-Augustins), Paris. Middle-class family. His father, subsequently a Counsellor at the Court, was then Chief Administrative Officer at the Ministry of Justice. His mother, Désirée Fournier, was daughter of one of Napoleon's diplomatic agents.

1839 At Canon Poiloup's preparatory school in the Vaugirard district.

1842 Boarder at the Collège Rollin. Schoolfellow of Antonin Proust, subsequently Minister of Fine Arts, with whom he took the special drawing course provided by the school. Also influenced by his uncle, Fournier, a connoisseur.

1848 His parents against his taking up art as a profession. He decides to go to sea and becomes a navigating cadet. Sails to Rio, Dec. 9, on the transport 'Le Havre et Guadeloupe.'

1849 June, back in Paris. Fails in the Naval School examination, in July. Lives at 6 rue du Mont-Thabor; takes piano lessons from Suzanne Leenhoff.

1850 January. Talks his father over into letting him enter the studio of Couture (rue de Laval), famous author of *Les Romains de la Décadence* (1847).

1856 Easter. Leaves Couture who has said to him disdainfully: "You'll never be more than the Daumier of your time." Rents a studio in rue Lavoisier, with Count Albert de Balleroy. Meanwhile he has been widening his knowledge by travels in Holland, Germany, Austria and Italy (autumn, 1853), where he studies the masterpieces; and by making copies, in the Louvre and art-galleries, of Titian, Tintoretto, Delacroix, Rembrandt, Filippino Lippi.

1859 Studio, rue de Douai. *The Absinthe-drinker* (Ny Carlsberg Glyptotek, Copenhagen). Despite Delacroix' backing, rejected at the Salon. Introduced to Baudelaire by Commandant Lejosne.

1861 His first exhibits at the Salon, the *Portrait of his Parents* (Coll. Mme E. Rouart, Paris) and especially his *Guitarrero* (Coll. W. C. Osborn, New York), which secures for him a medal and is enthusiastically praised by Gautier, are a great success. In the same year, paints *Concert in the Tuileries Gardens* (Tate Gallery, London), an open-air scene of contemporary life. Exhibition at Galerie Martinet.

1862 Studio, 81, rue Guyot. *La Chanteuse de Rues* (Coll. Mrs Sears, Boston), the model being Victorine Meurent who until 1875 remained his favourite model.
Aug. A troupe of Spanish dancers from Madrid is performing at the Hippodrome, and Manet makes several paintings of them, the most famous of which, *Lola de Valence,* was celebrated by Baudelaire in a quatrain. Sept. 25, death of his father.

1863 May 15. The Salon des Refusés creates an uproar. *Le Déjeuner sur l'Herbe* (Louvre. Plate, p. 7). Has great influence on the young painters at the Académie Suisse and in Gleyre's studio: the Impressionists-to-be. Oct. 6. Goes to Holland to regularize his marriage with Suzanne Leenhoff, with whom he has been living since 1852.

1864 June 19. Sea-fight between the *Kearsage* and the *Alabama* off the Cherbourg coast. Manet rushes to the scene and probably witnesses the actual engagement. Makes a large painting of it (J. J. Johnson Collection, Museum of Art, Philadelphia). Stays at Boulogne and Gennevilliers. Paints *Peonies* (Louvre) bought by Chocquet, Still Lifes of fish and fruit, exhibited at Martinet's and Nadart's galleries; also *Races at Longchamps* (Art Institute, Chicago). Settles at 34, boulevard des Batignolles.

1865 *Olympia,* a realistic nude inspired by Goya, painted in 1863 (Louvre), causes another uproar at the Salon. Exasperated by the malignity of the art critics, Manet goes to Spain for a fortnight; 'discovers' Velasquez, mets Théodore Duret at Madrid.

1866 Rejected at the Salon. Becomes the focus of admiration at the Café Guerbois, boulevard de Clichy; meets Zola, Cézanne, Monet. Zola devotes laudatory articles to him in *L'Evénement* and *La Revue du XIXe Siècle.*

1867 Does not exhibit at the World's Fair, but fixes up a one-man show of 50 canvases at the Place de l'Alma, near that of Courbet. Settles at 49, rue de Saint-Petersbourg.

1868 Exhibits *Portrait of Zola* (Louvre. Plate, p. 8) at the Salon; meets Berthe Morisot who sits for *The Balcony* (Louvre).

1869 Eva Gonzalès becomes his pupil and model. Summer at Boulogne. A week-end in London. Seascapes. Lithograph poster for Champfleury's *Les Chats.*

1870 Duel with Duranty. Central figure in Fantin-Latour's picture, *L'Atelier aux Batignolles* (Louvre); grouped round him are Zola, Monet, Renoir, Bazille. Stays at Boulogne; at St. Germain-en-Laye, with de Nittis. Lieutenant in the National Guard under Col. Meissonier's command.

1871 Feb. 12. Joins his family who have taken refuge at Oloron-Sainte-Marie in the Pyrenees. Feb. 20, at Bordeaux *Port de Bordeaux* (Private Coll., Berlin). Returns to Paris by slow stages, along the coast: Arcachon (March 1), Royan, Rochefort, Saint-Nazaire, Le Pouliguen (where he stays a month), Tours (May 10). Spends summer at Boulogne, with trips to Calais.

1872 Exhibits at the Salon *Le Combat du Kearsage et de l'Alabama.* Critics favourable. Swing-round of public opinion. Durand-Ruel buys his pictures to the tune of 51,000 francs. Fixes up a handsome studio for himself at 4, rue de St. Petersbourg. Four *Portraits of Berthe Morisot.* August, goes to Holland; much impressed by Hals.

1873 Great success at the Salon with his portrait of Belot the engraver, *Le Bon Bock* (C. J. Tyson Coll., Philadelphia). Studies from the *Bals Masqués* at the Paris Opera (March). Summer at Berck-sur-Mer: beach scenes, seascapes, watercolours. Sept., in Paris. Café de la Nouvelle-Athènes. Sells 5 pictures to Faure the singer. Meets Nina de Callias. First pastel: *Mme Manet,* in profile (Coll. Mme E. Rouart, Paris).

1874 Only two of four pictures sent in accepted at the Salon. Mallarmé, with whom he is friendly, protests. Manet refuses to take part in the First 'Impressionist' Exhibition in Nadar's studios, despite pressure by Degas and Monet.
Aug., stays at Gennevilliers, then at Argenteuil with Monet. Paints boating-scenes: *Argenteuil* (Tournai Museum. Plate, p. 27).
Dec. 22: Berthe Morisot marries his brother Eugène and ceases to sit for him. Publisher Poulet-Malassis hits on a 'device' for his bookplate, *Manet et Manebit.*

1875 Sept., visits Venice. Two *Views of the Grand Canal.*

1876 *Le Linge* (Barnes Foundation, Merion), a large open-air composition, and *The Artist in his Studio* (portrait of Marcellin Desboutin) rejected at the Salon. Invites the public to see them in his studio, April 15-May 1. Meets Mery Laurent at Fécamp in August. *Portrait of Mallarmé* (Louvre); of *Nana* (Kunsthalle, Hamburg).

1877 *Nana* rejected at Salon, exhibited in premises of Giroux, antiquarian, boulevard des Capucines.

1878 Obliged to quit his flat and, worse still, his beloved studio. Before leaving paints 5 pictures of the *Rue Mosnier.* Settles temporarily (July 1) into the greenhouse-studio, 70, rue d'Amsterdam, of a Swedish painter, Roser. Now begins painting 'naturalistic' subjects inspired by *brasseries* and *cafés-chantants La Serveuse de Bocks* (Tate Gallery, London).

1879 April 1, settles into No. 77 rue d'Amsterdam. First onset of illness that is to carry him off; he undergoes treatment at Bellevue.

1880 April, one-man show at *La Vie Moderne.* Again under treatment (for 3 months) at Bellevue, Still Lifes, watercolours. Returns to Paris in October. His studio becomes a great meeting-place for literary men, society people, men-about-town, and ladies of the street (whom he is coming to use more and more as his models and of whom he does pastel portraits).

1881 At the Salon, exhibits his *Portrait of Henri Rochefort* (Hamburg Museum) and the *Portrait of Pertuiset*, for which he is awarded a second-class medal. Series of pastels. Jeanne de Marsy sits for his *Spring* (Private Coll., New York), a charming evocation of the 'Parisienne,' and Mery Laurent for *Autumn* (Nancy Museum). Jul.-Oct. at Versailles. Antonin Proust, Minister of Fine Arts, has him awarded the Legion of Honour, Dec. 30.

1882 Exhibits *Bar aux Folies-Bergère* at the Salon (Tate Gallery, London). His illness is making rapid strides. At Rueil, where he spends the summer, he can hardly move; paints Still Lifes of fruit and flowers.

1883 Completely paralysed, confined to his bedroom, he paints only the flowers his friends send him. On March 25, Easter Eve, Mery Laurent sends him flowers; he makes a sketch in pastels of her maid, Elisa, who brings them; this is the last work of his life.
From April 6 he has to stay in bed. On the 18th his left leg is amputated. His death takes place at 7 p. m., April 30; the funeral on May 3. "He was greater than we thought," said Degas as the mourners left the little cemetery at Passy where he is buried. On May 5 Eva Gonzalès died.

BIBLIOGRAPHY

1. *Writings and Correspondence.*

E. Manet, *Lettres de Jeunesse*, Paris, 1929. J. Guiffrey, *Lettres Illustrées de Manet*, Paris, 1929 (Ed. in English, New York, 1944). A. Tabarant, *Une Correspondance inédite d'E. Manet : Lettres du Siège de Paris*, Paris, 1935.

2. *Catalogues.*

T. Duret, *Histoire d'E. Manet* (with catalogue), Paris, 1902 (new ed., 1919). Moreau-Nelaton, *Manet Graveur et Lithographe*, Paris, 1906. A. Tabarant, *Manet, Histoire catalographique*, Paris, 1931. Janot, Wildenstein, Bataille: *Manet*, 2 Vols., Paris, 1932. M. Guérin, *L'Œuvre gravé de Manet*, Paris, 1944. A. Tabarant, *Manet et ses Oeuvres*, Paris, 1947. (An indispensable work, catalogue and biography.)

3. *Monographs and Appraisals.*

E. Zola, *Manet, Etude biographique et critique*, Paris, 1867. E. Bazire, Paris, 1884. E. Waldmann, Berlin, 1910. A. Proust, *Souvenirs sur Manet*, Paris, 1913. J. E. Blanche, Paris, 1924. Moreau-Nélaton, *Manet raconté par lui-même*, 2 Vols., Paris, 1926. P. Jamot, Studies of Manet, *Gaz. des Bx-Arts*, 1927. P. Colin, Paris, 1932. Spec. numbers of *L'Am. de l'Art* and *Art vivant*, 1932. R. Rey, Paris, 1938. G. Jedlicka, Zurich, 1941. P. Courthion, *Manet raconté par lui-même et par ses amis*, Geneva, 1945. M. Florisoone, *Manet*, Monaco, 1947.

4. *Exhibitions.*

1861, 1863, March, 1865, Feb., Gal. Martinet; 1867, May, one-man show in a pavilion, Place de l'Alma, during World's Fair; 1880, April 10-30, one-man show in premises of *La Vie Moderne* organized by Charpentier the publisher (26 canvases); 1884, Jan. 5-28, Posthumous Exhibition at Ecole Nationale des Beaux-Arts, Paris (154 paint., 22 etchings, 5 lith., 13 drawings. Pref. by Zola); 1905, Oct. 18-Nov. 25, Retrospective Exh., Salon d'Automne (26 paint.); 1906, March, Gal. Durand-Ruel, Paris, Exh. of Manet's works in the Faure Collection (24 oils and watercolours); 1928, Feb.-March, Gal. Matthiesen, Berlin; 1928, Gal. Bernheim, Paris, Exh. for 'Les Amis du Luxembourg'; 1930, April. Exh. watercolours, drawings, lithographs, Gal. Sagot, Paris; 1932, Exposition du Centenaire, Orangerie, Paris (Pref. by Paul Valéry, Introd. by P. Jamot, Cat. by C. Sterling, 150 Exhibits).

MONET, Claude (1840-1926)

1840 Born in Paris, November 14. Son of a grocer. Spent childhood and youth at Le Havre.

1856 Begins by drawing caricatures. Taken up by Boudin, who encourages him to turn to landscape. Admires Daubigny, a picture by whom his aunt has given him.

1859 Comes to Paris in May. Troyon gives advice and encourages him to copy pictures at the Louvre. Frequents the *Brasserie des Martyrs* and the 'Suisse' Academy, where he makes friends with Pissarro, alongside whom he sets up his easel.

1860-61 Military service with the Chasseurs d'Afrique, in Algeria. 'Bought out' by his family after two years' service.

1862 Returns to Le Havre where he spends the summer in the company of Boudin and Jongkind. In November enters Gleyre's studio in Paris; meets Bazille, Renoir, Sisley.

1863 Shares with Bazille a flat in Place de Furstenberg, overlooking Delacroix' studio and they often watch him at work. Easter holidays at Chailly near Barbizon.

1864 With Renoir, Bazille, Sisley in Fontainebleau Forest. At Honfleur with Boudin, Jongkind, Bazille. Offers three canvases to Bruyas, the collector (Montpellier), but he declines them.

1865 Has success at the Salon with a seascape, praised by Mantz. Paints in Fontainebleau Forest a *Déjeuner sur l'Herbe*; then works with Courbet at Trouville.

1866 Another success at the Salon with the portrait *Camille* (Kunsthalle, Bern), bought by Arsène Houssaye. Paris scenes: *Saint-Germain l'Auxerrois* (Nationalgalerie, Berlin). At Ville d'Avray during summer, at Sainte-Adresse and Le Havre later in year. Meets Manet, whose influence he undergoes along with that of Courbet.

1867 His *Women in the Garden* (Louvre. Plate, p. 13) painted entirely in the open air, rejected at the Salon; bought by Bazille. Goes to Sainte-Adresse, where his mistress Camille gives birth, in July, to his son Jean. Penniless. His pictures seized and sold in lots of 50, at 30 francs a lot.

1868 At Etretat and at Fécamp, where he attempts to commit suicide.

1869 At Bougival with Renoir: scenes of the *Grenouillère* bathing-place (Metropolitan Museum of Art, New York), the first thoroughly impressionist pictures. Again at Etretat and Le Havre.

1870 Rejected at the Salon. In June marries Camille. Summer at Trouville (Plate, p. 18) and Le Havre, whence he embarks in Sept. for England.

1871 Meets Pissarro again in London. Daubigny introduces him to picture-dealer Durand-Ruel and goes with him to Holland. Seeks without success to show at the Royal Academy.

1872 Second trip to Holland. On his return settles in Argenteuil.

ARGENTEUIL 1872-1878

1873 Sets up studio in a boat and paints his masterpieces, regattas and river-bank scenes.

1874 Is acknowledged leader of Impressionism. Joined by Renoir, Sisley, Manet, Caillebotte, who work under his influence. At the first Group Exhibition shows 12 canvases, one of which, *Impression : Sunrise* (Coll. D. de Monchy, Paris), leads to the new painters' being called, mockingly, ' Impressionists.'

1876-77 *Gare Saint-Lazare* series (Plate, p. 28).

VÉTHEUIL 1878-1881

1878 Settles at Vétheuil, keeping a *pied-à-terre* in Paris. His second son, Michel, born in March. Financial straits.

1879 Death of Camille.

1880 One-man show at *La Vie Moderne*. Paints during this very hard winter his ' series ' *The Breaking-up of the Ice*, in which his style shows signs of systematization. For the last time exhibits at the Salon, and refuses to join in the Fifth Group Exhibition. Now begins a parting of the ways ; the Impressionist movement is falling apart.

1881 March, at Fécamp.

POISSY 1881-1883

Lives at Poissy near St-Germain-en-Laye from Oct. 1881 to May 1883, with Mme Hoschedé ; spends each summer at the seaside : Fécamp, Varengeville, Pourville, Dieppe.

GIVERNY (1883-1926)

1883 In April, settles at Giverny, near Vernon, where he is to live until the end of his life. When at last success brought prosperity, he bought the house (1891), laid out a flowergarden, a water-lily pool, and built a boathouse. One-man show in March. Le Havre. Etretat. Goes with Renoir to the Riviera in December.

1884 Bordighera, Jan. 18 to April 3 ; Menton, April 8-13. Lavish use of strong colour, akin to Fauvism. Etretat (Aug., Sept.).

1885 Joins in ' Exposition Internationale ' at Petit's Gallery. At Etretat (Oct.-Dec.).

1886 Visits Haarlem. In Belle-Isle, Sept.-Nov. Meets G. Geffroy.

1888 Antibes, Jan.-April. Admired by Mallarmé. " This is, I think, your finest hour."

1889 At Fresselines, with Maurice Rollinat (March-May). Two-man show with Rodin at Petit's.

1890 Beginning of his ' systematic ' series ; study of the effects of light on the same scene according to the hour, season, atmospheric conditions.

1891 *The Haystacks*. Visits London in the autumn.

1892 *The Poplars*. The *Rouen Cathedral* series (exhibited in 1895).

1895 Visits Norway ; snowscapes, northern light effects.

1904 Exhibits the series of London Views : Houses of Parliament, Waterloo Bridge, Charing Cross, begun in 1899. His supreme effort, these show the influence of Turner. Meanwhile he still paints the Seine banks (Port-Villers, Giverny, Vétheuil) and Normandy sea-beaches (Pourville, Varengeville, Dieppe).

1908 Venice. Here, as in London, he seeks to render luminous mists (series exhibited in 1912).

1909 *Waterlilies* series, begun in 1898, resumed in 1905. (Renderings of his water-garden at Giverny.)

1922 Operated on for cataract, recovers his sight.

1923 Gift to the Nation of a decorative *ensemble* with yet again the ' waterlilies ' motif, begun in 1915. This decorative work was installed after his death, in the manner enjoined by him, in the two oval rooms of the Musée de l'Orangerie.

1926 Died at Giverny, Dec. 6. For some time he had been living as a recluse, visited only by a few friends, the most eminent of whom was Clemenceau. His last years were darkened by bereavements (his second wife died in 1911, his son Jean in 1914), and by increasing doubts as to the value of his art and of an aesthetic theory which the younger generation so peremptorily rejected.

BIBLIOGRAPHY

Writings by the Artist and Interviews.

The voluminous correspondence with Durand-Ruel (411 letters from 1876 to 1926) has been published by L. Venturi : *Les Archives de l'Impressionnisme*, Paris, 1939. For letters of his youth to Boudin, see G. Cahen, *Boudin*, Paris, 1900 ; for those to Bazille, G. Poulain, *Bazille et ses Amis*, Paris, 1932. For letters to Manet, Tarabant, *L'Art Vivant*, May 4, 1928 ; to Chocquet, J. Joets, *L'Amour de l'Art*, April, 1935. Interviews : Thiebault-Sisson, *Le Temps*, Nov. 27, 1900 : L. Vauxcelles, *L'Art et les Artistes*, Dec., 1905 ; Duc de Trevise, *Revue d'Art Ancien et Moderne*, Jan.-Feb., 1937 ; M. Elder, *Chez Claude Monet à Giverny*, Paris, 1924.

Monographs and Appraisals.

O. Mirbeau, *L'Art dans les Deux-Mondes*, March 7, 1891 ; A. Alexandre, Paris, 1921 ; G. Geffroy, *Claude Monet, sa Vie, son Temps, son Œuvre*, Paris, 1922 ; R. Regamey, *La Formation de Claude Monet*, Gazette des Beaux-Arts, Feb., 1927 ; L. Werth, Paris, 1928 ; G. Clemenceau, Paris, 1928 ; M. de Fels, *La Vie de Claude Monet*, Paris, 1929 ; P. Francastel, *Monet, Sisley, Pissarro*, Paris, 1939 ; M. Malingue, Monaco, 1943.

Exhibitions.

1880, *La Vie Moderne*, Paris ; 1883, March, Gal. Durand-Ruel, Paris ; 1889, Exh. Rodin-Monet, Gal. Petit, Paris (Preface by O. Mirbeau) ; 1891, May, Gal. Durand-Ruel *(Les Meules)* ; 1892, Gal. Durand-Ruel *(Les Peupliers)* ; 1895, Gal. Durand-Ruel *(Rouen and Norway)* ; 1898, June, Gal. Petit ; 1904, Gal. Durand-Ruel *(London)* ; 1909, Gal. Durand-Ruel *(Waterlilies)* ; 1912, Gal. Bernheim-Jeune *(Venice)* ; 1931, Orangerie, Paris (Introd. by P. Jamot. 128 items) ; 1936, April 2-30,

Gal. P. Rosenberg, Paris (30 Items: Works 1891-1919); 1944, Orangerie, Paris; 1945, April-May, Wildenstein Gallery, New York.

PISSARRO, CAMILLE (1830-1903)

1830 Born July 10 at Saint-Thomas in the West Indies. Jewish parentage.

1841-47 Educated in a school in Passy (Paris), whose headmaster, Savary, an art-lover, has him taught drawing from nature.

1847-52 Back at Saint-Thomas, enters his father's business.

1852 Runs away to Caracas (Venezuela) with the Danish painter Fritz Melbye (1826-1869). Returns to Saint-Thomas in 1854.

1855 His father accepts his vocation and sends him to Paris, where he arrives in time to see the World's Fair and admires the works of Corot, whom he visits. Enters the studio of Anton Melbye (1818-1875), Fritz's brother. Lives in the country near Montmorency, but goes on painting West Indian scenes in an oriental style, *à la* Decamps.

1857 For a short time at the Ecole des Beaux-Arts. Discovers the Ile-de-France countryside.

1859 At the Académie Suisse; meets Claude Monet. Exhibits a landscape at the Salon.

1861 Rejected at the Salon. Meets Cézanne and Guillaumin.

1863 Exhibits three pictures at the Salon des Refusés, noticed by Castagnary. Birth of his eldest son Lucien (February 20).

1864 At Montfoucault, in the home of his painter friend Piette. La Varenne-Saint-Hilaire.

1866 Settles at Pontoise. His Salon picture praised by Zola.

1869 Louveciennes. Two pictures of the Seine bank at Bougival, with study of the play of light on water.

1870 At Montfoucault, then in England. Marries Julie Vellay, by whom he already has two children (he is to have seven in all, the five sons being painters). 'Discovers' Constable.

1871 Rejoins Monet, makes acquaintance of Durand-Ruel who buys two of his pictures. In June returns to Louveciennes. His studio looted by the Germans; "only some forty pictures left out of fifteen hundred."

1872 Returns to *Pontoise* (April) and there joined by Guillaumin, Cézanne, Vignon.

1873 Paints his *Portrait* (Louvre) and his first great works on the Hermitage motif. Imparts to Cézanne the aesthetic theories of Impressionism; his own works, however, strongly rooted to the soil, are more constructive than those of Monet.

1874 Takes part in the First Impressionist Exhibition and is to be the only member of the group exhibiting at all the seven following. Maturity of his style. Some pastels.

1875-76 Frequent stays at Montfoucault. Planned, strongly balanced, monumental, static compositions, akin to those of Cézanne.

1877 Again under Monet's influence. Light vibrations. *The Red Roofs* (Louvre).

1880 Introduces figures in his landscapes. Decorative tendencies. Does etchings with Degas and Mary Cassatt.

1883 One-man show at Durand-Ruel's. With Gauguin at Rouen.

1884 Settles at *Eragny*, near Gisors.

1885 Meets Signac and Seurat. Adopts their scientific theory of art.

1886 Year of thorough-going Pointillism. Succeeds in having Seurat and Signac accepted at the eighth and last Impressionist Exhibition. Meets Van Gogh.

1890 Desists from a technique which does not accord with his sensibility. Renews his stock of 'motifs' by a visit to London.

1891 Death of Seurat. Refuses to lead Neo-Impressionist movement and reverts to the free brushstrokes of his early phase. Spends his time between his Eragny and his Paris residences, 12, rue de l'Abreuvoir. Begins to find favour with picture-dealers.

1892 Exhibits at Durand-Ruel's (50 oil paintings, 20 gouaches). Financial success. Buys his house at Eragny. Spends summer in London; paints Kew Gardens.

1893 Begins his series of scenes of Paris viewed from above; crowds, traffic, vistas of avenues, seen from the windows of various hotels. Paints his *Rue Saint-Lazare*, where he now is living.

1894 Stays at Knocke (Belgium), where he meets Elisée Reclus whose anarchist theories he shares.

1896 At Rouen (spring and autumn).

1897 In London (May to July).

1898 Views of the *Théâtre Français*, Paris; and of *Rouen Cathedral*.

1899 Staying at 2-4, rue de Rivoli. Scenes of the *Tuileries Gardens* and *Le Carrousel*. At Varengeville in the autumn.

1900 At Bonneval near Dieppe. In Paris, 28, Place Dauphine: views of the *Pont-Neuf*.

1901 Moret (April-May). Dieppe (August-September).

1902 Again at Dieppe (July-September). "I am working on the Quai de la Poissonnerie; the range of colours is much like that at Rouen."

1903 In Paris; first, Place Dauphine, then at Hôtel Voltaire: *Pont-Royal* and *Quai Malaquais*. At Le Havre (July-September), where he paints the quays, harbour-scenes. In the intervals between his travels he goes on painting, at Eragny, the countryside, orchards in flower. Dies in Paris on November 13.

BIBLIOGRAPHY

1. *Correspondence*.
C. Pissarro, *Letters to his Son Lucien*, edited by John Rewald, New York, 1943 (477 letters between 1883 and 1903). The Letters to Durand-Ruel (86) and O. Maus (16) were published by L. Venturi in *Les Archives de l'Impressionnisme*, Paris, 1939; those to O. Mirbeau by G. Lecomte & Ch. Kunstler in *La Revue d'Art Ancien et Moderne*, March, 1930.

2. *Catalogues*.
C. Pissarro, son art, son œuvre, Paris, 1939. Indispensable. List compiled by L. R. Pissarro

the artist's son (1664 Items: 1632 Ill.) with an excellent appraisal by L. Venturi. A good bibliography. L. Delteil, *Le Peintre-Graveur Illustré*, Vol. XVII, Paris, 1923 (195 Items).

3. *Monographs and Critical Studies.*

O. Mirbeau. *L'Art dans les deux Mondes*, Jan. 10, 1891. G. Lecomte, *Pissarro*, Paris, 1922. A. Tabarant, *Pissarro*, Paris, 1924. C. Kunstler, *Pissarro*, Paris, 1930. J. Rewald, *Pissarro, his Work and Influence*, Burlington Magazine, June, 1938. P. Francastel, *Monet, Sisley, Pissarro*, Paris, 1939. J. Rewald, *C. Pissarro au Musée du Louvre*, Paris, 1939.

Exhibitions.

Galerie Durand-Ruel, Paris: May, 1883; Feb., 1892 (50 pictures & 21 gouaches; preface by G. Lecomte); March, 1893; March, 1894; April 15-May 9, 1893 (recent work: pref. A. Alexandre); June, 1898; Jan., 1901, April 7-30, 1904 (178 exhibits: pref. O. Mirbeau); May-June, 1907, Galerie E. Blot (pref. G. Lecomte); Salon d'Automne, 1911 (etchings and lithographs: pref. T. Duret); 1920, May, Leicester Gallery, London (pref. J. B. Manson); 1921, Durand-Ruel Gallery, Paris; Feb.-March, 1930, Orangerie, Paris, celebrating centenary of his birth (pref. A. Tabarant); Nov.-Dec., 1934, Bernheim Gallery, Paris, Pissarro and his Sons (pref. G. Kahn).

REDON, Odilon (1840-1916)

1840 Born at Bordeaux, April 20. His father, an explorer and 'squatter,' had married a Creole lady (of French descent) of New Orleans. A delicate child, he was brought up in the country, in charge of a nurse, on the family estate at Peyrelabade.

1847 First visit to Paris, where his aunt takes him to the museums.

1855 Resolves to become a painter. Lessons from the watercolour painter Gobin. A meeting with Clavaud the botanist has a decisive influence; Clavaud interests the boy in biology, makes known to him Delacroix' art and *avant-garde* literature: Baudelaire, Flaubert, Poe. He is very fond of music; also of country walks.

1857 Studies architecture at Bordeaux. Sits for the entrance examination of the Ecole des Beaux-Arts in Paris, but fails. Returns to Bordeaux, and takes to sculpture.

1858 At Paris, in Gérôme's studio.

1863 At Bordeaux becomes intimate with the romantic etcher Bresdin who is to have much influence on him; 'discovers' Rembrandt; first steps in etching.

1867 His first contribution to the Salon, an etching named *Landscape*.

1868 Art-critic of the newspaper *La Gironde* (May-July); articles on Fromentin, Courbet, Jongkind.

1870 Though exempted from military service, enlists as a volunteer. After 1870 lives mostly in Paris, in the Montparnasse district. Growing admiration for Delacroix, whom he has already copied at the Bordeaux Museum. Makes acquaintance of Corot, Courbet, and Fantin-Latour; works constantly with the last-named at the Louvre and learns from him lithography. Trip to Holland to see the Rembrandts.

1877 Summer at Barbizon.

1879 Publishes album of 10 lithographs, entitled (significantly) *Dans le Rêve.*

1880 May 1, marries Camille Fargue, a Creole from the Ile de Bourbon, who is to be for him, as he puts it, 'the lodestar of his life.'

1881-82 First exhibitions at *La Vie Moderne* and the office of the newspaper *Le Gaulois*. His work noticed by Huysmans and Hennequin.

1884 Exhibits at the first Salon des Indépendants, and presides at the gatherings preliminary to founding the *Société des Indépendants.*

1883-89 During this period — in which his first son, Jean, dies, and his younger son, Ari, is born — Redon does exclusively black-and-white lithography. Still little appreciated in France, has a better reception in Belgium and Holland.

1889 Takes part in exhibition of engraver-painters at Durand-Ruel's. Meets Mellerio, his biographer-to-be.

1891 Symbolist Banquet in honour of Jean Moréas. Redon now frequents writers, amongst them Jammes, Gide, Valéry, and especially Mallarmé, with whom he becomes very friendly. Frankly admits the 'literary' tendency of his art. "Painting is human beauty," he says, "with the prestige of thought superadded."

1899 Exhibition at Durand-Ruel's; *Hommage à Odilon Redon* (Bernard, d'Espagnat, Cross, Signac, Luce, van Rysselberghe, Ibels, Sérusier, André, Vuillard, Vallotton, Denis). Redon now leaves the Left Bank and settles in the Avenue de Wagram. Gradually gives up black-and-white (save for a short return to it in 1914) and goes back to painting, especially in pastel; his colour has now an almost incredible intensity. Flowers, portraits of women and children, and religious subjects are his favourite themes.

1909 Buys a small house at Bièvres. Lives a retired, studious and meditative life, propitious to the extreme originality of his visionary inspiration. "I have been led to this self-imposed isolation by the absolute impossibility of practising any other kind of art than that which I have always practised." In winter stays at Cannes or the Abbaye de Fontfroide (near Montpellier) with his friend Fayet, the collector, whose library he decorates.

1916 Dies, July 6, in Paris. Buried in the little graveyard at Bièvres.

BIBLIOGRAPHY

Writings by the Artist.

Like Delacroix, and likewise a brilliant writer, Redon kept up a fascinating 'Journal': *A soi-même* (1867-1915), Paris, 1922 (introd. by J. Morland). Also wrote articles (as a young man) in *La Gironde* (May-July, 1868) and the Preface to the Bresdin Retrospective Exh. at the 1908 Salon d'Automne. Some of his correspondence has been published: a Letter to E. Picard, *l'Art Moderne*, Brussels, Aug. 25, 1894; *Lettres d'Odilon Redon*, Paris, 1923; *Lettres à E. Bernard*, Brussels, 1942.

Monographs and Appraisals.

E. Hennequin, *Rev. Art et Lit.*, March 4, 1882; A. Salmon, *Art Décor.*, Jan., 1913; A. Mellerio, Paris, 1913 (new ed., Paris 1923. Cat. of black-and-white work); J. Douin, *Mercure de France*, July, 1914; A. Mellerio, *Gaz. des Beaux-Arts*, Aug.-Sept., 1920; W. Pach, *The Connoisseur*, Oct., 1920; C. Roger-Marx, Paris, 1925; C. Fegdal, Paris, 1929; M. and A. Leblond, Paris, 1941.

Illustrated Books.

G. Flaubert, *La Tentation de Saint Antoine*, Paris, 1935 (Les Amis de Redon); Paris, 1937, A. Vollard.

Exhibitions.

1881, *La Vie Moderne*; 1882, *Le Gaulois* (Drawings); 1894, March 29-April 14. Gal. Durand-Ruel, Paris (Pref. by Mellerio); 1898 and 1900, Gal. Vollard, Paris; March, 1903, Feb., 1906, Gal. Durand-Ruel; 1904, Salon d'Automne, Paris; 1908, Nov. 9-21, Gal. Druet, Paris; 1919, June-July, Winterthur, Museum; 1917, Gal. Bernheim-Jeune, Paris; 1920, May-June, Gal. Barbazanges, Paris; 1921, Gal. Giroux, Brussels; 1926, March, Musée des Arts Décoratifs, Paris (Introd. by J. Morland); 1929, May 23-June 13, Gal. Dru (Pref. by C. Roger-Marx); 1931, Feb. 1-March 2, Museum of Modern Art, New York, Exh. Lautrec-Redon. Forthcoming Redon exhibitions will, it is hoped, revela the eminence of an artist whose work is not yet sufficiently appreciated.

RENOIR, Auguste (1841-1919)

1841 Feb. 25, birth of Auguste Renoir. His father was a small tailor; there was a family of seven children (two died young).

1845 The Renoir family settles in Paris, in the rue d'Argenteuil, a street in the Carrousel quarter.

1849 Birth of Edmond, the youngest child. In the grammar-school, the music teacher, Charles Gounod, wants young Renoir to study music.

1854 But his parents send him to a china factory in the rue du Temple. This his first profession gives him a taste for decoration, for bright, translucent colours. Next, he paints fans, decorates blinds for Missions. Frequent visits to the Louvre, where he lingers in front of the old masters and Boucher's *Diane*.

1857 His grandmother dies; her portrait is his first known work.

1862 Ecole des Beaux-Arts, in Gleyre's studio, where he meets Monet, Sisley, Bazille.

1863 Stays at Chailly for Easter. Leaves Gleyre's atelier. Studies in the Louvre with Fantin-Latour.

1864 Meets Diaz in the forest of Fontainebleau. In the Salon exhibits an academic composition, *La Esmeralda* (which he later destroys).

1865 In the Salon exhibits a *Portrait* and *Soirée d'été*. Visits Marlotte.

1866 Stays with his friend Jules Lecœur. At Marlotte paints *Le Cabaret de la Mère Anthony* (Stockholm Museum), and reads with interest Zola's articles on the Salon. Refused admission to the Salon in spite of Corot's and Daubigny's intervention on his behalf.

1867 In the spring he paints views of Paris in Monet's company; Courbet's influence is obvious in the composition he submits to the Salon: *Diane Chasseresse*; it is rejected. Works in the forest of Fontainebleau, finds hospitality in Bazille's studio·

1868 *Lise* (Essen Museum), painted in the previous summer, is accepted at the Salon and attracts attention of Thoré-Bürger and Castagnary. Decorates a ceiling in Prince Bibesco's residence. Portraits of *Bazille* and *Sisley*.

1869 Spends part of the summer in the house of Lise's parents, at Ville-d'Avray, then joins Monet at Bougival. Together they paint boating scenes, and many versions of the *Grenouillère* (Stockholm Museum. Plate, p. 14) in a style already impressionist. In Oct. returns to Paris, to Bazille's studio.

1870 Sends to the Salon the *Baigneuse* (Basel Museum) and *Femme d'Alger* (Coll. Chester Dale, New York). Praised by Arsène Houssaye. Enlisted at Bordeaux in 10th Light Cavalry, he paints portraits of his captain, *Darras*, and of *Mme Darras* (Dresden Museum).

1871 Returns to Paris during the Commune; rue du Dragon. Roams the suburbs: Louveciennes, Bougival, Celle-Saint-Cloud. *Portrait de la Famille Henriot* (Barnes Foundation, Merion).

1872 His studio is in rue Notre-Dame-des-Champs. Influenced by Delacroix. Is intimate with Duret and the Clapissons. Views of Paris: *Le Quai Malaquais, Le Pont Neuf* (Marshall Field Coll., New York). Numerous visits to Monet who has just settled at Argenteuil.

1873 Durand-Ruel the dealer buys his pictures. He rents a large studio at 35, rue St-Georges and declares he has " achieved success."

1874 Takes part in the First Impressionist Exhibition at Nadar's, boulevard des Capucines (7 pict.). Stays at Argenteuil with Monet. Friendly with Caillebotte. His father dies at Louveciennes on Dec. 22.

1875 Disastrous sale at the Hôtel Drouot (March 24th), with Monet, Sisley, Berthe Morisot. Meets Chocquet, the connoisseur, who becomes his friend.

1876 Second Impressionist Exhibition (15 canvases). Rents a studio in Montmartre, in the rue Cortot. Floods figures and landscapes with brilliant light. During this memorable year paints the masterpieces of his impressionist period: *La Balançoire, Le Moulin de la Galette* (Louvre. Plate, p. 26), *La Femme nue* (Moscow Museum). Is intimate with the Charpentiers, the Daudet family and Jeanne Samary. Stays at Champrosay.

1877 Third Impressionist Exhibition (21 canvases). Publishes (in the fourth number of *L'Impressionniste*), on Apr. 28, a long article on " Contemporary Decorative Art."

1878 Stays at Pourville, near Dieppe. Paints his great composition: *Madame Charpentier et ses Enfants* (Metropolitan Museum, New York) which obtains considerable success at the 1879 Salon.

1879 From now on, Renoir deserts the Impressionists for the Salon, but without giving offence to his friends. In June, one-man show in the salons of *La Vie Moderne*, a review founded by his friends the Charpentiers, to which he contributes sketches. Is intimate with Paul Bérard who often invites him to Wargemont. Stays at Chatou and Berneval (Normandy).

1880 Period of uncertainties. Gradually breaks away from the Impressionists and returns to classical methods of drawing. Stays at Berneval, and at Croissy at Mère Fournaise's inn. His studio is in rue de Norvins.

1881 Travels in Algeria (March-April). New studio in the rue Houdon. In July at Wargemont. In autumn, starts for Italy, "to see the Raphaels." Venice delights him, but in Florence and Rome he is only interested in the museums. Enthusiastic about the Pompeii frescos.

1882 At Palermo, Jan. 15, paints his *Portrait de Wagner* (Louvre). On his return passes through l'Estaque and stays three weeks with Cézanne. Pneumonia. March-April, travels in Algeria, where his health is restored. Send in 25 pictures to the Seventh Impressionist Exhibition.

1883 Reading Cennini's *Traité de peinture* speeds up his technical evolution. One-man show in April at Durand-Ruel's (Preface by Duret). In Sept. travels to Guernsey. Suzanne Valadon sits for *The Dance* (Durand-Ruel Coll.). Dec. 10-26, travels with Monet from Marseilles to Genoa; visits Cézanne at l'Estaque.

1884 Plans a league of "Irrégularistes." Paints in La Rochelle, remembering Corot.

1885 Birth of Pierre Renoir, his eldest son. Preparatory studies for *Grandes Baigneuses* (Carroll J. Tyson Coll., Philadelphia); close study of line which marks the beginning of his "Ingresque" period. In July stays at Wargemont: in Nov. at Essoyes in the Aube, his wife's country; Sept-Oct. at La Roche-Guyon where Cézanne joins him.

1886 Refuses to join in the last Impressionist Exhibition, but contributes to the New York exhib. organized by Durand-Ruel; to the XX group exhibition in Brussels, and to the "Exposition Internationale" at Georges Petit's (May-July). In July at La Roche-Guyon; from Aug. to Sept. at Saint-Briac.

1887 Success of the *Grandes Baigneuses* at the next Internat. Exh. at Petit's.

1888 Welcomed by Cézanne in Jan. at Le Jas de Bouffan; stays at Martigues from February to March.

1889 With Cézanne again at Aix; rents for several months the estate of Cézanne's brother-in-law, M. Conil, at Montbriand near Aix, whence Cézanne painted his views of the Vallée de l'Arc.

1890 Exhibits at the Salon for the last time. Lives at 11, boulevard de Clichy. "Mother-of-pearl" period.

1891 Travels to Tamaris, Feb., March, with Teodor de Wyzewa; in April at Le Lavandou, then at Nîmes. Short stay at Mézy (Seine-et-Oise) at Berthe Morisot's; travels in Spain.

1892 Exhib. at Durand-Ruel's. First sale to the State. Another journey to Spain, with Gallimard. In August works in Brittany, at Pornic; in Sept. at Pont-Aven. Decorative panels for Durand-Ruel's flat.

1893 Birth of Jean, his second son. Spends winter at Beaulieu, returns to Pont-Aven in Aug. There he engages a maid, Gabrielle, who becomes his favourite model.

1894 Caillebotte dies (Feb. 21), leaving his collection to the State; Renoir is his executor. Another transformation of his style, which is moving towards its superb maturity.

1895 Goes to London, then to Holland.

1896 His mother dies (Nov. 22). New exh. at Durand-Ruel's. His studio is now at "Château des Brouillards," Montmartre.

1897 Stays again at Berneval. Buys a house at Essoyes, where he goes every summer.

1899 Renoir is suffering from severe rheumatism and decides to move South. He now discovers Cagnes. On April 15th he is back in Paris, at 39, rue de la Rochefoucauld. In Aug. he goes to Acqui for a 'cure.' Exhibits 41 pictures at Durand-Ruel's; presents a canvas to his native town, Limoges. In Dec. on the Riviera at Grasse, Nice, Monte-Carlo.

1900 Stays at Grasse till April. Goes to Saint-Laurent-les-Bains to undergo treatment, passing through Avignon and Aix. In Aug. stays at Louveciennes, where he learns that he has been made Chevalier de la Légion d'Honneur. Back at Grasse in Now.

1901 Birth of Claude, "Coco," his third son, whom he paints in various poses. Interrupts his stay at Grasse with brief excursions to Le Trayas and Cannes. Redon visits him and finds him "suffering a great deal, but keeping the flag flying splendidly." Cure at Aix-les-Bains. Spends the summer at Essoyes; back at Paris in Sept.

1902 "Wonderful quarters" at Le Cannet, a suburb of Cannes. Albert André is with him.

1903 In March, leaves Le Cannet for Cagnes; lives in the Maison de la Poste, then rents "Les Collettes." From now on, Renoir spends the winter in Cagnes and the summer at Essoyes, with short stays in Paris between trips. His rheumatism is getting worse.

1904 'Cure' at Bourbonne-les-Bains in Sept. The 'retrospective' exhibition at the Salon d'Automne (35 pictures) is a triumph.

1905-09 His suffering increases. Besides rheumatism he suffers from stomach-troubles, hernia, bronchitis. Walks with two sticks, gives up a journey to Italy. Maillol makes his bust at Essoyes; connoisseurs, dealers and friends visit him.

1910 Improved health enables him to go to Munich where he stays with Thurneyssen. Paints many portraits. Publishes a preface to Cennini's *Treatise*.

1911 Buys a car for the journeys Cagnes-Paris-Essoyes.

1912 His legs and arms are paralysed by a stroke (in January). Undergos an operation in August; the Legion of Honour "Officer's" cross is brought to him in bed. He now has his brush strapped to his hand, and goes on painting.

1913 Exh. at Bernheim's (Preface by Mirbeau).

1914 The war. Pierre and Jean are at the front.

1915 Pierre is wounded. Madame Renoir, already ill, rushes to see him at Gerardmer and comes back only to die, June 28.

1916 Illness, bereavement, solitude cannot keep Renoir from painting, with ever-rising fervour. He has just discovered a new model, Dédée, by whom he is dazzled, and who inspires him to some hundred pictures, certain of which may be deemed his greatest works — the series of the *Grandes Baigneuses* (Stockholm Museum. Plate, p. 44).

1919 In July at Essoyes. In Aug. asks to be taken to the Louvre. Goes through the galleries in his wheel-chair, venerable and venerated, "like the pope of painting." Returns to Cagnes, where he dies Dec. 3.

BIBLIOGRAPHY

Writings, Correspondence.

Cennino Cennini : *Le Livre d'Art* with Renoir's prefatory letter, Paris, 1911. The letters written to Durand-Ruel (212) and to Octave Maus (9) were published by L. Venturi in the *Archives de l'Impressionnisme,* Paris, New York, 1939. Letters to Mme Charpentier and to Duret were pub. by Florisoone in *l'Amour de l'Art,* Feb., 1938. Letters to Chocquet were pub. by J. Joets in *l'Amour de l'Art,* April, 1935. Letters to A. André are to be found in the *Bull. des Exp.,* Nov., Dec., 1932. Selections from letters to Bazille reproduced by G. Poulain in *Bazille et ses amis,* Paris, 1932 and some letters to Monet in G. Geffroy : *Monet, sa vie, son œuvre,* Vol. II, Paris, 1924.

Catalogues.

The bulk of Renoir's enormous output has not yet been catalogued (this task was begun by L. Venturi). The most valuable sources are A. André and M. Elder : *l'Atelier de Renoir,* Paris, 1931 (716 reprod.). The Cat. of the Exhib. at Bernheim's (40 insets, notices by Forthuny ; important Pref. by Mirbeau). Cat. of the Gangnat Sale, Paris, June, 1925 (161 reprod., introd. by R. de Flers and E. Faure). Cat. of the Exhib. at the Orangerie, June, 1933, by C. Sterling (126 pict., 23 pastels, watercolours and drawings) with Pref. by P. Jamot, Cat. of the Exhib. at the Metropolitan Museum, New York, May-Sept., 1937 (139 pict. and five sculpt., all reproduced) with a Pref. by H. B. Wehle. For the engraved work, see L. Delteil : *Le Peintre-Graveur Illustré,* Vol. XVII. For Sculpture, P. Haesaerts : *Renoir Sculpteur,* Brussels 1947.

Biography, Witness Accounts.

T. Natanson : Renoir, *Revue Blanche,* June 15, 1896. W. Pach : Interview with Renoir, *Scribner's Magazine,* 1912. O. Mirbeau : Renoir, Paris, 1913. A. Vollard : Renoir, Paris, 1919 and 1920, G. Rivière : *Renoir et ses amis,* Paris, 1921. A. André : *Renoir,* Paris, 1919 and 1928. A. Alexandre : Renoir sans phrases, *Les Arts,* Paris, 1920. Th. Duret : Renoir, Paris, 1924. G. Besson : Auguste Renoir, Paris, 1929. M. Bérard : *Renoir à Wargemont, Souvenirs,* Paris, 1938.

Monographs and Appraisals.

J. Meier-Graefe : *Renoir,* Munich, 1911, Leipzig, 1929 (407 reprod.) ; fundamental work. *L'Amour de l'Art,* special number, Feb. 1921. P. Jamot, *G. B. A.,* Nov.-Dec., 1923. G. Duthuit : Renoir, Paris, 1923. F. Fosca : Renoir, Paris, 1923. *L'Art Vivant,* special number, July, 1933. L. Venturi : l'*Arte,* 1933, pp. 458-489. A. Barnes and V. de Mazia : *The Art of Renoir,* Paris, 1944. M. Drucker, Renoir, Paris, 1944, new. ed. 1949 (Pref. by G. Bazin). J. Rewald : Renoir Drawings. New York, 1946. M. Raynald, *Renoir,* Geneva, 1949.

Exhibitions.

Exhib. : Durand-Ruel, Gal., Paris, April, 1883 (cat. and Preface by Th. Duret) ; May, 1892 (11 n°, cat. and Pref. by A. Alexandre) ; May-June, 1896 (42 n°) ; June, 1902 (40 n°) ; June, 1912 (58 portraits) ; Jan., 1917 (18 n°) ; Feb.-March, 1918 (28 n°) ; Apr., 1919 (35 n°). Exhib. at the *Vie Moderne,* June, 1879. Salon d'Automne, 1904, Renoir Room (35 n°). Thannhauser Gal., Berlin, Jan.-Feb., 1913 (41 pict.). Bernheim-Jeune Gal., Paris, March, 1913 (42 n°), Pref. by O. Mirbeau.
Retrosp. : Durand-Ruel Gal., Paris, Nov.-Dec., 1920 (76 n°) ; April, 1921 (31 watercolours, 33 pastels, 78 drawings). Durand-Ruel Gal., New York, Feb., 1920 (41 n°) ; Jan., 1924 (23 n°) ; March-April, 1939 (portraits). Salon d'Automne, 1920. 1921, Feb.-March, Nasjionalgalleriet, Oslo (44 n°). 1923, Feb., Druet Gal. Paris (85 n°). 1927, Feb.-March, P. Rosenberg Gal. *50 Renoir, choisis parmi les nus, les fleurs, les enfants.* 1928, Oct.-Nov., A. Flechtheim Gal., Berlin (60 n°). 1932, Nov., Braun Gal., Paris. 1933, Musée de l'Orangerie, Paris, *Exp. Renoir* (149 n°), cat. by Ch. Sterling, Pref. by P. Jamot. 1934, Jan.-Feb., P. Rosenberg Gal., Paris (53 n°, from the last years). 1934 (Oct. 15-Nov. 10), Gal. des Beaux-Arts, Paris : *L'œuvre gravé et sculpté de Renoir* (Introd. by A. Vollard and R. Cogniat). 1937, May-Sept., Metropolitan Museum, New York : *Renoir, special Exh. of his paintings* (139 pict. and 5 sculpt. American coll., introd. to the cat. by H. B. Wehle). 1938, June-July, Bernheim-Jeune Gal., Paris, *Renoir portraitiste* (47 n°). 1941, Duveen Brothers Gal., New York : *Renoir Centennial Exh.* 1943, Feb.-March, Basel, Kunsthalle : 102 pict. and sanguines, drawings, watercol., bronze stat. 1948, June, Lefèvre Gal., London.

ROUSSEL, Ker Xavier (1867-1944)

1867 Born at Lorry-les-Metz, son of a doctor. Studies at the Lycée Condorcet, where he strikes up a lasting friendship with Vuillard, his schoolfellow, who leads him towards painting ; he marries Vuillard's sister, Mary, in 1893.

1888 After studying at Diogène Maillard's studio, he enters the Académie Julian and becomes a member of the 'Nabis' group, initiated, under Sérusier's guidance, into Gauguin's 'synthesism.'

1891 Contributes, with his friends, to exhibitions at Le Barc de Boutteville's. Paints Still Lifes in dark colours and 'intimate' scenes, but also peasant studies and landscapes inspired by country life.

1901 Shows for the first time at the Salon des Indépendants.

1906 Pays a visit to Cézanne, accompanied by Maurice Denis, who brings him back to neo-traditionalism. From that date he delights in scenes from mythology, in oil, tempera, pastel, gouache ; and in big decorative compositions. (Curtain of the Théâtre des Champs-Elysées, 1913.)

1944 Dies at l'Etang-la-Ville, where he had lived since 1905.

BIBLIOGRAPHY

T. Leclerc, *Art et Décoration*, 1921. F. Fosca, *Am. de l'Art*, 1922. L. Cousturier, Paris, 1929. L. Werth, Paris, 1930.

Exhibitions.

Gal. Maratier, Paris ; 1942, Jan. 15th-Feb. 5th, Gal. Carré, Paris (Mythological scenes) ; 1947, Gal. Charpentier, Paris (Retrospective. Notes by L. P. Fargue, F. Jourdain, C. Roger-Marx, J. Salomon).

SÉRUSIER, Paul (1863-1927)

1863 Born at Paris. His father was manager of the Houbigant perfumery. He did very well at school (Ecole Fénelon and Lycée Fontanes). Bachelor of Letters and of Science.

1888 Exhibits his *Breton Weaver's Workroom* at the Salon. Student-in-charge at the Académie Julian. After beginning with academic realism and sombre tones he now makes the acquaintance of Gauguin, at Pont-Aven and, on his advice, paints a '*Bois d'Amour*,' which he calls his ' talisman ' and proudly shows on his return to his fellow-students at Julian's : Bonnard, Vuillard, Roussel, Denis and Ranson.

1889 At his instance they form a group, the ' Nabis.' Their meeting-place is a little restaurant in the Passage Brady ; their discussions turn chiefly on philosophy and religion.

1889-90 Stays at Le Poilu in Brittany with Gauguin, Filiger, Meyer de Haan.

1891 Gauguin leaves for Tahiti. Sérusier meets Verkade under whose influence he takes up theosophy.

1892 At Pont-Aven with Verkade, Bollin, Rassetti (the ceramist) and Ranson ; then at Heulgoat.

1893 Collaborates in the Théâtre de l'Oeuvre now founded by Lugné-Poë. Spends winter in Paris (studio, rue de Hauteville) and the summer at Châteauneuf-du-Faou in Brittany.

1895 Travels in Italy with Maurice Denis : Giotto, Sienese art, Fra Angelico.

1897 After the collapse of a love-affair travels in Central Europe. Meets again Jean Verkade, now a monk at the Beuron Monastery.

1899 Second stay at Beuron ; meets Père Didier, founder of the School of Religious Art, based on the theory of the ' holy measures.'

1903 His mother dies. Another stay with Maurice Denis at Beuron. Buys a house at Châteauneuf-du-Faou.

1904 Travels in Italy with Maurice Denis : Rome, Monte Cassino ; interview with Père Didier ; Naples and Pompeii.

1907 Goes to Munich ; meets Verkade again.

1908 With Denis teaches at the Académie Ranson (R. de la Fresnaye and Goerg amongst his pupils). Hieratic and mathematical painting.

1912 Marries one of his pupils. Honeymoon at Florence.

1914-27 Lives a retired life in Brittany ; more and more interested in Celtic mediaeval tapestry. Decorates his house and Châteauneuf Church. Stays at Kermouster with Henry Joly ; at Perros-Guirec with Maurice Denis.

1927 Dies of a stroke at Morlaix and is buried in Breton soil, his " true home, since he was spiritually born there."

BIBLIOGRAPHY

By Himself : A. B. C. de la Peinture, inspired by the aesthetics of Père Didier, whose pamphlet *Les Saintes Mesures* he had translated in 1905. Paris, 1921 (republ. 1942).

Monographs and Appraisals.

M. Denis, *L'Occident*, Dec., 1908. J. Dupont, *Art Sacré*, Jan., 1937. E. de Thubert, *Art et Décoration*, 1932. M. Denis, *Sérusier, sa vie, son œuvre*, Paris, 1943.

Exhibitions.

Galerie Druet, Paris : 1907, 1914, 1919 Nov. 10-26 (Preface by M. & A. Leblond). Brussels, 1914. 1947 Retrospective, Musée Galliera, Paris (86 paintings).

SEURAT, Georges (1859-1891)

1859 Born Dec. 2, in Paris, rue de Bondy. Son of a bailiff in La Villette. A small-bourgeois, bigoted family. Schooling until 16. An obedient, earnest, rather reserved lad.

1875 At the Municipal School of Design near the church of St-Vincent-de-Paul, presided over by a sculptor, Justin Lequien, who had won a *Prix de Rome*. Became close friend of a fellow-student, Aman-Jean.

1877 Haunts museums and libraries. Copies Holbein, Ingres, Poussin, Raphael. Much enthusiasm for the writings of the Goncourt brothers.

1878 With Aman-Jean enters Ecole des Beaux-Arts, where their master is Henri Lehmann, who imparts to them the principles, now rather insipid, of Ingres. Studies Chevreul's treatise on the *Harmony and Contrast of Colours* and Charles Blanc's *Grammar of Painting and Drawing*.

1879 Nov. Leaves the studio he has been sharing with Aman-Jean in rue de l'Arbalète and does his term of military service at Brest in a line regiment. First contact with the sea. Does many sketches.

1880 Nov. Returns to Paris. Lives at No. 19, rue de Chabrol.

1881-87 Devotes himself to drawing in well-defined masses of blacks and whites, with contrasts and shadings ; also to studying Delacroix' colour technique. He practises the ' optical mixture ' and the use of complementary colours. Often visits the Chapelle des Saints-Anges (Saint Sulpice), decorated by Delacroix. In 1882 paints his first pictures with small separate touches and also large weeping strokes that give the effect of broken gleams.

1883 His *Portrait of Aman-Jean* (Stephen C. Clark Coll., New York), a Conté crayon life-size drawing, is accepted at the Salon and praised by Roger-Marx, as being " an excellent study in chiaroscuro." Seurat now paints his first big picture based on the ' contrast of colours', *Une Baignade à Asnières* (Tate Gallery, London) ; he uses the technique of the division of tones, but in a free manner, resembling that of Impressionism. For this picture he made a number of sketches from nature, jotted down on the little panels of his painter's box, which he called " croquetons " (Plate, p. 53) — this method he adopted for all his later compositions.

1884 Rejected at the official Salon, *La Baignade* was shown at the first Salon des Indépendants (May 15-July 1), along with contributions by Redon, Angrand, Dubois-Pillet, Cross and Signac. These artists now got to know each other and decided to found a *Société des Artistes Indépendants* and have another exhibition in December. The group meetings took place every Monday at Signac's studio and in the evening at the Café d'Orient or the Café Marengo. Seurat was especially friendly with Angrand and Signac.

1885 Prompted by Signac who had much fondness for all things maritime, he goes in the summer to the little seaport of Grandcamp, near Le Havre, and makes his first seascapes. Through Signac, too, he comes to know Pissarro, who now joins the ranks of the 'Divisionists.' Paints his *Sunday Afternoon on the Island of La Grante Jatte* (Art Institute, Chicago) — a sort of ' manifesto ' of the new technique, for which he made elaborate preparations in no less than 38 painted studies and 23 drawings. Many months went to its making, his mornings being spent on the Island itself, while in the afternoons he worked in his studio.

1886 Thanks to Pissarro's insistence, Seurat and Signac appear at the 8th and Last Impressionist Exhibition (May 15-June 15). Monet, Renoir, Sisley, hostile, stand out. Degas insists on the omission of the word ' impressionist ' on the poster. Seurat sends in 6 landscapes, 3 drawings and his *Grande Jatte*, which rouses a storm of protests. With the exception of Verhaeren and Félix Fénéon (who publishes an excellent critical appraisal of the picture in *La Vogue*, reprinted in his famous *Les Impressionnistes en 1886*), most artists and connoisseurs are disgusted with this picture. Seurat becomes very friendly with Fénéon, who persuades him to come to the gatherings of the Symbolists in the office of the *Revue Indépendante*. He becomes the official exponent of ' Neo-Impressionism.' The *Grande Jatte* is shown this same year at the exhibition organized by Durand-Ruel in New York and at the Second Salon des Indépendants. Seurat spends the summer at Honfleur (seascapes) and exhibits at Nantes with Pissarro.

1887 Feb. Goes to Brussels for the opening of the ' XX ' exhibition, to which Octave Maus has invited him. Has sent 6 Honfleur landscapes and the *Grande Jatte* which is the subject of heated discussion, Verhaeren strongly commending it in *La Vie Moderne*. Fénéon publishes another article in *L'Art Moderne*, explaining in detail Seurat's theories and technique ; Seurat, recognized leader of the group, jealously safeguards his prerogatives.

1888 Fourth Salon des Indépendants. 8 drawings and 2 new compositions, his masterpieces : *Parade de Cirque* (S. C. Clark Collection, New York) and *Les Poseuses* (Barnes Foundation, Merion). Pointillist technique, contrasts of tones and colours, attempt to bring even the frame into harmony with the lay-out. Spends summer at Port-en-Bessin, a small seaport near Bayeux (Plate, p. 55). Reads scientific works on optics : N. O. Rood, David Sutter, C. Henry.

1889 Leaves Paris in the spring and goes to Le Crotoy a seaside resort in Picardy, where he paints nine seascapes which lead Angrand to remark : " He is the first to render the emotion the sea inspires on calm days." Seurat stays in Paris every winter, working at a large-scale composition and goes every summer to the seacoast to paint from nature and to " wash his eyes clean of the days spent in the studio." Exhibits with the ' XX ' at Brussels and the Indépendants in Paris, drawings and paintings made at Port-en-Bessin and Le Crotoy. Pissarro breaks with Pointillism.

1890 Stays at Gravelines, exhibits at the Indépendants, *Le Chahut* (Rijksmuseum Kröller-Müller, Otterlo), based on the contrast of lines (it was bought by Gustave Kahn), and *Jeune Femme se poudrant* (Courtauld Coll., National Gallery, London), in consequence of which such terms as ' static ' and ' lifeless ' come to be applied more and more to his work. Seurat made a complete mystery of his private life and it was only after his death that his friends discovered that the *Jeune Femme* of the picture was his mistress, Madeleine Knobloch. He had begun by painting his own face reflected in a mirror hanging on the wall — the only self-portrait he ever made —but, in consequence of a remark about this from one of his friends, who was quite unaware of the liaison, he replaced it with a flower-pot. His studio this year is at No. 39, Passage de l'Elysée-des-Beaux-Arts.

1891 Feb. Present at the famous ' Symbolist Banquet ' presided over by Mallarmé, and attended by Gide, France, Renard, Barrès, Gauguin, Mirbeau, Redon, de Régnier.
March. Helps with the installation of the Exposition des Indépendants, whose opening day is March 10. At it he shows 4 views of the *Chenal de Gravelines* and his last, unfinished work, *Le Cirque* (Louvre). A sore throat followed by an access of fever obliges him to take to his bed. He died in his mother's house, on the boulevard de Magenta, on March 29. On April 1, Pissarro wrote to his son : " I went to Seurat's funeral yesterday. I saw Signac there ; he was terribly cut up by the loss of his friend. I think you're right, Pointillism has had its day ; but I suspect that it will have effects of much importance on the future of art. Seurat obviously has made a definite contribution."

BIBLIOGRAPHY

Writings and Correspondence.

Hitherto unpublished notes on Delacroix, by Seurat, *Bull. de la Vie Artistique*, April, 1922. Extracts from Seurat's letters have been published by R. Rey : *La Renaissance du Sentiment Classique*, Paris, 1931 (letter to

Beaubourg, dated Aug. 20, 1890, gives a full exposé of his theories). O. Maus: *Trente Années de Lutte pour l'Art*, Brussels, 1926. J. Rewald, *Seurat*, New York, 1943, 1946: Paris, 1947.

Catalogue.

Until his death in 1944, F. Fénéon was working on a catalogue of Seurat's works, a studio-inventory of which he had made with Luce and Signac. "The list included some 170 small paint-box panels, 420 drawings, 6 sketch-books and some sixty canvases (figures, sea-scapes, landscapes), five of which were several square yards in size and might be reckoned as masterpieces." (*Entretiens Politiques et Littéraires*, Vol. II, No. 13. Quoted by J. Rewald, *Seurat*, 1947, p. 158).

Monographs.

J. Christophe, Paris, 1890; A. Salmon, Brussels, 1921; L. Cousturier, Paris, 1921; A. Lhote, Rome, 1922 and Paris, 1947; W. Pach, New York, 1923; Coquiot, Paris, 1924; G. Kahn, Paris, 1926 (2 Vols. with reproductions); W. George, Paris, 1928; C. Roger-Marx, Paris, 1931; D. C. Rich, Chicago, 1935 ("La Grande Jatte"); Rewald, New York, 1943 and Paris, 1947 (Indispensable; based on Fénéon's records); J. de Laprade, Monaco, 1945; D. Cooper, London, 1946 ("La Baignade"); H. Bertram, Copenhagen, 1946; G. Seligman, New York, 1947 (Illustrations).

Articles in Magazines.

F. Fénéon, *L'Art Moderne*, Sept. 19, 1886 and 15 March, 1888; E. Verhaeren, *La Vie Moderne*, Feb. 26, 1887; P. Signac, *Le Cri du Peuple*, Feb. 9, March 24, 1888; E. Verhaeren, *Société Nouvelle*, Apr., 1891; G. Kahn, *L'Art Moderne*, Apr. 5, 1891; J. Christophe, *La Plume*, Sept. 1, 1891; T. Natanson, *Revue Blanche*, 1900; Bissière, *Esprit Nouveau*, Oct. 15, 1920; A. Ozenfant, *Cahiers d'Art*, Sept., 1928; J. Helion, *Burlington Magazine*, 1936; P. Mabille, *Minotaure*, 1938; G. Duthuit, *Labyrinthe*, Dec., 1948; L. Venturi, *Gazette des Beaux-Arts*, Sept., 1947; René Huyghe, Bull. des M. de France, Aug. 1947.

Exhibitions.

Retrospective at Salon des Indépendants in 1892 and 1905 (44 pictures); *La Revue Blanche*, 1900 (organized by Fénéon); Gal. Bernheim-Jeune, Paris, 1908-09 and 1920; J. Brummer Gal., New York, 1924; Renaissance Society of the University of Chicago, Feb., 1935 (24 pictures and drawings); Gal. P. Rosenberg, Paris (129), 1936, Feb. 3-29.

SIGNAC, Paul (1863-1935)

1863 Born in Paris, Nov. 11. His father kept a saddlery shop in the rue Vivienne. The family lived in Montmartre (Ave. Frochot).

1880 His parents wish him to become an architect, but a visit to the Monet Exhibition in the premises of *La Vie Moderne* "settles his career." He writes to Monet, who gives him advice, and Guillaumin, who has seen him painting on the Seine bank, also encourages him to persevere.

1883 Attends Bin's 'Académie Libre.' Great admiration for Huysmans and Jules Vallès.

1884 Shows his *Pont d'Austerlitz* at the first Salon des Indépendants. Meets Cross and Seurat with whom he strikes up a friendship — a decisive factor in his career. Gives up the impressionist palette and decides to paint solely with the colours of the spectrum, employing Seurat's scientific 'Pointillism.' Has an exuberant, forthright temperament, revels in controversy and bold innovations. Every Monday his friends forgather in his studio and hold debate far into the night. He becomes the theoretician of the group. Lives near Seurat in Montmartre.

1885 Shares studio in rue de Steinkerque with Henri Rivière. Sub-editor of periodical *Le Chat Noir.*

1886 First experience of the South, at Collioure.

1888 Invited to show in Salon of the 'XX' Group at Brussels. Became a member of it in 1891.

1889 Visits Van Gogh at Arles. Friendly with C. Henry, the physicist.

1892 As much a sailor as a painter; always cruising off the coast, from Brittany to the Mediterranean. Sailed in no less than 32 yachts at one time or another. In summer 1892, sailing South, discovers Saint-Tropez, and instals a small house there, *La Hune*, to which he returns yearly. His technique changes, he gives up the 'point' for a square mosaic-like spot and aims at violent colour harmonies. His watercolours (of which he paints many after 1900) remain wonderfully simple and spontaneous.

1899 Publication of his technical treatise *D'Eugène Delacroix au Néo-Impressionnisme.* Travels abroad: Holland 1896, 1898, 1906; Italy 1904, 1905, 1907, 1908; Constantinople, 1907.

1935 Dies in Paris. Had been President of the Salon des Indépendants since 1898.

BIBLIOGRAPHY

Writings.

Series of articles in *Le Cri du Peuple*, March, 1888; *Art et Critique*, Feb. 1890; Study of *Jongkind*, Paris, 1927; *D'Eugène Delacroix au Néo-Impressionnisme*, Paris, 1899; Preface to the Exhibition '*Seurat et ses Amis*,' Paris, 1933-34; 'Les Besoins individuels et la Peinture,' *Encyclopédie Française*, Vol. XVI, Ch. 2, Paris, 1935; *Fragments du Journal de Signac*, Arts de France, Jan. 1947; Extracts from unpublished Letters, published by J. Rewald, *Seurat*, Paris, 1948.

Monographs and Appraisals.

F. Fénéon, Paris, 1890; L. Cousturier, Paris, 1922; G. Besson, Paris, 1934; C. Roger-Marx, Paris, 1924; J. Guenne, *L'Art Vivant*, March, 1925; J. de Laprade, *L'Art Vivant*, 1935; L. Deshairs, *Art et Décoration*, 1923; G. Besson, *Arts de France*, Jan., 1946.

SISLEY, Alfred (1839-1899)

1839 Born in Paris, October 30, of English parentage. His father was a business man trading with South America.

1857 Sent to London to learn English and to qualify for a commercial career.

1862 On his return to Paris works at Gleyre's studio, where he meets Monet, Renoir, Bazille.

1863 Signs a petition against a change being made in the statutes of the Ecole des Beaux-Arts lowering the age-limit for competing for the Prix de Rome from 30 to 25.

1865 Paints in Renoir's company in Fontainebleau forest, at Marlotte.

1866 Exhibits two landscapes at the Salon. *L'Allée de Châtaigniers à la Celle-Saint-Cloud* shows Courbet's and Daubigny's influences. In his group, *At the Inn of Mère Anthony* (Stockholm Museum), Renoir places Sisley in the foreground, reading *L'Evénement*.

1867 In July at Honfleur, where Bazille makes his portrait. Accepted at the Salon as "Corot's pupil."

1869 Often visits the Café Guerbois. *View of Montmartre* (Grenoble Museum. Plate, p. 17).

1871 During the war and the Commune, in London, where he is in contact with Durand-Ruel. His family is ruined. None the less he decides to devote himself wholly to painting — hitherto he has painted only as an amateur — and is prepared to face suffering, both mental and material, for his art's sake.

1872-80 His best work is done in this period. He paints in the neighbourhood of Paris, at Marly, Louveciennes, Bougival, Sèvres, Saint-Cloud, Meudon, following in the wake of Monet whom he often visits at Argenteuil; but he never wavers in his allegiance to the Corot tradition. Devoting himself exclusively to landscape, he is the painter *par excellence* of the Ile-de-France. The most modest, least self-assured of the Impressionists, he is, in his happy moments, the purest and the most poetic. He is especially successful with snowscapes. He took part in the first three group exhibitions and in the auction sale of 1875 (price fetched by his canvases, from 50 to 70 francs each). Married, father of two children and wretchedly poor, seeks aid of Duret in 1878. Had only brief contracts with dealers Durand-Ruel and Petit.

1881 Stays in the Isle of Wight.

1882 Veneux-Nadon. Settles at Moret in September.

1883 One-man show at Durand-Ruel's (June). Settles in the autumn at Les Sablons, near Moret, as usual on the outskirts of Fontainebleau forest, which he rarely leaves, and only for short trips (Normandy in 1894 and Wales in 1897). Endures poverty and loneliness, without the consolation of the renown which at last is coming to his friends. In his last canvases, all inspired by the town of Moret and the banks of the Loing, his painting becomes systematized, strained, lacking the spontaneous charm of his early work.

1899 Dies Jan. 29 of cancer of the throat, without having succeeded in obtaining the French nationality for which he had applied four years earlier. Funeral attended by Monet, Renoir, Cazin, Tavernier.

BIBLIOGRAPHY

Correspondence.

Sisley's ideals are expounded in a letter he wrote to Tavernier, published in *L'Art Français*, May, 1893. Letters (16) to Durand-Ruel and to O. Maus (5) in L. Venturi, *Les Archives de l'Impressionnisme*, Paris, 1939. Hitherto unpublished letters in *Formes*, Nov., 1931. Letters to Duret in *La Revue Blanche*, March 15, 1899.

Catalogues.

No catalogue of the paintings extant. His few etchings have been listed by L. Delteil, Vol. XVII, Paris, 1923.

Monographs and Appraisals.

No comprehensive monograph has so far been published (Ole Vinding has one in preparation). H. Heilmaier, *Die Kunst für Alle*, 1930-31. F. Watson, *Sisley's Struggle for Recognition*, The Arts, Feb.-March, 1921. G. Geffroy, Paris, 1923. E. D. de Montcorin, *Moret à travers l'Histoire*. Account of Sisley, Moret, 1932. L. Venturi, *Parnassus*, Oct., 1939. C. Sisley, *The Ancestry of Sisley*, Burlington Mag., Sept., 1949, pp. 348-352. G. Jedlicka, Bern, 1949.

Exhibitions.

Gal. Durand-Ruel, Paris, June, 1883; Gal. Boussoud & Valadon, Paris, 1893; Gal. G. Petit, Paris, Feb. 1897 (with notes by Roger-Milès); Gal. Bernheim, Paris, (14 pict.) Feb., 1899; Gal. Bernheim-Jeune, Paris, 1907, Dec. 2-4, 'L'Atelier de Sisley' (note by A. Tavernier); Gal. Durand-Ruel, Paris, Jan. 23-Feb. 18, 1922; Gal. Braun, Paris, Jan. 31-Feb. 18, 1933; Gal. Durand-Ruel, Paris, Jan. 23-Feb. 13, 1937; Gal. Durand-Ruel, New York (Centenary Exhibition), 1939.

TOULOUSE-LAUTREC, Henri de (1864-1901)

1864 Born November 24, at Albi. Son of Alphonse de Toulouse-Lautrec Monfa and Adèle Tapié de Celeyran. A direct descendant of the famous Counts of Toulouse, ennobled under Charlemagne. Precocious talent for drawing.

1872 Comes to Paris with his family. Brilliant studies at Lycée Fontanes (Lycée Condorcet of to-day), completed by private tuition under the guidance of his mother, a highly cultured person, who played a great part in his life. A delicate lad. Treatment at Amélie-les-Bains. A schoolfellow at the Lycée, Maurice Joyant, is his bosom friend; later, his biographer.

1878-79 In two successive accidents, at Albi in 1878, and some months later during a 'cure' at Barèges, he breaks both thighs. This infirmity prevents his leading the normal life of a country gentleman, and throws him back on painting. Seeing in art a possible compensation for his physical deformity, his parents encourage him.

1880-81 His first teachers are René Princeteau, a painter of military and sporting scenes, then Lewis Brown and Bastien-Lepage. His first pictures, *Artilleur sellant un Cheval* (Albi Museum), *Le Mail-Coach à Nice* (Petit-Palais, Paris), show his brilliant craftsmanship, his extraordinary virtuosity in drawing, and his taste for 'modern' subjects.

1881-83 Despite his success, Lautrec decides to recommence his art education from the beginning and after passing his baccalauréat at Toulouse in 1881, he enters, in 1882, Bonnat's studio (Bonnat finds his drawing "atrocious"!); then, Cormon's studio.

1884-85 Is influenced by Willette, Forain; makes a parody of the *Bois-Sacré* (Puvis-de-Chavannes), discovers and admires the art of Manet, of Berthe Morisot and above all that of Degas, who liberates him from his academic prepossessions and leads him towards naturalistic themes.

1886-88 During one of his rare attendances at Cormon's studio he meets Van Gogh who has just come to Paris. He rents a studio at the corner of rue Tourlaque and rue Caulaincourt, where he remains till 1897. Lives in the heart of Montmartre, whose nightly activities supply him with subjects till 1893. Frequents *Le Mirliton*, Bruant's famous "Cabaret artistique," and *Le Moulin de la Galette*, where he becomes friendly with the floor dancers, Grille d'Egout, La Goulue, Jane Avril.

1889 His first exhibition at the Indépendants.

1891 Draws his first poster for the Moulin-Rouge, and at once proves himself a master of this form of art. The elliptical technique of the poster, with its clean-cut, flat planes, reacts on his painting.

1893 On Joyant's initiative, exhibits with Charles Maurin at the Goupil Gallery. Invites Degas, who looks at the pictures in silence and, on leaving him, says: "Well, Lautrec, I can see you're one of our trade!"

1894 Arsène Alexandre launches *Le Rire* and invites the collaboration of Lautrec, who is already drawing for *L'Echo de Paris*, *L'Escarmouche*, and *Le Figaro Illustré*. Visits Brussels. The Boulevards and Champs-Elysées become his new sector of observation.

1895 Decorates the *La Goulue's Booth* (Louvre). Makes a trip to London where he meets Oscar Wilde, Beardsley, Arthur Symons, Conder. Discovers Whistler; detests the Pre-Raphaelites; admires Primitives in the the National Gallery: Giotto, Uccello, Piero della Francesca.

1897 Moves from rue Tourlaque to a new studio in Avenue Frochot. Gives up poster painting and concentrates on colour lithography, which both calls for subtler treatment and gives him more scope. Frequent stays at Villeneuve-sur-Yonne, with his friends the Natansons, founders of *La Revue Blanche*. Other subjects now appear in his works: brothels, the circus and sporting events, nudes, medical scenes, pictures of animals, interiors, numerous portraits.

1898 Goes to London during his exhibition at the Goupil gallery. His health is seriously impaired by his insatiable appetite for night-life and heavy drinking.

1899 Confined from February to May in the Saint-James clinic at Neuilly where attempts are made to break him of his disastrous habits. It is here that he paints his admirable series, *Le Cirque*. Released as a result of a press campaign launched by his friends, he breaks his stays in Paris with trips to Arcachon, Bordeaux, Le Havre and Malromé.

1901 Starts drinking again and his health deteriorates rapidly. A paralytic stroke immobilizes him at Taussat, where he is under treatment. Foreseeing the end, he asks to be taken to his mother, and he dies at the Château de Malromé on Sept. 9th, aged 37, like Van Gogh, after a very different but no less feverishly agitated life. His mother collected all the works in his studio and presented them to the town of Albi; they are housed in the Toulouse-Lautrec Museum, which was inaugurated on July 30, 1922, in the episcopal palace of La Berbie.

BIBLIOGRAPHY

The basic work (biography and catalogue) is that of Maurice Joyant: *H. de Toulouse-Lautrec*, 2 vols., Paris, 1921. See also: L. Delteil, *Le Peintre-Graveur Illustré* (Vols. X and XI), Paris, 1920; and E. Julien: *Catalogue of Albi Museum*, Albi, 1939.

The chief monographs are: H. Esswein: *Moderne Illustratoren, H. de Toulouse-Lautrec*, Munich, 1904; G. Coquiot, Paris, 1913; T. Duret, Paris, 1920; P. de Lapparent, Paris, 1927; F. Fosca, Paris, 1928; G. Jedlicka, Berlin, 1929; P. MacOrlan, *Toulouse-Lautrec, peintre de la Lumière Froide*, Paris, 1934; Schaub-Koch: *Psychanalyse d'un Peintre Moderne*, Paris, 1935; G. de la Tourette, Paris, 1939; E. Julien, *Les Dessins de Lautrec*, Monaco, 1942; W. Rotzler, *Affiches de Lautrec*, Paris, 1946; H. Delaroche-Vernet Henraux, Paris, 1948: G. Schmidt, Basle, 1948. Among articles from reviews: Th. Natanson, *La Revue Blanche*, Feb. 16th, 1893 and *Labyrinthe*, June 1, 1946; A. Salmon, *l'Art Vivant*, Sept 15th, 1931; *l'Amour de l'Art*, Special N°, April, 1931; H. Focillon, G. B. A., June, 1931; A. D'Eugny, *l'Amour de l'Art*, 1946, p. 188-195; L. Venturi, *Les Arts Plastiques*, Brussels, 1947, pp. 3-14.

Illustrated Books: G. Geffroy, *Album d'Yvette Guilbert*, Paris, *l'Estampe originale*, 1894 (16 lith.); G. Clemenceau, *Au pied du Sinaï*, Paris, Floury, 1898 (10 lith., 6 culs-de-lampe); J. Renard, *Histoires Naturelles*, Paris, Floury, 1899 (22 lith.); E. de Goncourt, *La Fille Elisa*, Paris, Librairie de France, 1931 (16 watercolours and facsimile drawings).

Exhibitions: In his studio, Avenue Frochot, in 1898 and 1900; at Boussod and Valadon's, Paris, 1893; Goupil Gallery, London, 1898; Retrospective in 1902 at the Indépendants (60 Items) and at *La Libre Esthétique*, Brussels (45 Items); at the Salon d'Automne, 1904 (24 Items); 1902 (May 14-31) at the Durand-Ruel Gal., Paris (200 Items, Pref. by A. Alexandre); 1904, Dec., 1905, Jan., Musée National du Luxembourg, Paris, Lithographs (68 Items); 1908 (Oct. 12-24), Bernheim-Jeune Gal., Paris (23 Items); 1909, Nov., Petit Gal., Paris (36 Items); 1910, Musée des Arts Décoratifs, Paris (97 Items); 1914 (Jan.-Feb.), P. Rosenberg Gal., Paris (46 Items); 1914 (June 15th-July 11th), Manzi et Joyant Gal. (201 Items. Pref. by A. Alexandre); 1924 (Nov. 10-Dec. 10), Matthiesen Gal., Berlin (46 Items); 1925, Wildenstein Gal., Paris (14 pictures); 1930 (Dec. 23-Jan. 18, 1931), Art. Institute, Chicago (Cat. D. C. Rich); 1931 (Apr. 9-May 17). Musée de l'Orangerie, Paris (Pref. Tristan Bernard, 427 Items); 1937 (Nov. 15-Dec. 11), Knoedler Gal., New York; 1938

(March) Knoedler Gal., Paris; 1946 (Oct. 23-Nov. 23), Wildenstein Gal., New York (127 Items); 1947 (July-Aug.), Municipal Museum, Amsterdam; (Nov.), Palais des Beaux-Arts, Brussels (Pref. G. Dortu, 247 Items).

VALLOTTON, Félix (1865-1925)

1865 Born, Dec. 28th in Lausanne (Switzerland), of a French Protestant family of the Jura, who came to live in Vallorbe when the Edict of Nantes was revoked. In Lausanne attends evening drawing-classes, and is passionately fond of reading and music.

1882 Paris. He is 17. After a brief stay at the Académie Julian, passes rapidly through the Ecole des Beaux-Arts (Jules Lefèbvre's studio). Frequent visits to the Louvre, admires Courbet.

1885 Exhibits in the Salon. *Portrait de M. Ursenbach.* In the 1886 Salon, *Portrait de Mme X.* Copies Dürer, Leonardo, Antonello da Messina.

1887 At the Salon, *M. Jasinsky* (Helsingfors Museum), a portrait of a Polish engraver, shocks public opinion. Some say: " Deliberate revolt against the School "; others hail it as a masterpiece. Works with a picture-restorer. Also in 1887, *Portrait de mes Parents* (Lausanne Museum).

1889 Travels to Vienna, Venice. Makes friends with Charles Cottet, and Charles Maurin, inventor of a new lithographic process, " le crachis "; also numbers Toulouse-Lautrec amongst his friends. The milliner, Hélène Chatenay.

1890-1900 Specializes in black-and-white, for material reasons. Woodcuts.

1890-95 Art critic to the *Gazette de Lausanne.*

1891 Stops showing at the Salon after contributing for 7 years. Exhibits for the first time at the Salon des Indépendants. From 1891 to 1894, and from 1901 to 1909, collaborates in *La Revue Blanche.* Artists' and writers' portraits (T. Natanson, Mirbeau).

1893 Exhibits his " Masks " at the Indépendants. In October exhibits at Le Barc de Boutteville's with Roussel, Vuillard, Bonnard, Denis, Ranson, Ibels and Sérusier.

1894 Second group exhibition in the Paris office of *La Dépêche de Toulouse.*

1899 With Thadée Natanson at Cannes. In Paris, lives in the rue de Milan.

1900 June 3rd. Vallotton acquires French nationality. Exhibits at Zurich.

1902 A number of *L'Assiette au Beurre* (" Crimes et Châtiments ") meets with great success.

1903 Exhibits at Salon d'Automne; lives in Paris, rue des Belles-Feuilles.

1904 Hébrard, the founder, casts four of Vallotton's statues: *Femme qui marche, Femme à l'amphore, Femme à la chemise, Maternité.* Abandons small-scale works for big compositions.

1906-10 Period of Nudes: *L'Enlèvement d'Europe, La Baigneuse au Rocher.*

1908 Breaks his sojourns at Honfleur with annual visits to Lausanne and to his friends and admirers, the Hahnlosers, at Winterthur.

1913 Travels in Russia, Italy, Germany.

1921-22 Stays at Cagnes. Landscapes.

1925 Dies in Paris, on Dec. 28th (by an odd coincidence, he was born on Dec. 28th). His last work, a picture of the Bois de Boulogne under snow.

BIBLIOGRAPHY

Writings.

Vallotton contributed to the *Gazette de Lausanne*, and wrote several books, amongst which his *Journal*, a play, *L'homme fort*, Paris, 1907, and an autobiographical novel: *La Vie Meurtrière*, Lausanne, 1930 (Preface by A. Thérive).

Catalogue.

Vallotton himself compiled his *Livre de Raison*, a descriptive list of 1379 pictures.

Monographs and Appraisals.

J. Meier-Graefe, Paris, Berlin, 1898. A. Thérive *l'Amour de l'Art*, 1921. Ch. Fegdal, Paris, 1931. L. Godefroy, *L'Oeuvre gravé de F. Vallotton*, Paris, 1936 (basic work).

Illustrated Books.

Jules Renard, *La Maîtresse*, Paris, 1896 (26 drawings). R. de Gourmont, *Le Livre des Masques*, Mercure de France, Paris, 1896 (30 drawings). R. de Gourmont, *Le Deuxième Livre des Masques*, Mercure de France, Paris, 1898.

Exhibitions.

Gal. Druet, Paris, Jan. 10-29, 1910 (Preface by O. Mirbeau); 1912, Jan. 22-Feb. 3; 1914, May 4-16; 1929, Apr. 22-May 3; 1927, Oct., Nov., Kunsthalle, Bern; 1938, Aug. ,Sept., Kunstmuseum, Lucerne; Nov., Dec., Kunsthaus, Zurich.

VAN GOGH, Vincent (1853-1890)

1853 March 30, birth of Vincent Willem Van Gogh at the parsonage of Groot-Zundert, a small village in Dutch Brabant, south of Breda, near the Belgian frontier. Eldest son of Pastor Theodorus, who came of an ancient, much respected Calvinist family, amongst whom we find clergymen, sailors, business men and patrons of art. Three of Vincent's uncles were art-dealers. His mother, Anna Cornelia Barbentus, was daughter of a Court bookbinder at The Hague.

1857 May 1. Birth of Theo, Vincent's favourite brother, who is to be his moral and material stand-by to the end of his days.

1865-69 Studies at a Provily boarding-school, then at the neighbouring town of Zevenbergen.

1869 July 30. Employed at the Goupil art-gallery at The Hague, then in Brussels. Reads much and visits museums.

1872 Begins exchanging letters with Theo.

1873 June 18. Transferred to the London branch while Theo enters the Brussels office.

1874 June. Wants to marry the daughter of his landlady, Ursula Loyer, with whom he is wildly in love, but she rejects him. Bitter disappointment. Oct., in Paris; Dec., returns to London.

1875 May. Transferred to headquarters in Paris. Quarrels with the Goupil staff and with customers. His obsession with the Bible begins.

1876 March. Loses his post in Paris. Returns to England, and is a schoolmaster at Ramsgate, then at Isleworth. Dec., comes home to Etten for Christmas.

1877 Jan. 21-Apr. 30. Clerk in a bookshop at Dordrecht. But Vincent is more and more obsessed by his religious vocation. May 9, goes to Amsterdam to study for admission to the theological college.

1878 July 22, fails to pass the examination, and abandons his studies. Home again. In August begins a three-months' course at an evangelical training-college in Brussels. On Nov. 15 sent on a mission as lay-preacher to the miners in the Borinage. Lives in a hawker's house in Les Pâturages, a townlet near Mons. Shows immense zeal, nurses the sick, sleeps on bare boards.

1879 Jan. Temporary pastor at Wasmes, in the heart of the black country. July, relieved of his duties. Complete destitution, equally complete despair. Tramps the roads aimlessly in August. Stops at Courrières, intending to visit Jules Breton, but dares not knock at his door.

1880 July. During those anxious months, the darkest of his life, he glimpses his artistic vocation. Writes to his brother Theo the long, emotional letter in which he announces his decision. Lives with M. Decrucq in the rue du Pavillon, Cuesmes, near Mons.

Dutch period (1880-1885).

1880 *Borinage* (Cuesmes). Drawings of miners, copies from Millet.

1880-81 Brussels (Oct. 1880-Apr. 1881). Lodges at a small hotel, 72, bd du Midi. Meets and makes friends with the painter Ridder van Rappard (1858-1892), with whom he corresponds for five years. Private lessons in anatomy and perspective. First monetary aid from Theo, who is now working for Goupil in Paris.

1881 Etten (Apr.-Dec.). With his parents. Conflicts with his father about his artistic career. Another ill-fated love-affair, with his cousin "K."

1882-83 *The Hague* (Dec. 1881-Sept. 1883).

1882 Jan. Picks up in the street a drunken — and pregnant — prostitute, Christine (whom he calls Sien), who serves him as model and companion for twenty months. Asks advice of his cousin the painter Mauve, who, sensing his genius, helps him in his work, gives him lodging, but with whom he quarrels almost at once. He suffers from feeling that others see in him a nonentity, a feckless, unpleasant crank; yet, he protests, "there is in me harmony, calm and music." In his first paintings the tones are sombre, the impasto very thick. Feb., in hospital. Meets Breitner, the painter. Given his first and only order: for 12 pen-and-ink sketches, views of the town. Takes walks to Scheveningen, Woorburg, Leidschendau. Watercolours, lithographs; studies of peasants, fishermen, seascapes, landscapes.

1883 *Drenthe* (Sept., Nov.). Stays at Hoogeveen, in a land of moors and peat-bogs. Studies of heath-land, thatched cottages, hamlets, peasants at work.

1883-85 *Nuenen* (Dec. 1883-Nov. 1885).

1883 Dec. Returns to his parents' house at Nuenen, where his father has been appointed pastor. Sets up his studio in the vicarage barn. Works hard, reads Dickens, Carlyle, Beecher-Stowe.

1884 Aug. Short idyll with a local girl, Margot, who tries to commit suicide.

1885 March 27. Sudden death of his father. Still Lifes, peasants, weavers, studies of heads. *The Potato Eaters* (April-May 1885); *Tête de Paysanne* (June, 1885, Plate, p. 62) "You won't find any silvery tones in my present work; only browns — bitumen, sepia, and the like."

Antwerp period (Nov. 1885-Feb. 1888).

1885 Nov. 23. Starts for Antwerp. Studio at 194, rue des Images. 'Discovers' Rubens and Japanese prints. Enters the Academy and works under Sieber and Verlat, whose conformist outlook gets on his nerves.

1885 End of Feb. Suddenly decides to start for Paris.

Paris period (Feb. 1886-Feb. 1888).

1886 March. Theo welcomes him enthusiastically and puts him up, first in the rue Laval (now rue Victor-Massé), then at 54, rue Lepic. Enters Cormon's studio where he meets Toulouse-Lautrec. Frequents the Louvre but is also influenced by the Impressionists. Often visits Père Tanguy's shop and the Cabaret du Tambourin. Meets Pissarro, Degas, Seurat, Signac and Gauguin. Adopts the pointillist technique for a time.

1887 April. Makes friends with Emile Bernard. June, works with Bernard at Asnières. His palette gradually grows brighter and his style is completely changing. More than 22 pictures date from this Paris period: self-portraits, Still Lifes, views of Montmartre, studies of the outskirts of Paris, interiors. *Intérieur de Restaurant* (Summer, 1887. Plate, p. 61).

1888 Feb. 21, leaves suddenly for Arles, on Lautrec's advice. "It's in the South that the studio of the future must be set up."

Arles period (Feb. 1888-May 1889).

1888 Feb. Puts up at the Restaurant Carrel, in rue Cavalerie. March. Plans a colony of artists. Long exchange of letters with Theo. Death of Mauve. April. Spring landscapes: *Les Vergers en Fleurs*. May. Settles in a small house, 2, rue Lamartine, "a yellow house with a tiny white studio." June. Stays a week at Saintes-Maries de la Mer. Enraptured by this first sight of the Mediterranean. *Barques sur la Plage*. At Fontvieille pays a visit to his friend the Belgian painter Boch. July. Drawings of La Crau, near Montmajour. August. Becomes very friendly with the household of the local postman, Roulin; makes portraits of him. *The Sunflowers*. Sept. Nightscapes. *Le Café à Arles le Soir*. Oct. 20. Arrival of Gauguin, who has a great influence on him. Three months of life in common, during which the tension grows between these two men of fiercely opposed natures. Now., with Gauguin visits Montpellier to see the works bequeathed to the Museum by Bruyas. Dec. 23. The crisis. Van Gogh attempts to kill Gauguin, then cuts off his own ear. Gauguin hurries back to Paris. Theo arrives. Two weeks' confinement in hospital.

1889 Jan. 7. Vincent returns to his house. *Portrait of the Man with the Cut Ear. Still life with Onions* (Plate, p. 64). *La Berceuse* (Plate, p. 68). Feb. Hallucinations. Hostility of the neighbours. The police are called in, and he is again put into confinement, until the end of March. March. Signac visits him. April 17. Theo's marriage. 200 pictures are painted during this period, the most important and copious of his career.

Saint-Rémy period (May 1889-May 1890).

1889 May 9. At his own request, Vincent is admitted to the asylum at Saint-Rémy, a small town near Arles. Dr. Rey takes care of him. Has two rooms at his disposal. Comparative freedom. Long intervals of lucidity between spells of madness.

1890 Jan. Birth of Theo's son: Vincent Willem. First article dealing with his work: Albert Aurier's enthusiastic appreciation, in the *Mercure de France*.
March. One of Vincent's pictures, *La Vigne Rouge* is sold for 400 francs at the exhibition of 'Les XX' in Brussels; it is the only picture sold during his lifetime.
May 16. Comes to Paris, visits Theo.
150 pictures painted during this period of feverishly intensive productivity: amongst them *Les Cyprès, Les Moissons, The Hospital Yard*, self-portraits, portraits of the asylum staff. *On the edge of the Alpines*, May, 1890 (Plate, p. 65). About thirty copies from Millet, Delacroix, Daumier, Rembrandt, Doré.

Auvers-sur-Oise Period (May-July 1890).

1890 May 21. Arrives at Auvers. Becomes the patient and friend of Dr Gachet, whose portrait (Plate, p. 67) he paints. Puts up with 'Père' Ravoux, Place de la Mairie.
July 1. Spends some days in Paris: at Theo's meets Lautrec, Albert Aurier. Returns to Auvers and paints "three huge canvases, three far-flung wheatfields, under lowering skies"; also, on July 14 *La Mairie d'Auvers*.
July 27. In the evening, when in the open country, shoots himself.
July 29. Dies, aged 37, with faithful Theo at his side. His last words were: "There'll never be an end to human misery."

1891 Jan. 25. Theo dies. The brothers lie side by side in the little cemetery of Auvers.

BIBLIOGRAPHY

1. *Correspondence.*

His correspondence remains our main source of information on Van Gogh's life and work, and his letters are amongst the most moving ever penned. *Brieven aan zijn broeder* (letters to Theo), Complete Dutch ed. with Pref. by J. Van Gogh, Bonger, 3 vols., Amsterdam, 1914, 2nd. ed. 1923-24; English ed. London, 1927 and 1929; *Selected Letters*, A. Hamilton Barr, New York, 1935; French ed., selected by G. Philippart, Paris, 1937 and 1947. *Lettres de Vincent van Gogh à Emile Bernard*, Paris, 1911. *Briefe an E. Bernard und Paul Gauguin*, Basel, 1921. *Brieven van Vincent Van Gogh aan A. G. A. Ridder Van Rappard*, 1881-1885, Amsterdam, 1937. *Letters to Emile Bernard*, edited, translated, with a foreword by Douglas Lord, London, 1938. H. Thannhauser: *Van Gogh and John Russell, An Unpublished Correspondence*, Burlington Magazine, Sept. 1938. See also *Les Lettres de Theo à Vincent*, Amsterdam, 1932. A collection of the entire correspondence, with some hitherto unpublished letters, is being compiled for publication by P. Cailler, Geneva.

2. *Catalogues.*

J. B. de la Faille: *L'Œuvre de Van Gogh.* Catalogue raisonné. 4 vols., Paris and Brussels, 1928. W. Vanbeselaere: De Hollandsche periode in het werk van V. Van Gogh, Antwerp, Amsterdam, 1937. A. M. Hammacher: Rijksmuseum Kröller-Müller, Catalogue van 264 werken van Vincent Van Gogh, Otterlo, 1949.

3. *Monographs and Appraisals.*

G. A. Aurier, *Les Isolés : Van Gogh*, Mercure de France, Jan. 1890; E. Bernard; *V. Van Gogh*, Amsterdam, 1915; J. Meier-Graefe, *Vincent*, Munich, 1921 (transl. J. Holroyd Reece, London, 1936); L. Pierard, *La Vie tragique de Vincent Van Gogh*, Paris, 1924; R. Fry: Van Gogh, *Transformations*, London, 1926; J. B. de la Faille, *Les faux Van Gogh*, Paris and Brussels, 1930. M. Florisoone: *V. Van Gogh*, Paris, 1937; Special numbers of *L'Amour de l'Art* and *Renaissance*, 1937; W. Ueberwasser: *Le jardin de Daubigny*, Basel, 1936; W. Uhde: *Van Gogh*, Vienna, 1936; J. de Breucken, *V. Van Gogh, un Portrait*, Liège, 1938, Brussels, 1945; R. Huyghe: *Van Gogh (Dessins)*, Paris, 1938; W. Nigg: *V. Van Gogh*, Bern, 1942; *Swedish Van Gogh Studies*, Konsthistorick Tidskrift XV, Stockholm, 1946; W. Muenstenberg, *V. Van Gogh, Drawings, Pastels*, London and Paris, 1947; *Van Gogh raconté par lui-même et par ses amis*, Geneva, 1947; G. Schmidt: *V. Van Gogh*, Bern, 1947; A. M. Hammacher, *V. Van Gogh*, Amsterdam, 1948; C. Nordenfalf, *V. Van Gogh*, Amsterdam, 1948; Mark Trabault, *V. Van Gogh in zijn Antwerpsche Periode*, Amsterdam, 1948; G. Duthuit, *V. Van Gogh*, Lausanne, 1949.
For a complete bibliogr. see: C. M. Brooks: *V. van Gogh. A Bibliography comprising a catalogue of the Literature published from 1890 through 1940*, New York, 1942.

Exhibitions.

1891: Retrosp. at the Salon des Indépendants and at the Exh. of the 'XX' group in Brussels; 1905 (July-Aug.), Municipal Museum, Amsterdam; 1924 Kunsthalle, Basel (March, April); Kunsthaus, Zurich (July-Aug.); 1925, Marcel Bernheim Gallery, Paris; 1928 (Dec.), 1929 (Feb.), National Gallery, Berlin; 1930 (Sept. 6-Nov. 2), *Vincent Van Gogh and his Contemporaries*, Municipal Museum, Amsterdam; 1937 (June-Oct.), Paris (Cat. by M. Florisoone); Oct. 1946-Jan. 1947, Brussels, Mons (171 Nos. Cat. by E. Langui); 1947 (Jan.-March), Paris (Pref. by R. Huyghe, 172 Nos.); 1947 (March-April), Geneva, Rath Museum, (177 Nos); 1947 (July-Aug.), Boymans Museum, Rotterdam, drawings and watercolours (115 Nos); 1947 (Oct.-Nov.), Kunsthalle, Basel; 1948 (Oct.-Dec.), Municipal Museum, The Hague (Pref. by J. de Gruyter); 1948 (Nov. 3-Dec. 12), Cleveland Museum of Art (50 Nos); Oct. 21, 1949, Metropolitan Museum of Art, New York.

VUILLARD, Edouard (1868-1940)

1868 Born Nov. 11th at Cuiseaux (Saône et Loire). Son of a former officer and tax-collector, who dies in 1883. His father is 27 years older than his mother, Marie Michaud, who survives him for forty-five years, dying after devoting her whole life to her son Edouard. Edouard is the youngest of the family, which includes Marie (the eldest child) and Alexandre who becomes a pupil at the Ecole Polytechnique.

1877 The family settles in Paris. Edouard begins his studies at the Marist School (Ecole Rocroy).

1883 Death of the artist's father. Edouard continues his studies at the Lycée Fontanes (now Lycée Condorcet). He makes friends with K. X. Roussel, his future brother-in-law. The family lives in the rue Daunou, where Mme Vuillard, to supplement her income, opens a corset factory. It is said that this special atmosphere of workgirls handling multi-coloured clothes and silks under artificial light, influenced the artist's sensibility.

1886 His devotion for Roussel makes him give up studying for the Ecole de St. Cyr, and turns his thoughts towards painting. Both friends work in various studios; first at Maillard's where they meet Cottet. Through Lugné-Poë, a former pupil of the Lycée and future director of the Théâtre de l'Œuvre, they make the acquaintance of Maurice Denis.

1888 Académie Julian. Our young painters meet Bonnard, who, with Vuillard and Roussel, are working under Bougereau and Robert Fleury.

1889 Sérusier, student-in-charge at Julian's, and Denis prevail upon Ranson, Piot, Ibels, then Bonnard and finally Vuillard to form an association to be called the 'Nabis.' At the Ecole des Beaux-Arts Vuillard works in Gérôme's studio, but leaves it before long. Paints *La Femme endormie* (1890). Opposed to academic art and also to Impressionism. Simplified forms, small patches of colour, broken tones. Painting on cardboard; influenced by Japanese art.

1891 First exhibition in the offices of *La Revue Blanche*, which the Natanson brothers have just launched. Vuillard, Bonnard, Denis and Lugné-Poë, stage-manager of the Théâtre Libre, share a studio at 28, rue Pigalle.

1892 Exhibition at Le Barc de Boutteville's. Vuillard meets Verlaine and Mallarmé. Roger-Marx the critic and Jos. Hessel the dealer are their first admirers and patrons.

1893 K. X. Roussel marries Marie Vuillard. Foundation of the Théâtre de L'Œuvre by Lugné-Poë. According to him, it is Vuillard who is most interested in the theatre; he is also the best general adviser, is good at finding titles and plays an active part in the rehearsal and staging of the first performed play: Ibsen's *Rosmersholm*.

1894 First great decorative composition (in 9 panels): *Jardin des Tuileries* (Musée d'Art Moderne, Paris).

1896-99 Decorative work for Dr Vaquez (Petit-Palais, Paris), for the novelist Claude Anet, for Princess Bibesco. Vuillard now lives in the rue Truffaut. His art has reached its climax. Stays at the Natansons' in Villeneuve-sur-Yonne.

1900 At Romanel, with Vallotton. Paints Vallotton's portrait.

1900-10 *Paysages de Paris*. Simplification, bareness, gravity. Still paints on cardboard.

1908 Moves to rue de Calais, facing Place Vintimille. Leaves this house only in 1927, when he finds a new home in Square Vintimille. Teaches for a while in Ranson's Academy, with Roussel and Denis.

1903-14 Summer holidays in Brittany and Normandy with the Hessels and their friends; at Vasouy, Anfreville, Criquebœuf, Loctudy, Le Pouliguen.

1913 Goes to London and, with Bonnard, to Holland.

1914 Vuillard is mobilized for a time as a signaller in the Army Reserve.

1917-24 Stays at Clos Cézanne, Vaucresson.

1918 Vuillard's 50th birthday falls on Armistice day, Nov. 11th, and his friends celebrate both together. Returns to realism and tradition.

1924-40 Stays at Château des Clays (Seine et Oise).

1930 Travels in Spain with Prince Bibesco.

1930-37 Many commissions, society portraits: *La Parisienne*, 1930, *Mme L. Marchand*, 1931, *Mme de Noailles*, 1932, *Comtesse de Polignac*, 1932, *Simone Berriau*, 1934, *Mme Henraux*, 1937, *Elvire Popesco*, 1937, *Dr Viau*, 1937.

1938 Decorates the Palais de Chaillot. Elected member of the Institute.

1939 Decorates the Palace of the League of Nations, Geneva.

1940 Dies in La Baule on June 21.

BIBLIOGRAPHY

T. Leclerc, *Art et décoration*, 1920. F. Fosca, *l'Amour de l'Art*, 1920. R. Coolus, *Art vivant*, 1938. A. Lhote, N. R. F., March, 1941. B. Dorival, *Revue des Beaux-Arts de France*, 1942. J. Salomon, Paris, 1945. C. Roger-Marx, *Vuillard et son Temps*, Paris, 1945. A. Chastel, Paris, 1946. Vuillard's unpublished notebooks will be opened in 1980 only.

Exhibitions.

Bernheim-Jeune, Paris (exh. every year from 1907 to 1913, except 1910); 1906, Dec., Gal. P. Rosenberg, Paris, Bonnard and Vuillard Exh.; 1932 (May 29-July 3rd), Kunsthaus, Zurich, Bonnard and Vuillard Exh.; 1938 (Jan., Feb.), Gal. Bernheim-Jeune, Works from 1890-1910; 1938 (May-July), Retrosp. in Musée des Arts Décoratifs, Paris (315 Nos.), organized with the artist's help; 1946, Brussels, Palais des Beaux-Arts (67 Nos. Pref. by C. Roger-Marx); 1948, Gal. Charpentier, Paris (165 Nos. Pref. C. Roger-Marx and J. Salomon); 1948, June, Wildenstein Gal., London (66 Nos. Pref. C. Roger-Marx); 1949 (March 26-May 1), Kunsthalle, Basel (260 Nos.).

SELECTED BIBLIOGRAPHY

I. General

A. Fontainas, *Hist. de la Peint. Française au XIXe S.*, Paris, 1906 (new ed. 1922). W. H. Wright, *Modern Painting*, New York, 1915. E. Faure, *Hist. de l'Art*, Vol. IV, L'Art Moderne, Paris, 1921. R. Fry, *Transformations*, London, 1926. F. J. Mather, *Modern Painting*, New York, 1927. H. Focillon, *La Peint. aux XIXe et XXe S.*, Paris, 1928. W. Pach, *Masters of Modern Art*, New York, 1929. R. Rey, *La Peint. Francaise à la Fin du XIXe S.*, Paris, 1931. J. Klein, *Modern Masters*, New York, 1938. R. Huyghe, *Les Contemporains*, Paris, 1939 and 1949. R. H. Wilenski, *Modern French Painters*, New York, 1940 (new ed. 1947). B. Dorival, *Les Etapes de la Peinture Française Contemporaine*, Paris, 1945. L. Venturi, *Peintres Modernes*, Vol. II (printing).

II. Pre-Impressionism and the Honfleur School

G. J. Aubry, *Boudin*, Paris, 1922. G. Poulain, Pré-Impressionnisme, *Formes*, Nov. 1931. ' Les origines de l'Impressionnisme,' Special Number, *Beaux-Arts*, Brussels, June-Sept. 1935. 1934, July 12-Sept. 9, Exh., Musée Municipal, Honfleur, *Honfleur et ses Peintres* with notes by Lavedan and Joubin. 1937, May, Gal. des Beaux-Arts, Paris, *La Naissance de l'Impressionnisme* (Exh. with pref. by A. Joubin ; cat. by R. Cogniat).

III. Impressionism

1. Sources and documents : Duranty, *La Nouvelle Peinture*, Paris, 1876 (new ed. M. Guérin, Paris, 1945). T. Duret, *Les Peintres Impressionnistes*, Paris, 1878. J. K. Huysmans, *L'Art Moderne*, Paris, 1883. G. Moore, *Confessions of a Young Man*, London, 1888, Reminiscences of Impressionist Painters, Dublin, 1906. J. E. Blanche, *Propos de Peintres*, Paris, 1919. A. Vollard, *Souvenirs d'un Marchand de Tableaux*, Paris, 1937. J. Rewald, *Cézanne, sa vie, son œuvre, son amitié pour Zola*, Paris, 1939. A. S. Hartrick, *A Painter's Pilgrimage through Fifty Years*, Cambridge, 1939. L. Venturi, *Les Archives de l'Impressionnisme*, Paris, New York, 1939. C. Pissarro, *Letters to his Son Lucien*, New York, 1943.

2. Historical Studies : G. Lecomte, *L'Art Impressionniste*, Paris, 1892. G. Geffroy, *Histoire de l'Impressionnisme*, Paris, 1894. C. Mauclair, *The French Impressionists*, London, 1903. T. Duret, *Histoire des Peintres Impressionnistes*, Paris, 1906 (new ed. 1939). C. L. Ragghianti, *Impressionismo*, Turin, 1944. J. Rewald, *The History of Impressionism*, New York, 1946 (Ital. ed. 1949). G. Bazin, *L'Epoque Impressionniste*, Paris, 1947.

3. Critical Studies : J. Meier-Graefe, *Manet und sein Kreis*, Berlin, 1902 ; *Entwicklungsgeschichte der modernen Kunst*, 3 Vol., Stuttgart, 1904 ; *Impressionisten*, Munich, 1907. V. Pica, *Gl'Impressionisti Francesi*, Bergamo, 1908. W. Weisbach, *Impressionismus*, 2 Vol., Berlin, 1910-11. L. Venturi, in *L'Arte*, March, 1935. P. Francastel, *L'Impressionnisme*, Paris, 1937. W. Uhde, *Les Impressionnistes*, Vienna, 1937. R. Huyghe, in *Prométhée*, Feb. 1939. L. Venturi, in *The Journal of Aesthetics*, 1941. E. Scheyer, in *The Art Quarterly*, VI, 2, 1943. *L'Amour de l'Art*, Spec. No., 1947 (G. Bazin, J. Leymarie, M. Florisoone).

Exhibitions : Eight Group Exhibitions (1874, 1876, 1877, 1879, 1880, 1881, 1882, 1886). 1886, April-May, Exhibition organized at New York by Durand-Ruel with the American Art Association. 1904, Feb.-March, La Libre Esthétique, Brussels (Pref. by O. Mirbeau). 1905, Grafton Galleries, London. 1908 ; Kunsthaus, Zurich. 1922, July, Brussels, *Les Maîtres de l'Impressionnisme et leur Temps*. 1924, Gal. A. Flechtheim, Berlin and Frankfurt. 1929, Feb., Lucerne. 1934, Museum of Art, Toledo. 1935, Palais des Beaux-Arts, Brussels. 1935-1936, Museum of Art, Baltimore. 1936, Museum of Fine Arts, Washington. 1936, Albany Institute of History and Art. 1947, Musée du Jeu de Paume, Paris. 1948, Biennale, Venice. 1949, Kunsthalle, Basel.

IV. Neo-Impressionism

F. Fénéon, *Les Impressionnistes en 1886*, Paris, 1886. P. Signac, *D'Eugène Delacroix au Néo-Impressionnisme*, Paris, 1899. G. Coquiot, *Les Indépendants*, Paris, 1921. E. Verhaeren, *Sensations*, Paris, 1927. P. Signac, *Le Néo-Impressionnisme*, Documents, Gaz. des Beaux-Arts, 1934. J. Rewald, *Seurat*, New York, 1946, Paris, 1948. J. Rewald, F. Fénéon, Gaz. B. A., 1947-48.

Exhibitions : Gal. Braun, Paris, 1932, *Le Néo-Impressionnisme* (Pref. O. Maus) ; Dec. 1933-Jan. 1934, Gal. des Beaux-Arts, Paris, *Seurat et ses Amis* (Intro. by Signac ; Cat. R. Cogniat) ; Same exh. Wildenstein Gal., London, Jan.-Feb., 1937. Dec. 1936-Jan. 1937, Musée Boymans, Rotterdam, *De Divisionisten*. Dec. 1942-Jan. 1943, Gal. de France, Paris, *Les Néo-Impressionnistes*.

V. Gauguin and the Pont-Aven Group

G. A. Aurier, *Œuvres Posthumes*, Paris, 1893. E. Bernard, *Notes sur l'Ecole dite de Pont-Aven*, Mercure de France, Dec. 1903. C. L. Hind, *The Post-Impressionists*, London, 1911. C. Chassé, *Gauguin et le Groupe de Pont-Aven*, Paris, 1921. E. Bernard, *Souvenirs Inédits sur l'Artiste P. Gauguin et ses Compagnons*, Lorient, 1941.

Exhibitions : 1889, Impressionist and Synthesist Group Exhibition at the Café Volpini, Paris. Feb.-March, 1934, Gal. des Beaux-Arts, Paris : *Gauguin, ses Amis, l'Ecole de Pont-Aven et l'Académie Julian* (Pref. by M. Denis, Notes by R. Cogniat).

VI. Symbolisme and the Nabis

A. Aurier, *' Le Symbolisme en Peinture,' Mercure de France*, 1891. A. Mellerio, *Le Mouvement Idéaliste en Peinture*, Paris, 1896. R. Barré, *Le Symbolisme*, Paris, 1911. M. Denis, *Théories*, Paris, 1913. A. Segard, *Les Décorateurs*, Paris, 1913. M. Denis, *L'Epoque du Symbolisme*, G. B. A., 1934. H. Hahnloser-Buhler, *F. Vallotton et ses Amis*, Paris, 1936. A. Armstrong Wallis, *The Symbolist Painters of 1890*, Marsyas, 1941. J. R. Goldwater, ' Symbolist Art and Theater,' *Mag. of Art*, 1946. C. Roger-Marx, *Vuillard et son temps*, Paris, 1945. C. Chassé, *Le Mouvement Symboliste*, Paris, 1948.

Exhibitions : Exp. des Peintres Impressionnistes et Symbolistes, Le Barc de Boutteville, 1891-1897. Other group exhibitions at Vollard's (1897-98) ; at Bernheim-Jeune's 1900 and 1907 ; others in the premises of *La Revue Blanche* and *La Plume* ; in 1899 ' Hommage à Odilon Redon ' at Durand-Ruel's. 1917, Exh. of Nabis at Kunsthaus, Zurich ; 1936, Paris, Exp. *Peintres de la Revue Blanche* organized by Bolette Natanson ; *Cinquantenaire du Symbolisme* at Bibliothèque Nationale, Dec. 1949, Orangerie, Paris : *Carrière et le Symbolisme*.

PICTURES MENTIONED IN THE TEXT

This list enables the reader to trace at once all references to these, for purposes of comparison or documentation.

WRITERS AND CRITICS

Instead of giving a mere list of names in alphabetical order, followed by page references, we have sought to facilitate research-work by inserting after the name of each writer that of the artist on whom he has written. Thus the reader need only turn to the bibliography of the artist in whom he is interested, to elicit all the information he may require.

GENERAL INDEX

Our Index has been arranged in the simplest possible way, so as to enable all references to be traced with the maximum of rapidity. This lists the names of places and persons, the chief events and most significant dates cited in the text.

PRINTED IN SWITZERLAND

THIS EDITION
OF THE FIRST VOLUME OF THE COLLECTION

PAINTING ○ COLOUR ○ HISTORY

WAS PRINTED BY L'IMPRIMERIE LA CONCORDE, LAUSANNE
FINISHED ON THE TWENTY-FIFTH OF AUGUST
NINETEEN HUNDRED AND FIFTY-ONE

THE PLATES WERE ENGRAVED BY
GUEZELLE ET RENOUARD, PARIS

THE PAPER WAS SUPPLIED BY BLUM ET ROCHAT, GENEVA

BINDING BY ROGER VEIHL, GENEVA
AND MAYER ET SOUTTER, LAUSANNE